Black Religion / Womanist Thought / Social Justice
Series Editors: Dwight N. Hopkins and Linda E. Thomas
Published by Palgrave Macmillan

"How Long this Road": Race, Religion, and the Legacy of C. Eric Lincoln
Edited by Alton B. Pollard, III and Love Henry Whelchel, Jr.

African American Humanist Principles: Living and Thinking Like the
Children of Nimrod
By Anthony B. Pinn

White Theology: Outing Supremacy in Modernity
By James W. Perkinson

The Myth of Ham in Nineteenth-Century American Christianity:
Race, Heathens, and the People of God
By Sylvester Johnson

Loving the Body: Black Religious Studies and the Erotic
Edited by Anthony B. Pinn and Dwight N. Hopkins

Transformative Pastoral Leadership in the Black Church
By Jeffery L. Tribble, Sr.

Shamanism, Racism, and Hip Hop Culture: Essays on White Supremacy and
Black Subversion
By James W. Perkinson

Women, Ethics, and Inequality in U.S. Healthcare: "To Count Among the Living"
By Aana Marie Vigen

Black Theology in Transatlantic Dialogue: Inside Looking Out,
Outside Looking In
By Anthony G. Reddie

Womanist Ethics and the Cultural Production of Evil
By Emilie M. Townes

Whiteness and Morality: Pursuing Racial Justice through Reparations and
Sovereignty
By Jennifer Harvey

Black Theology and Pedagogy
By Noel Leo Erskine

Black Religion and the Imagination of Matter in the Atlantic World

James A. Noel

First published in 2009 by
PALGRAVE MACMILLAN®
in the United States—a division of St. Martin's Press LLC,
175 Fifth Avenue, New York, NY 10010.

Where this book is distributed in the UK, Europe and the rest of the world,
this is by Palgrave Macmillan, a division of Macmillan Publishers Limited,
registered in England, company number 785998, of Houndmills,
Basingstoke, Hampshire RG21 6XS.

Palgrave Macmillan is the global academic imprint of the above companies
and has companies and representatives throughout the world.

Palgrave® and Macmillan® are registered trademarks in the United States,
the United Kingdom, Europe and other countries.

ISBN-13: 978–0–230–61506–9
ISBN-10: 0–230–61506–6

Library of Congress Cataloging-in-Publication Data

Noel, James A., 1948–
    Black religion and the imagination of matter in
  the Atlantic World / James A. Noel.
        p. cm.—(Black religion, womanist thought, social justice)
    Includes bibliographical references and index.
    ISBN 0–230–61506–6
    1. Blacks—Religion. 2. Africa—Religion. 3. African Americans—Religion.
4. Long, Charles H. I. Title.

BL2400.N64 2009
200.89′96—dc22
                                                                2008043012

A catalogue record of the book is available from the British Library.

Design by Newgen Imaging Systems (P) Ltd., Chennai, India.

First edition: April 2009

10 9 8 7 6 5 4 3 2 1

Printed in the United States of America.

To my wife, Diana Nieves Noel and
my children: Michelle, Kaiya, Daniel, and Amada;
My deceased brother, Rodney Noel;

my Pastor, the late Rev. Dr. H. Eugene Farlough, Jr.;

my teacher, Dr. Charles H. Long;

and the Saints where I served as Pastor at:
St. Andrew Presbyterian Church in Marin City, CA;
Sojourner Truth Presbyterian Church in Richmond, CA, and
New Liberation Presbyterian Church in San Francisco, CA.

Contents

Introduction

The phrase "imagination of matter"[1] was coined by Charles H. Long and is central to the conceptual framework that informs the methodology of the many students in the history of religions, African American studies, and the study of black religion. Long was Professor in the History of Religion Department at University of Chicago's Divinity School along with his colleagues Mircea Eliade and Joseph Kitagawa. His book, *Significations: Signs, Symbols, and Images in the Interpretation of Religion* (1986), was reprinted in 1995 and is treated as a classic by many scholars in the History of Religions field. It is slowly dawning on scholars that Long's thought is indispensable for understanding the nature of religion in the modern period.[2]

This book while exploring the nature of black religion is also the first sustained discussion and application of Long's thought by a single author and is envisioned as an initial contribution to a more sustained project that investigates the nature of black religion within the Atlantic World's geo-temporal framework. This book attempts to describe the way modernity was constituted and brought into being by new modes of imagining materiality that occurred within and during the period of the Atlantic slave trade. I understand modernity to be something that emerges from the reciprocal interaction of global economic exchanges, technological advances, cultural symbols and expressions, epistemological categories, and subjectivities/identities that differentiated themselves in Western Europe beginning in the long sixteenth-century conquest, colonialism, and slavery were integral to this process. Race was one of modernity's epistemological categories that materialized into white, black, and other identity formations. But, since the category of race presupposes an entire world view concerning how the cosmos or world is and ought to be ordered it is not isolated from what we call "religion." Broadly conceived, religion is not separate from matter. The gods were imagined through primary material forms. In turn, religion determines how matter is conceived. In Long's thought, materiality is the entire network of contacts and exchanges that humans have with each other, nature, and the invisible forces of the cosmos. This is also the way I am describing religion. Racial identity represents a new mode of being human in the world and, therefore, will be conceived of as a new mode of materiality. Religion is implicated in this because the racialized groups that appear in modernity imagine their selves and the cosmos through religious symbols. The category of "race" that was imposed on racialized groups was initially a religious construct as much as anything else. Thus, the imagination of matter encompasses the self and the cosmos. It is a religious act that operates at the archaic level of consciousness. Since the archaic is not amenable to direct observation, its description requires interpretation—a hermeneutic. This book concerns itself with the original consciousness that constituted religious subjects in the historical space of the Atlantic World.

This book's central argument is that the religious subject and the religious object make their phenomenological appearance simultaneously and the hermeneutical problem in the study of black religion is that of apprehending and describing their mutual appearance. This task is further complicated by the fact that the religious subject has been objectified and signified by the Other's epistemological discourse. In this discourse, the West has posited non-whites and colonized peoples as primitives and, therefore, as the inferior—the dialectical opposite of the West as civilized and superior. But the conquest, slavery, genocide, and colonialism that structured the primitive/civilized dichotomy has been denied and silenced. This is what Long calls the "negative structure of concreteness" and another way he thinks about "materiality." The origin of race and the origin of religion are connected to these materialities and the Atlantic World is the geo-political space where these materialities make their historical appearance.

The nature of the task assumed by this book requires a more circular than linear approach. My contention is the methodological problem in the study of black religion has to do primarily with the issue of how one understands the religious subject and object and only secondarily with other matters. I explore the way black religion and its exemplars are constituted through the imagination of matter on both sides of the subject-object epistemological framework of Western culture. Black folks were imagined as objects through the discursive practices of their oppressors, and they overcame objectification through their own imagination and religious practice. To intuit what was involved in this process, we must circle around the problem because religious experience is not directly observable or amenable to linguistic description. In placing the genesis of black religion within the historical framework of the "long sixteenth century," I am viewing it as one of modernity's fundamental components. It is an essential component of modernity's epistemological categorizations and subjectivities. Although the chapters of this book are not sequenced linearly but approach the study of black religion from various angles of vision, there are certain categories that are applied in each chapter: contact and exchange, imagination, materiality, opacity, silence, and signification. The interrelated meta-questions are: Under what conditions do black people first appear?—to themselves?—to others? How was God perceived during this appearance through their various modes of cultural expression?

In chapter one, "Studying Black Religion: Contacts/Exchanges and Continuities/Discontinuities," I assert a thick description of black people's religious experience that indicates black identity or, if you prefer,—black consciousness—was constituted through their religious experience. Phenomenologically speaking, black religion and black people appeared simultaneously. Black people are visible and material; their religious consciousness is not. The material aspect of blackness required something immaterial—black religion—to make it manifest. Therefore, black religion is involved and implicated in the manifestation of the new form of materiality represented by black people themselves. This appears in the midst of the contacts and exchanges of the Atlantic World. Chapter two, "The Age of Discovery and the Emergence of the Atlantic World" provides an historical overview of the way the Atlantic World was constituted through the slave trade. In chapter three "The Imagination of Matter in the Atlantic World's Political Economy," I discuss Long's concept of the imagination of matter by showing how his is distinct from his former colleague Mircea Eliade's. I attempt to demonstrate how this was played out in Western history by focusing on the Roman Church's understanding of grace and the way Luther's attack on Indulgences affected the Church's material base. I discuss Karl Marx's definition of the commodity in *Capital* as a form of fetish before discussing William Peitz's study of the history of the concept of the fetish as something that arose out of the contacts and exchanges between Portuguese and West African traders during the end of the fifteenth and early sixteenth centuries. In chapter four, "Being, Nothingness, and the 'Signification of Silence' in African American Religious Consciousness," I utilize several categories from the Christian mysticism such as the "Dark Night of the Soul" and "the Cloud of Unknowing" in conjunction with the Hegelian notion of "Non-Being" to explore the Middle Passage experience and tie it in with Long's notion of the "signification of silence." My description and exploration of nothingness in the black experience relies heavily on Martin Heidegger. This chapter understands the categories of "silence" and "nothingness" in the black experience to demarcate and constitute the hyphen in continuity-discontinuity discussed in chapter one and African American discussed in relation to Du Bois's notion of "double consciousness."

In chapter five, "Epistemologies Opaque: Conjuring, Conjecture, and the Problematic of Nat Turner's Biblical Hermeneutic," I argue that by relegating African slaves to the realm of materiality the West rendered them opaque. And thus their ways of knowing and experiencing the world was made opaque to the West's epistemological gaze. What Long terms the "empirical Other" becomes exempt from Western knowledge. This is evident when we try to understand Nat Turner's Confession. This chapter attempts to make the unintelligibility Turner's biblical hermeneutic intelligible. In chapter six, "The Mulatto as Material/Sexual Site of Modernity's Contacts and Exchanges," I describe how black people make their appearance in modernity through discursive practices that relied heavily upon the U.S. legal apparatus. We can observe the imagination of matter through legal minds that succeeded in determining the boundary between blacks and whites by focusing on the category of the "mulatto." In chapter seven, " 'The Signification of Silence' Revisited: African American Art and Hermeneutics," I argue that African American art is one of the most productive sites for excavating the "archaic" in African American consciousness. It is only in this sense that African American art can function as "text." Perhaps we should substitute the term "site" instead. "Archaism," according to Long, "is predicated on the priority of something already there, something given. This 'something' may be the bodily perceptions, as it is for Alfred North Whitehead and Maurice Merleau-Ponty, or *a primal vision of aesthetic form*, as it is for the artist" (my emphasis). In chapter eight, "The Meaning of the Moan and Significance of the Shout in Black Worship and Culture and Memory and Hope," I posit a phenomenology of the African American worship experience that is comprised of two modalities existing in a dialectical relationship with each other: the moan and the shout. I even assert that these two modalities—the moan and the shout—are present in and characteristic of all African American cultural expressions. I also extend this phenomenological analysis to discuss African American consciousness and identity in terms of the modalities of memory and hope. Memory is to hope what the moan is to the shout. In chapter nine, "The Salsa/Jazz/Blues Idiom and Creolization in the Atlantic World," I trace the African roots of the salsa music genre as an example of how creolization happens in the Americas. In so doing, I offer an approach to a nonessentialist understanding of African American identity, religion, and culture as a mode of subjectivity.

I hope the sequencing of these chapters will make historical and phenomenological sense to the reader. We notice that chapter one begins historically in Africa and addresses the issues of retentions, and continuities/discontinuities between Africa and the Americas. Chapters two and three situate the study within a description of exchanges constituting the Atlantic World. Chapter four has the Middle Passage as its foci explored phenomenologically under the categories of "nothingness" and "silence." Chapter five moves from "nothingness" and "silence" into what is revealed in one of black religion's manifestations—Nat Turner's Confession—but remains, nevertheless, "opaque." Chapter six moves from the opacity of black religion to the indeterminacy of blackness as signified in the appearance of the mulatto. Chapter seven revisits the notion of "silence" through its signification in African American cultural expressions—art. Chapter eight can be seen in continuity with the preceding chapter with regard to signification; only in this case the discussion is of the "moan," "shout," "memory," and "hope." Chapter nine posits the Afro-Caribbean music genre "salsa" as a model of "creolization" that can serve as an analogue for studying African American identity, religion, and culture. All the chapters in this study, while probing the nature of black religion, arrive at the reality of "opacity," and "Otherness."

Studying Black Religion: Contacts/Exchanges and Continuities/Discontinuities

I should like to begin this reconsideration and critique through the recovery of the literal and metaphorical meaning of matter and materiality. In one way or another, all of our pressing problems might be subsumed under some notion of materiality. Whether we are talking about ecology, gender, or ethnicity, the issue of matter or materiality is to the fore. We have, however, in the modern western world thought of matter as inert or neutral or have relegated it to the realm of commodities and commodity exchanges. But whether we are speaking of our bodies (personal or social) or the issue of economics, or of the spirit, in one way or another we are speaking of matter, of that which forms the relationship among and between ourselves and other human beings and the create world. I am placing the locus of matter and materiality precisely at the point of relationships, contacts, and exchanges between and among human beings and between human beings and all other forms of life and meaning. We are speaking of how our bodies are embodiments of this fact ought to cause us to have regard for human matter and its place in the universe. (Charles H. Long, "Matter and Spirit: A Reorientation" p. 5)

Introduction

It is important at the onset to say something about one of the most important and provocative concepts in Charles H. Long's thinking—that of materiality. I attempt to elucidate materiality in terms of the way matter is imagined in the next chapter. Indeed, we will be coming at this term from numerous angles through this book because no single definition can exhaust the full range of meanings it invokes or do justice to what it represents about Long's intuition of the way human experience is constituted through religion. The term, materiality, is in no way related to the similar sounding term, materialism. Materialism refers to an epistemological stance that presumes all one can know about reality through one's experiences of matter. Long employs the term materiality to challenge our common sense assumptions about so-called matter as distinguished from whatever we regard as nonmatter—spirit falls also under this category.

Contacts, Exchanges, and Materiality

Materiality is not, therefore, the opposite of spirituality. Hence, religion is also encompassed by this term. From the earlier quotation, we can see that Long places the locus of materiality "at the point of relationship, contacts, and exchanges between and among human beings and between human beings and all other forms of life and meaning." Materiality includes the total process, products, and modalities constituting human exchanges—the entire matrix. We cannot grasp the notion of materiality without coordinating that term with two others: "contact" and "exchange." To be human means to be involved in some sort of contact and exchange with other humans, nature, and the invisible realm. And from these contacts and exchanges there always arises a surplus or something extra. Therefore the question to ask about human exchanges, as we study them in various times and places, is what happens to the surplus?

Sometimes, the surplus appears as religious phenomena; religion, in turn, supplies meaning to this surplus. At other times, however,—as in the case of the commodity—this surplus appears elsewhere under the veil of so-called secular meanings. The term materiality discloses the cunning way the surplus assumes this new guise and exposes its hidden religious content, connotation, and meaning. This is not by any means to reduce religious phenomena to "the economic base." For Long, religion and the gods appear as phenomena during and through human exchanges. When Long talks about contacts and exchanges we must understand that his thinking about this is heavily indebted to Marcel Mauss's study of gift-exchange in his book *The Gift*. Long's thinking about contacts and exchanges has also been heavily influenced by his study of the cargo cult phenomenon that he devoted a chapter to in *Significations*.

The gift and cargo constitute another way of speaking about the excess or surplus. It is also another way of conceptualizing and speaking about divinity. Although Long is adamant about not being a theologian, his thought has profound theological implications. Long's theology, like the rest of his thought, is based on his notions of materiality, contact, and exchange—particularly, gift-exchange. Christianity discloses the revelation of God's gift of God's divinity to humanity in Jesus whose salvific act on the cross can be seen as a form of divine-human exchange. We likewise can study Indigenous African religions and black religions in the New World in terms of exchange. However, black religions in the New World were determined by new modes of exchange elaborated in the Atlantic World through the commodification of black bodies. This brings us to consider the problem of continuity and discontinuity in the study of black religion.

One of the significant differences I have with treatments of the black religious experience by many black theologians is that they presume the presence of a people with a black identity before their having undergone the religious experience these theologians seek to describe. However, a thicker description of black people's religious experience would indicate how black identity or, black consciousness, was historically constituted through religious experience. Hence, phenomenologically speaking, black religion and black people appear simultaneously. Black religion is involved and implicated in the manifestation of the new form of materiality represented by the concreteness black people represent. White religion, of course, is also implicated—it helped fashion white identity vis-à-vis the discursive modes that went into the construction of blackness. In this scenario, matter and consciousness become inextricably related. This point will be addressed more extensively later. What needs to be indicated is the connection between religious experience and the "imagination of matter."

Long situates his reflection on this way of understanding religious experience at the beginning of the sixteenth century to discern how Africans and other enslaved and conquered peoples imagined matter as one world was disintegrating and another possible world was being posited through the symbolic forms of their consciousness. How did their bodies as matter become imagined collectively as community even in the midst of being subjugated and exchanged as commodities or cargo? Black religion and the black consciousness arose within the framework of a particular historical/geographical context or—to speak in more dynamic terms, we could say—political economy. That context and its political economy are what we wish to invoke by the related terms Atlantic World and modernity.

The Atlantic Ocean always existed. Peoples existed in African, Europe, and the Americas since time immemorial. The difference justifying naming the Atlantic World as something new is that beginning in the long sixteenth century these three areas were connected through contacts and exchanges for the first time in history and suddenly become a part of the same world. According to M. Malowist:

> The period from 1500 to 1800 was to witness the establishment of a new Atlantic-oriented geo-economic system, with its triangular trading pattern linking Europe, Africa, and the Americas. With the opening up of Atlantic trade, Europe—particularly Western Europe—gained ascendancy over the Americas and African societies. Henceforth, Europe was to play a leading role in the accumulation of capital generated by trade and plunder on a worldwide scale. The emigration of Europeans to trading settlements in Africa and the territories of North and South America gave rise to the establishment of supporting overseas economies. These were to play a decisive long-term role through their contribution to Western Europe's rise to power over the rest of the world.[1]

Europe, Africa, and the Americas became interconnected through commercial networks that in the words of Bernard Bailyn were "polycentric and dynamic." Spain dominated Atlantic exchanges during the first century of colonization. It was not long, however, before the Portuguese, English, French, and Dutch entered into the picture. Bailyn points out that New England was dependent upon the African slave trade. Caribbean sugar plantations were the major consumers of New England's agricultural products. The South produced rice and tobacco. The former product was traded in markets that extended from Peru and Argentina and as far as the Black Sea. Tobacco also was exchanged through numerous channels throughout the Atlantic. What emerged was "an immensely complex and regionally differentiated Euro-Afro-American labor system." According to Bailyn the Atlantic World was one wherein: "Information as well as trade and people moved in stable routes, which in their entirety formed a communication system that, however erratically, bound Peru to Seville, Rio de Janeiro to Lisbon, Appalachia to Ireland, Scotland to Barbados, the Rhineland to Pennsylvania. The interpenetrations were deep."[2]

These exchanges were not benign to say the least. They lacked reciprocity and the meanings or legitimations of their outcome resulted in new estimations of human value and notions of self among those who were made to participate in them. Europeans began to form a new sense of themselves in relation to the other peoples with whom they made contact through trade, conquest, enslavement, and colonization. African and other discovered, conquered and/or colonized peoples became signified in the West's discourse about itself. One of the dichotomies where this form of signification is evident is in the notions of primitive and civilized peoples. To the West accrued the collective sensibility of being the planet's civilized peoples in contrast to the backward, primitive, and inferior peoples that it found everywhere else. Europeans in North America very quickly developed a sense of being "white people" distinct and apart from blacks whom they enslaved. This sensibility achieved expression and permanence through the concept and category of race. In the chapter in *Significations* titled "Primitive/Civilized: The Locus of the Problem," Long writes:

> The problem defines our hermeneutical situation. Since the beginning of the modern period in the West the primitives have been understood as religious and empirical "others," empirical from the point of view of those disciplines and sciences which take these people and their cultures as the data of inquiry—for example, anthropology, ethnology, and history of religions. These others are religious in two senses. In the first sense, the primitives form one of the most important bases of data for a non-theological understanding of religion in the post-Enlightenment West. In the second sense, the "primitives" define a vague "other;" their significance lies not in their own worth and value but in the significance this other offers to civilization when contrasted with it. The primitives operate as a negative structure of concreteness that allows civilization to define itself as a structure superior to this ill-defined and inferior "other."[3]

Blackness, therefore, has a density and concreteness that is proportional to historical description of contacts and exchanges that make it appear as a phenomenon. It is from this dark matter that black religion and black consciousness begins to appear in our description of the Atlantic World's ligaments and sinews. But blackness does not arise by itself. It is not inert. Blackness has intentionality as a form of consciousness and signifies a world view determined by and, as well, transcending its historical context.

> Religious experience is that mode of experience which apprehends and discovers the sacredness of the forms of the world...The symbol expresses the imaginative experience through which a new form of the world is discovered by the human consciousness. In this

experience the subject and the object are so inextricably interwoven that they seem identical.[4]

Blackness can become a mode of reflection on the temporal structures in which it appears. We are cautioned however against thinking we can gain access to this mode of being in the world through the epistemological categories generated by Enlightenment discourse because these are the very categories that signified blacks in the first place as the "empirical other." As V. I. Mudimbe points out, the naïve assumption that one has a privileged access to the black experience by virtue of being defined by that category is false. The understanding we are seeking must entail a hermeneutical method—"a form of the archaic critique, or, if you will, a kind of crawling back through the history that evoked these experiences."[5]

Contacts, Exchanges, and the African Gods

With regard to the role religion played in the aforementioned contacts and exchanges that constituted the Atlantic World, Bailyn observed that it "played a major role in forming and maintaining these networks." He went on to state:

> While we have long known of the elaborate structure of the Catholic Church in Spanish America—its far-flung parochial system and the subsystems of regular clergy which together penetrated into all the corners of the settled territories and linked them to the hierarchy of the metropolitan Church—we have not as clearly seen the Atlantic networks of the Protestant churches. They too, in different, more diverse ways, spread across and bound together elements of the Euro-American world.[6]

As we have already seen, however, the Euro-American world of which Bailyn speaks is one that has been brought into intimate contact with Africans and indigenous Americans. Our question then is how to study the African religious element within this context. At this point we need to discuss the African gods who reappear among slaves in the Americas.

A lot has already been written about this phenomenon—for example, Santeria in Cuba and Puerto Rico, *Macumba* and *Candomble* in Brazil, Voudu in Haiti, and so on—going back to Melville Herskovits's *The Myth of the Negro Past*. Current African American Theologians and Religious Scholars engaged in the interpretation of black religion have revisited the "Herskovits thesis." Unfortunately, in handling the data, many of these efforts by African American scholars to get back to Africa demonstrate a lack of methodological sophistication and historical depth. For the most part, too much is assumed, by way of interpretation, from the mere fact that one can make a correlation between the gods in Africa and those found among its Diaspora in the Americas. This never addresses the question as to the conditions within which the gods made their hierophany or appearance in Africa and the Americas. Not addressing this more difficult question results in a depiction of Traditional African Religions that is romantic, static, and a-historical.

Indeed, when we examine African Traditional Religions in historical depth, we see that their gods have always appeared within the historical framework characterized by the same thing we have already been discussing—contact and exchange. The gods of Traditional African Religions emerged out of the complex system of contacts and exchanges that occurred between various African groups. For instance, we must pay close attention to the role of blacksmiths as both religious specialists and traders, particularly, among the *Mande* speaking group in the Senegambia region of West Africa.[7] The conjunction between the role of blacksmith, trader, and religious specialist within the same person or lineage functioned not only to facilitate the spread of elite religious systems via migration, but also to make the migrating religious system subject, through contact and exchange, to profound metamorphosis. We see this taking place in the nineteenth century, at the height of the slave trade, with the *Agbala* of *Awaka* and *Ibini Okpube* (Long Juju) oracles of the Igbo. The *Agbala* oracle was spread by the *Awaka* blacksmiths who had migrated throughout Igbo territory and the Niger Delta. The *Aro* traders spread the influence of the oracle they presided over, the *Arochukwu*. In their middleman role as slave dealers, "*Aro* traders established settlements and markets throughout Igboland and used the utterances of the oracle to procure slaves."[8] This is one illustration of how the gods who accompanied Africans on the Middle Passage were already undergoing rapid and radical reinterpretation before and concomitant with the exchanges that made them slaves. The study of black religion should not conceive of African Religions in static cultural categories that are then contracted with the disruption of the Middle Passage. Even though the Middle Passage was something unimaginable and something that inflicted a radical experience of discontinuity on its victims, it—in and of itself—is not what initiated religious and cultural change among Africans. Religious change is inherent in the gradual evolution of West African society—the use of iron, the conquest of new stretches of forest land, expansion in the savannah belt, the rise of villager communities and towns—mastery of the rivers, lagoons and seas, all had their implications for Traditional Religion. So did the rise of empires, the pressures from Islam, and the contacts with European traders and missionaries. What is significant in the Middle Passage is the nature of its contacts and exchanges. These determined what was expedient to retain or abandon during Africans adaptation to their New World environments. This can be further illustrated in the following example.

In *Lemba, 1650–1930. A Drum of Affliction in Africa and the New World*, John M. Janzen says that within the Lemba cult "the exchange of material goods...should be considered under the same rubric as the "symbolic" exchanges...All goods, services, and symbols exchange hands within one and the same social matrix. There are not two economies, but rather a single social structure in which numerous media get exchanged to create or maintain statements of value."[9] Paralleling the *Lemba* cult was the *Gaan Tata* that made its appearance between 1880 and 1920 among the Bush Negro and Maroon tribes of Surinam and French Guiana. The Bush Negro and Maroon tribes played the role of middlemen in the river traffic necessitated by the discovery of gold in their areas of habitation. This introduced a lot of wealth among the Bush Negro and Maroon tribes that could have potentially polarized and stratified their society. "The *Gaan Tata* cult brought about an increased vigilance for a stronger morality, a more generalized, even universal, ethic, supported by a new and centralized high-God cosmology...the universalizing ethic...was the outcome of the cult's oracle to protect the entrepreneurs from kin envy...to establish anti-witchcraft standards of social life. Thirty to forty percent of goods received were channeled to kinsmen: another substantial portion was dumped at *Gaan Tata's* shrines. Only a minimal portion was 'used' by an elite."[10]

In studying the *Lemba*, Janzen is trying to work at a fundamental theoretical problem for Africanist. He wants to compare the preconditions for cult formation and change with those—that is, trade, economic surplus, human migration, warfare—which have been associated with state formation. "My concern," says Janzen, "is...with the apparent lack of discussion between those who study state formation and those who study cult cycles, and the failure of these persons to address the question of why such similar preconditions as both groups often consider give rise in the one case to a "state," and in the other to a "cult."[11]

Continuities and Discontinuities

Some phenomenological remarks need to be made regarding the observed continuities between African and African American religion in a way that allows for us to account for this continuity historically. African American religion exhibits the indelible characteristics of modalities found in West Africa. The intensity and density of these modalities, however, have been differentiated and mutated under the exigencies of the challenges Africans encountered in the Americas. How New World Africans met these challenges depended upon a number of variables and always entailed, to some degree or another, the creative employment of spiritual, psychic, and cultural strategies derived from their places of origin which, in turn, were pragmatically combined with extraneous elements so as to facilitate African's adaptation to the new environment. Achieving this presupposes a unity or similarity underlying the apparent diversity of cultures and regions from which the African Diaspora was drawn. In light of the devastating impact the Middle Passage had on its human cargo, this presupposition is required to account for the continuity of things African in the religious constitution of African Americans. On the other hand, the commonality of the new environment in which the African Diaspora found itself also helped to structure similarities into its religious constitution.

The early research of Melville Herskovits lends credence to this first presupposition. He argued that the coast of West Africa and its hinterland could be seen as a "culture area" or, at least, several very closely related "culture areas."[12] This culture area emerged through a long process of culture diffusion brought about through complex interethnic interactions involving migrations, conquests, state formations, trade networks, and so on. The problem with this notion of culture area, as subsequent anthropologists have noted, is that it has a tendency to connote a static entity. The criticism of John Thornton is pertinent here:

> All too often...specialists in the history of the Americas have not fully grasped the dynamic of pre-colonial African societies. Frequently they have studied African culture through the medium of modern anthropology rather than the careful study of contemporary documents.

> Because anthropologists' knowledge is based on fieldwork in contemporary <usually mid-twentieth-century> Africa...their statements about earlier times were based on theoretical presuppositions...that Africa did not change.[13]

We need, therefore, to guard against a static usage of the concept of culture area. Regarding the commonality of the New World environment, Charles Wagley applied the term "Plantation America" to the context that defined the social relations of the African Diaspora.[14] This culture sphere "extends spatially from about midway up the coast of Brazil into the Guianas...throughout the Caribbean...and into the United States." Linking the culture area of West Africa with that of Plantation America is the research of Bastide cited in Price. Focusing on Brazil, Bastide discovered that some New World expressions of ritual kinship originated not in the continent but, rather, were forged on the slave ship during the Middle Passage.[15] From this we might infer that Africans began to make a self-conscious discovery of their common cultural-religious identity during the Middle Passage and not, as is usually supposed, only after they arrived to the New World.

The above remarks, however, are not meant to imply that the study of African American religion should concern itself exclusively with the continuity of African cultural-religious traits or "survivals" in the New World—identifying their existence does little to explain the dynamism of African American religion. What is more relevant to this book is, in Smith's words, the elucidation of the process of "acculturation rather than the simple identification or attribution of elements."[16] Price, for example, concluded from his research on maroon societies that the important issue in the study of African American culture is the identification and description of "deep-level organizational principles" rather than individual traits. Deep-level organizational principles, according to Price, represent a more important mode of cultural continuity. Indeed, "one of the most striking features of West African cultural systems is their internal dynamism, their ability to grow and change." The success of Maroon societies rested on this "fidelity to 'African' principles on these deeper levels...rather than on the frequency of their isolated 'retentions.'"[17] We may also be justified in attributing the success of non-Maroon African American societies to their fidelity to the same principles.

Such fidelity, however, took more than one form, and a number of variables influenced the various forms it took. One of the most significant variables was demographic and had to do not just with the total African population in a given area but, more importantly, the ratio of blacks to whites and the intermediate class of free persons of color. Other variables were the colonial power's nationality and the manner by which it sought to impose its will on its colonies. Yet another variable was the religion dominant in any particular colony and the presence, or lack thereof, of agencies charged with the task of spreading the Gospel to slaves. Finally, another variable, which determined the number of slaves with immediate recollections of Africa, was the slave trade's longevity in a given colony.

Given the caveats stated earlier regarding religious change in Africa, we can safely make the following broad generalizations about the West African world view that can serve as a heuristic base line in determining continuities. What the New World survival of various African deities evidence is a particular religious orientation toward the world. In this orientation, material existence is seen to be permeated with life, energy, spirit, or force which, through proper combination of gestures and utterances, can be manipulated by those adept in the esoteric knowledge this feat requires. This force exists not only in nature but also in its active form in certain unique individuals. Although this force or power is potential present in all humans, priests, priestesses, diviners, mediums, and healers operated in African societies as specialists in the practice of techniques able to influence these forces for benevolent or malevolent purposes. Initiation into particular cults usually entailed an extensive period of apprenticeship of varying lengths depending on the cult. Spirit possession by particular gods occupied a central place in African religions. The experience was regarded as a type of death. Among the Fon in southern Dahomey and Togo female initiates are termed a *"Vodunsi"* from *Vodun we si* or *Vodun* (God) has killed his wife. How to bring about, maintain, and manipulate the phenomenon of possession is one of the most closely guarded secrets of African religious cults.[18] In Haiti the term *vodusi* becomes *"hu-si,"* in Guyana by the term *"asi,"* and in Cuba by the term *"hijos del santo."*[19] A hierarchy is structured into the cosmology of African societies. God occupies the apex of this hierarchy followed in turn by the lesser gods, ancestors, humans, animals, and nature that are all connected in a "chain of being," so to speak. The order of the cosmos is balanced through the dialectical interaction of the attributes of different forces. Among the Dahomeans, for example, the Godhead was conceived as a trinity: Vodu, *Mawu*-corresponding with the night, moon, west, female principle, earth-, and *Lisa*-corresponding with the day, sun, east, male principle, sky.[20] The *Mawu* cult "*correspond aux cults nago d'Olou, d'Oduwa ou Duduwa, d'Ajaguna*" and those of *Lisa* with *Obatala*, which is the androgynous divinity of "*la brujeria afrocubana.*"

Fa (*Ifa*), the idea of destiny or fate, was counterbalanced with Legba, a trickster figure who creates chaos and mischief. *Legba* (*Eshu, Elegbara*) can be seen as personifying the notion of chance or accident. He also functions in the role of messenger and, hence, sacrifices must be made first to him to appease the gods. Humans, however, must know their fate before deciding if it needs altering. This knowledge is acquired through the art of divination.

The complexity and metaphysical sophistication of African divination systems can be appreciated from Herskovits's description of the Dahomean practice: "The bokono employs sixteen palm-kernels and a carved rectangular board on which powdered white clay has been sprinkled. Holding these palm-kernel in his closed right hand, he brings this hand down on the palm of his outstretched left hand, and, quickly raising the hand with the kernel in it, leaves one or two seeds in the other. If one kernel remains, he makes a double mark on the powdered white clay, if two are left, he makes one mark. This operation is repeated sixteen times, there being, therefore, many possible combinations of these marks, each being termed a Du...sixteen principle ones each 'ruled' by the spiritual force or forces...as having an 'emissary'...The technique of the bokono, therefore, consists in knowing the several hundred mythologies associated with these principle and subsidiary Du, and interpreting each in the light of the Du identified with the destiny of the individual for whom Fa is being consulted."[21]

The origin of this practice is shrouded in mystery. According to one account, the technique originated at Ile-Ile and spread from there to the rest of Yorubaland and Dahomey. Shortly after the conquest of the plateau of Abomey, the kings of the *Aladaxonu* dynasty sold the indigenous *Djetovi* priests of the *Sagbata* gods, river gods, and gods of the silk-cotton trees into slavery. However, as the Sagbata cult could not be eliminated completely, King Agadja introduced the Fa divination system to delegitimate the indigenous *bokanto* diviners.[22]

From the earlier discussion, we can appreciate the complexity involved in describing both the continuities and discontinuities between the two locations where African gods are found—on the African continent and in the Americas. Interpreting the significance of African gods in the Americas must entail, among other things, some appreciation of how the gods first made their appearance in Africa and how their initial appearance underwent constant mutation. This cannot be done in a linear, evolutionary fashion or by merely moving from the African context to the African American context as so many have tried to do. For this reason, I have situated my analysis in the waters of the Atlantic World at the beginnings of modernity. From the contacts, exchanges, and imagined meanings that arise there in the Atlantic, we can move back and forth to examine the relationship between Spirituality and Materiality not only in Africa but, as well, in Europe and the Americas.

Therefore, from a functionalist perspective, African American religion facilitated the overcoming of these junctures and discontinuities through rituals and cultic practices whose rhythms, intonations, and utterances were multivalent in meaning. The multivalent significations of African American religion enabled it to structure and sustain the community's sanity by simultaneously evoking three realities into being: Africa, America, and the space in the Atlantic Ocean and the Americas where black bodies embodied the hyphenation between their places of origin and present location. This is the phenomenology behind African American religion's syncretism. *Shango*, for example, in Cuba, Puerto Rico, and Brazil, simultaneously or alternately represents the Yoruba deity and Saint Barbara; *Shango* also, however, rides his saints and speaks through them while they are possessed.[23] Of the thousands of other divinities known to Africans before their importation to the Americas, only a few were able to be recollected subsequent to the Middle Passage and the seasoning process in the New World. Roman Catholicism unwittingly facilitated in the survival of African belief systems due to the affinity between its saints and the divinities Africans recollected in the New World. In areas where Protestantism was the dominant religion conditions for such survivals were less favorable. We can conjecture that African divinities became identified, initially, with Old Testament figures in the United States, and finally, with Jesus. On the other hand, in places such as Cuba, Brazil, and Haiti the Roman Catholic saints referred to by the names of African deities and function according to those assigned roles or the African deities enjoy autonomous cultic provinces.

The appearance of African gods in the New World doesn't only represent a form of continuity. Their appearance is also a radical critique of the oppression Africans underwent and experienced as a form of discontinuity. Black religion exhibits a longing for what was lost, but it also exhibits an eschatological orientation toward something that will be attained in the future. The black body and black consciousness are both structured by this dialectic that gives rise to black religion. Black religion, as I argued elsewhere, oscillates between the poles of collective memory and hope, which might be viewed, respectively, as analogues to continuity and discontinuity.

Conclusion

Accounting for African American religion, therefore, entails much more than a mere description of how blacks were acted upon as the objects of Christian missions; it involves the narration of how African American religion was constituted in the midst of all the aforementioned historical forces that helped shape it and, in turn, were shaped by it. For had Africans not survived the horrors of the Middle Passage and slavery the colonies could not have prospered and, as Eric Williams asserted, the capital accumulation that formed the basis for the Industrial Revolution would have proven more difficult to amass. But African survival in the New World was due to more than the sturdiness of their physical stock; it was also due, in no small measure, to their capacity to live life "anyway, anyhow" with a sense of transcendent meaning in the meager, ordinary data of experience. African Americans derived this capacity from religious sources. Though religiously derived meanings facilitated black survival and, in so doing, the exploitation of their labor as well, African American's religion did not legitimate their oppression and functioned, alternately, as a vehicle for both adaptation and resistance to the slave regime. Yet, whether adapting, resisting, or doing both simultaneously, in African American religion was envisioned a freedom not lodged in property, or persons as property, or property as persons—formal, civic freedom—but something else derived from the inarticulate sensibility of those incarcerated in the realm of unfreedom. In Britain's former North American colonies slave's sang songs that certainly had counterparts in the Caribbean and Latin America: "0 Freedom!...And before I'll be a slave, I'll be buried in my grave and go home to my Lord and be free."

2

The Age of Discovery and the Emergence of the Atlantic World

The beginnings of the study of religion as an academic discipline must be seen in light of the beginnings of modern globalization and its origins in the formation of the Atlantic world. Religion from this perspective no longer defines an intimacy of meaning but is objectified in time, space, and cultural ideology in various modes of distantiation.[1]

—Charles H. Long

Introduction

In this chapter, I will be constructing a framework for viewing the simultaneity of: (1) Roman Catholic Reform, the Protestant Reformation, and the Counter Reformation in Europe; (2) European global expansion through the Atlantic Ocean; (3) decimation and colonization of indigenous Americans; and (4) the enslavement of African during the "long sixteenth century." This, I assert, is the preferred site for studying religion in the modern period as distinct from more typical approaches to the subject that treat these occurrences sequentially and independently. In so doing the false impression is conveyed that these historical happenings are incidental to one another with the consequent incomprehension of how modernity is comprised of their simultaneous interactions

The Sinews of the Atlantic World

We need not discover new facts to write a different kind of religious history in the modern period. All is required is for us to decide where the story properly begins and then to rearrange the component parts constituting the conventional narrative. Once this is done the narrative as a whole will suffer fragmentation at many points and indicate the places where different stories can to be told. Church history textbooks generally follow the convention of using the Protestant Reformation as the event demarcating the transition from the medieval to the modern period in world history. The Protestant Reformation that began with Luther's nailing of his Ninety-five Theses against church abuses on the door of the cathedral at Wittenberg certainly can be privileged as the date that instigated a series of interrelated events resulting in the Roman Catholicism's loss of hegemony in Western Europe vis-à-vis princes, newly developing nation states, and economic agents of change. However, Europe's history during this period of what Ferdinand Braudel termed the "long sixteenth century" was not unfolding solely within the confines of its own territory but also in other hitherto unknown parts of the world. The events that were occurring in other parts of the world outside of Europe proper are as important in understanding how what we term the "Modern Period" unfolded as those that occurred within Europe. Indeed, those newly formed nation states that were most successful in becoming autonomous entities were those that entered the Atlantic and acquired colonies that bolstered their mercantilist economies. After Spain and Portugal's initial success at conquest and colonization of distant lands and peoples, England, France, and the Netherlands followed suite in fierce competition with one another in exercising control over commerce and colonies. European conquest and colonization of non-Europeans in other parts of the world is not just a part of its political/economic history but its religious history as well. The wars of religion in Europe are connected with the wars fought over colonies outside of Europe. Religious identity—either Roman Catholic, Eastern Orthodox, Lutheran, Calvinist, or Anglican—was involved in the development of national identities that in turn legitimated the colonialist projects of European nations by linking colonization and evangelization.

The present state of the world cannot be fully comprehended if these connections are seen as only incidental. The critique of modernity must consider the fact that the ages of religious reform and intellectual Enlightenment were also—and not just incidentally—ages of colonization, slavery, and insipient religious warfare. So too, technological and scientific innovation was in no small measure stimulated by the necessity of European states to find better, more efficient ways to defend themselves and/or kill their enemies. Wars had to be financed. The relation between warfare, finance, and commercial innovation was a key component in the modernization process that gave Europe a decided advantage over other parts of the world.[2] If, in light of these observations, we chose to Martin Luther as our initial focal point in studying World Christianity in the modern period we will have a very difficult time explaining what exactly makes the period modern in comparison with the preceding Medieval Period. So too, we will find it very difficult to explain how something we are terming the "world" makes its appearance. On the other hand, if we privilege the Age of Discovery as our initial focal point in studying World Christianity in the modern period we are able to see it as what occasions the appearance of the "world" and, as well, "modernity" which both serve as the broader context in which Roman Catholic Reform and the Protestant Reformation were dialectical components. We then begin to discern how those structures—epistemological as well as political and economic—emerged that now defines the reality we term alternately "global" and "modern." Such discernment will make us aware of continuities as well as discontinuities between the past and the present.

It is quite amazing, however, to encounter so many Church History textbooks that treat the Age of Discovery as only incidentally related to that of narrating the history of Christianity. These textbooks move from Martin Luther to Zwingli to Calvin and then to The English Reformation before crossing the Atlantic with the Puritans. Then the First Great Awakening is described sometimes in relation to the Pietistic Movement in Germany and sometimes not. This is sort of narrative structure hardly qualifies as World Christianity because there is no world per se. There is only the fiction of one branch of Christianity existing as a coherent organism. But in this narrative structure there is no Africa. There is no Caribbean. There is no South America. There is no India. There is no China. There is no Japan. There is no Korea. There are no Africans in the British colonies. The other peoples are out there somewhere but will be encountered much later—incidentally. Their presence does not constitute one of modernity's defining features and, therefore, Europeans and Euro-Americans discern no need to ponder the nature of their encounters with these peoples in understanding themselves. They are already understood negatively through the Christian epistemological category that justified their being conquered and colonized or instigates them being uplifted. But this is getting too far ahead of us.

If we think along these lines it is not difficult to see that although it is difficult to move from Luther's nailing of his Ninety-five Theses to the cathedral door at Wittenberg in the early sixteenth century to events in the Caribbean in the same century, it is easy to move from the Caribbean back in the other direction. Eric Williams pointed out in his *From Columbus to Castro: The History of the Caribbean*:

> Spain, lord of the New World monopoly, was the center of the Counter-Reformation in Europe. Spain's wealth from the Indies represented the mainstay of Catholic strength in Europe. Spain's armies and Spain's hegemony in Europe were financed by Spain's mines and trade in the Caribbean and America. It became, therefore, a matter of vital policy for the Protestant powers to sap Spain's strength and drain Spanish resources by diversionary expeditions over the ocean...The battlefield of the Wars of Religion was not only Germany but also the Caribbean.[3] (p. 78)

Spain was by no means the only European state that exploited the resources of the New World. Portuguese, French, Dutch, and English would also become what came to termed "maritime powers" by acquiring the sufficient naval, military, and financial institutions to extract their share of the wealth that was to be gained from participating in what had become an international economy. The underlying question Europe's theologians, jurists, and political economist sought answers to was how to legitimate the most ideal relationship between the king, aristocrats, nobles, clergy, and the like for assuring the greatest accrual of wealth to one's "nation." The legitimation came first in the form of papal bulls and further legitimations followed later in the form of various political theories elaborated by Hobbs, Locke, and others.

bull Inter caetera divinae and Patranado Real

The Portuguese and Spanish ventures into the Atlantic were motivated by a number of related factors. The Ottomans had captured Constantinople in 1453 making them even more dangerous a threat to European ships sailing in the Mediterranean to purchase silks, spices from India and China from Venetian and Genoese merchants who operated as middlemen. Europe's gold supply originated in the area called Guinea in West Africa and reached Europe through trans-Sahara trade routes. Prince Henry the Navigator (1394–1460) sought a way to reach African gold supplies and India and China via the sea to bypass the Muslim middlemen and the Venetian and Genoese merchants who controlled the land routes to the East. New navigation techniques and methods of ship design allowed the Portuguese to push further and further down the African coast beginning in the early fifteenth century. The Portuguese conquered Ceuta in 1415. By 1419, they had reached the Madeira Islands and from there they advanced into the Azores between 1427 and 1431. In 1433, Gil Eannes sailed beyond Cape Bojador. As the Portuguese sailed down the western African coast they established trading posts and began to trade in gold dust and African slaves even though there was only a slight demand for the latter. One of the forts, Sao Jorge da Mina, was built in 1482. The gold obtained from Africa allowed Portugal to mint its first gold coin—the crusado—in the 1440s. By 1460, they had reached Guinea and in 1472 they were able to cross the equator. Bartolomeu Dias (1450–1500) reached the Cape of Good Hope in 1487. Vasco da Gama (1460–1524) reached Calicut on May 22, 1498. His trip yielded a profit of more than sixty times the value of the goods exchanged by the Portuguese. Upon his return to Portugal, Vasco da Gama was proclaimed "Lord of the Conquest, Navigation and Commerce of Arabia, Persia, and India" by King Manuel II. He indeed lived up to this title by ravaging, burning, and pillaging whatever villages offered any signs of resistance to Portuguese control over the spice trade. From their Indian bases the Portuguese continued eastward. Alfonso de Albuquerque established the capital of Portuguese operations in Goa between 1509 and 1511. In 1509 also they reached the Straits of Malacca, Amboina, and the Spice Islands. Jorge Alvarez reached Canton in 1513. In 1556, the trading operation at Macao was established.

Portugal's neighbor, Spain, was preoccupied with expelling the Moors from their last stronghold in Grenada during the last part of the fifteenth century. However, on the same eve of Ferdinand and Isabella's victory over the Moors they entered into an agreement with Christopher Columbus to finance his attempt to reach the Indies by sailing west across the Atlantic. He set sail on August 3, 1492 with three ships and ninety sailors. Columbus reached Barbados on October 12, then Cuba, and then Hispaniola (modern Haiti and Dominican Republic). Columbus made three journeys in total. Upon Columbus's return from his first voyage, conflict arose between Portugal and Spain over the latter's claim to the lands he discovered. Conflict had already arisen between the two nations over their mutual claims to the Canary Islands that had been discovered by Genoese sailors in the early fifteenth century. Spain tried unsuccessfully to settle the matter by sending an expedition in 1478. In 1479 the treaty that ended the war between Spain and Portugal recognized Spain's claim to the Canaries in return for its recognition of Portugal's right to the kingdom of Fez, Madeira, and the Azores. It was not until 1482 that Ferdinand and Isabella succeeded in establishing control of the Canaries that would later serve as a staging point for their American ventures. It was Ferdinand and Isabella's practice during both the Reconquista and the settlement of the Canaries to make contracts, called "capitulations," with leaders of military expeditions defining how spoils were to be divided, conquered lands settled, and titles awarded to leaders of military expeditions as "Mercedes" or reward for services rendered. Ferdinand and Isabella's care in preserving their rights as sovereigns over new territories illustrated in its agreement with Columbus. But this "capitulation" had to rest upon some foundation. That foundation took the form of papal bulls that need to be situated within the context of Ferdinand and Isabella's strategy for exercising control over ecclesial benefices to appreciate their importance.

If Ferdinand and Isabella were to consolidate their political control over Spain, they could not allow the church's power to operate autonomous to their own. Although the practice was in place for them to nominate lesser benefices, the crown had to compete with the Cathedral Chapter and the pope when it came to the more important benefices. To challenge direct papal appointments Ferdinand and Isabella summoned an ecclesiastical council at Seville in 1478 to define Spain's position and intercede with the pope. When the see at Cuenca became vacant in 1479, the monarchs used this opportunity to insist on their royal prerogatives and Pope Sixtus IV was forced to capitulate in this instance. The matter was settled formally in 1482. As the Reconquista was nearing completion, Ferdinand and Isabella were in a good position to press their claims in this matter once again. They pressed for royal patronage over all the churches to be established in the reconquered areas of Grenada. Pope Innocent VIII who needed Ferdinand's help in pursuing the church's ambitions in Italy extended royal patronage to Spain over churches established in Grenada in a papal bull of December 13, 1486. This was monumental in that nothing of this nature existed on the European continent outside of Grenada and set the precedent and model for any churches that were to be established in the New World. In capitalizing on the similarity between the land recovered in the Reconquista and those discovered in the New World, the Spanish monarchs were able to obtain royal patronage over all churches in the Americas from Pope Alexander VI in the bull Inter caetera divinae.[4] Thus, this and similar papal bulls must be understood to have had ramifications not only pertaining to political control of territories in the Americas but also to ecclesiastical control of church appointments in Spain as well as the Americas. This helps explain why the pope was sought to adjudicate the competing claims of Portugal and Spain over their territorial discoveries—both countries were seeking not only to legitimate their claims to new territories but to acquire royal patronage as well to strengthen their political authority.

Potential conflict between Portugal and Spain over their so-called discovered lands was adjudicated and legitimated through a series of papal bulls—Treaty of Alcacovas (March 6, 1480); Inter caetera divinae (May 4, 1493); Dudum siquidem (1493); Treaty of Tordesillas (June 7, 1494) which endowed Spain with the same rights in the Americas enjoyed by Portugal in Africa and Asia. These later bulls were structured after the pattern of earlier ones which legitimated Portuguese claims along the western coast of Africa among which were: Dudum cum nos (1436) and Rex Regum (1443); Divino amore communiti (1452) and Rex Pontifex (1455); Inter caetera (1456); and Aeterni Regis (1481) of Eugene IV, Nicolas V, Callistus III, and Sixtus IV, respectively. Through these aforementioned bulls, Portugal gained the "right" to title of ownership of any territories it discovered and occupied, to make ecclesial appointments in those lands, collect tithes, propagate Christianity, and enslave the indigenous peoples inhabiting the newly discovered territories. Bull Inter caetera divinae clearly links Spain's claim to territories in the Americas with the reconquista completed in 1492.

> Alexander, Bishop, servant of the servants of God, to our beloved son in Christ, King Fernando, and to our beloved daughter in Christ, Isabel, Queen of Castilla, Leon, Aragon, Sicilia, and Grenada, greetings and apostolic blessings...understanding you to be true Catholic Sovereigns and Princes...as your expeditions restoring the kingdom of Grenada from the tyranny of the Saracens do plainly declare...We are informed that lately you were determined to seek and find certain isles and mainlands remote and unknown (and not heretofore found by any other) with the intention of bringing their inhabitants to honor our Redeemer and to profess the Catholic faith...we exhort...to bring the people of said mainlands and isles to the Christian religion...And that being authorized...we...do give, grant, and assign to you, your

heirs and successors, all the mainlands and isles found or to be found, discovered or to be discovered...all those lands and islands, with their dominions, territories, cities, castles, other places, and villages with all the rights and jurisdictions and all their belongings to you, your heirs and successors to be lords with full and free power, authority, and jurisdiction.

From a global standpoint, this is the most important document of the long sixteenth century. It links Christianization and colonization as no previous document had previously done and enshrines the ideological underpinning of Spain's New World conquests. "The Christian religion," in other words, "becomes the official ideology for imperial expansion."[5] This bull also provoked Spain's main Protestant rival England to seek to found its imperial ambitions on another basis. Therefore, we should be more specific and say, Inter caetera divinae served as the official Roman Catholic ideology for Spain's imperial expansion since Protestant England would contest Spain's understanding of its divine mission. Queen Elizabeth I stated that she "could not be convinced that [the Indies] were legitimately owned by Spain by decree of the pope of Rome, in whom I do not recognize any prerogatives in such matters, much less that he can oblige Princes who do not owe him any obedience."[6] For Elizabeth and other's who came after her "England's...providential role was to defend the achievements of the Reformation and to oppose the power of Spain, which was identified as the bulwark of papist superstition, both in Europe and beyond."[7] Of course, the wars of religion in Europe and their extensions into the Atlantic were not strictly determined by Roman Catholic/Protestant division. King Francis I of France, where Roman Catholicism was also the official religion, also questioned Spain's divine mission as articulated in the above mention papal bull when he commented in 1540: "The sun shines for me as it does others...I would be pleased to see the clause in Adam's testament that excludes me from a share in the globe."[8] Along with the Dutch conversion to Protestantism during their rupture from Spanish hegemony came the entry of their sailing vessels in the Mediterranean and Caribbean waters at an increasing rate between the late sixteenth and mid-seventeenth centuries. It would take some years before European colonialism could be founded upon a mutually agreed basis of "International Law" principles. Europe is still at a loss to articulate a self evident rationale for dominion over lands that are already occupied.

Theological Excursus

The West's Christology was implicated in these historical developments because it was forced to address the issue of whether the Indios were fully human when certain friars such as Fray Antonio de Montesinos asked in 1511: "Are they not men?" A full-fledge debate on this question occurred in 1550 between Las Casas and Sepulveda. The same question was pondered among Protestants as they applied higher critical tools to the creation account in Genesis. Roman Catholic tried to understand their relationship to the Indian and African other within the framework of Thomistic Theology. Protestants had to figure thing out within a biblical framework because it was the Bible that allowed Protestants to break with Roman Catholicism and its secular supporters such as Spain. One biblical scholar contends that race "started out as a theological problem in the early modern period" when Protestants debated the contending theories of monogenesis and polygenesis.[9] However, the main divisive theological controversy between Protestants and Roman Catholics and within their respective ranks had to do with soteriology rather than Christology in the form of the Armenian controversy among Protestants and Jansenism among Roman Catholics. Both Protestants and their Roman Catholics counter parts in the Old and New Worlds were oblivious to the relationship between the issue of Christ's humanity articulated in the Caledonian Creed and the question regarding the humanity of Indios and African being articulated negatively through their colonization and enslavement. Had Protestants embraced the Armenian position that allowed for the will's participation in the reception of God's grace and Roman Catholics embraced the Jansenist position regarding the irresistibility of God's grace, the two branches of the church might have been able to establish a theological basis for reconciliation. However, for indigenous Americans and Africans God's grace was being imposed through the structures of their colonization and enslavement. Thus, we arrive at the appalling notion of God's Providence operated through human oppression. This notion could not be stated so plainly and therefore had to be repressed until it could be articulated in Adam Smith's theory of political-economy and later Hegel's theory of history—both secularized versions of Calvin's theology of Divine Providence.

As we shall see Amerindians and enslaved Africans were readily able to articulate their own notions of how the divine economy should function via their petitions, religious expressions, and rebellions that occurred up until and beyond their formal emancipation.

Portuguese and Spanish Occupations and Missions

The religious or theological issue involved in the expansion of Europeans into the Atlantic pertained not only to the legitimization of its territorial claims but also to its treatment of the peoples it encountered in the newly appropriated and settled land. As stated earlier, evangelization was one of the stated purposes for European expansion. The nature of European encounters with non-Europeans during the long sixteenth century established enduring social patterns and epistemological structures that still persist in modernity—namely, the idea of European superiority. The Spanish Historian Joseph Fontana wrote:

> All people define themselves by looking in the mirror of "the others"... But this, so simple for communities that speak the same language and share lifestyle and customs, was not so simple for Europeans, especially after the sixteenth century, when religious unity had been broken and literary use of the various tongues was on the increase. The Treaty of Utrecht in 1714 was the last European document to be drawn up in terms of the republica Christiana. This now plural people looked at itself from this moment in a more complex set of mirrors in order to make out what identifying marks it had within its diversity... The new way in which Europeans thought about themselves was born out of an awareness that no longer had to do with religion, but was based on a belief in moral and intellectual superiority. The new term of reference on which this image was elaborated was that of the inferior nature of non-Europeans. Yet the mirror they looked into when seeking to define themselves had two surfaces. In one of them racial differences were seen and the savage showed his face; in the other, reflecting a Eurocentric view of history, the primitive was displayed. Out of the first there emerged genocide and the slave trade; out of the second imperialism.[10]

At each place where Europeans landed in their voyages, they formed certain attitudes that defined their self-understanding vis-à-vis the non-European "Other." These attitudes were not based on objective observations of those they encountered but were determined by the nonreciprocal nature of those primal encounters. In short, the people who served as the objects of European colonization and Christianization were deemed inferior to their benefactors. Thus, non-Europeans had not only to be Christianized but "civilized" as well to receive and enjoy the benefits of the Gospel. This was the underlying logic of bull Inter caetera divinae that linked conquest and Christianization. Since non-Europeans lacked the sense to know they needed the Gospel, they needed to be subdued for their own benefit. The means Portuguese, Spanish, English, and Dutch missionaries employed to this end varied. In the Americas "reducciones" was the model for Christianizing the indigenous peoples; slavery was the model for Christianizing peoples taken from Africa. In Asia the model differed in India, China, Japan, and Korea depending upon the existence and viability of local polities and whether how closely missionary endeavors were associated with western military might. In the Americas, the patranado made it impossible for Christian missions to operate independent of the state's administrative structures. Franciscans and other mendicant orders therefore found themselves having to work within Spain's imperialist framework even when advocating for humane treatment of their Indian charges.

The bases and routes established by Portuguese explorers and merchants were used by missionaries in their endeavors. The Portuguese made a number of half hearted and unsuccessful attempts to introduce Christianity to the various ethnic groups and polities it interacted from its thirty forts established by the mid-eighteenth century along the west coast of Africa. The Kongo Kingdom was the exception. The Portuguese reached the Kongo in 1483. Mbemba Nzinga or King Alfonso became king in 1506 and ruled the Kongo until his death in 1543. Christianity became the states official cult and would have thrived as an indigenous form of Christianity had it not been for the slave trade that disrupted the economic and political stability of the kingdom. In 1500 the Portuguese crossed the Atlantic and reached Brazil that due to its protrusion beyond the longitudinal line separating Portuguese from English territories could be legitimately claimed and occupied by Portugal.

In Asia the most famous Portuguese missionary was Francis Xavier (1506–1562). He left Rome for the East in 1541 at the invitation of King John III. Portuguese missions were legitimated and organized according to the "padroado" that was stipulated in a series of papal bulls and briefs promulgated between 1452 and 1514. As discussed earlier, the padroado gave the crown the right to appoint all benefices in its territories in exchange for financial support. At his death in 1552 he had baptized 700, 000 in his work among the natives of Goa, Travancore, and Malacca. Xavier had also traveled to Japan. When he died on the island of Chang-Chuen, he was hoping to extend his missionary work to China.

Hispaniola was fully under Spain's control by 1508. Santo Domingo was one of Spain's first colonies in the New World and used as a base for explorations into Florida, Mexico, Panama, Yucatan, Guatemala, and Nicaragua. Santiago de Cuba was founded in 1514 and Havana in 1519. 1519 is also the year that Hernan Cortes (1485–1547) set sail from Cuba with 600 soldiers to conquer the Aztec Empire. In 1533 Francisco Pizarro (1470–1541) conquered the Inca Empire in Peru. In 1513 Vasco Nunez de Balboa (1475–1517) reached the Pacific Ocean by crossing the Isthmus of Panama. Ferdinand Magellan (1480–1521) set out to reach the Indies by sailing around the southern tip of South America. He died in skirmishes with indigenous peoples in the Philippines but the surviving 15 out of 280 sailors were able to return to Spain.

In the Americas, the crown deliberately prevented the conquistadors from obtaining direct control of land and Indian labor by declaring that the Indios were also its subjects. Land was issued only on the crowns terms through the mechanism of temporary grants called the "encomienda." The encomienda assigned to a recipient specified amounts of tribute and labor from the Indios in return for their Christianization. The crown sought to create in the Americas a two-tiered segregated society of encomienderos and Indios with Spanish officials serving as the buffer between these two groups. The crown abolished Indian slavery in 1542 to strengthen their policy designed to maintain settler dependence on the crown for Indian labor. This prohibition was not carried out in practice in a number of areas where Spanish authority was weak and caused conflict between the encomienderos and the Franciscan, Dominican, and Jesuits who sought the welfare of the Indios. No such prohibition applied to Africans who were imported in increasing numbers to augment the declining native population at a rate that is stupefying.

Demographics

Determining exact numbers of deaths of indigenous Americans through European conquest and colonization and Africans through the slave trade is impossible to determine due to the lack of exact statistical records to substantiate the estimates of what we could label the "high counters" and the "low counters." Politically speaking, the higher the count the greater the blame and shame accruing to Europe; the lower the count, the lower the blame and shame. I am choosing to err in the more conservative direction because beyond a certain threshold the returns in adding numbers diminish—the magnitude of the horror and extent of human genocide is not increased because it has already even in the conservative estimates reached absolute proportions. Therefore I will not engage in a long argument to rationalize these numbers. An estimated 25 million people and 6 million people comprised pre-Hispanic Mesoamerica and the Inca Empire respectively. Some give much higher figures totaling 80–100 million. After one century of European colonization the indigenous population had declined to 10 million.[11] By 1650 the Mesoamerican area's population had declined to 1.6 million people and the Inca area's population in the Andes had declined less than 300,000 by the late eighteenth century![12] In 1492 Hispaniola's population was between 200,000 and 300,000. It declined to 60,000 in 1508; then to 46,000 in 1510; then to 20,000 in 1512; and then to 14,000 in 1514. By 1548 only two Indian villages remained.[13]

The number of Africans transported to the Americas on slave ships is conservatively estimated to be anywhere from 12 to 20 million. The mortality rate of those placed on Portuguese, Dutch, and British slave ships averaged between 20 and 25 percent. To this number, we must calculate the number of Africans who never boarded the slave ships because they died during the violence entailed in their capture or thereafter during the travail of their march to the Atlantic coast. We arrive at a number far exceeding 6 million—the benchmark quantitative figure for measuring human atrocity based on estimates of deaths during the Jewish Holocaust.

English Occupations in the Caribbean and North America

The Americas were regarded as a sacred space for the unfolding of God's design for the English as well as the Spanish. Hakluyt, Purchas, and other theorist wrote to refute Spain's claim to "dominium" based on papal bull and to found English prerogatives in the Americas on a different basis.[14] In 1702 Cotton Mather reflected in his *Magnalia Christi Americana*, "The overruling Providence of the great God is to be acknowledged, as well in the concealing of America for so long a time, as in the discovering of it, when the fullness of time was come for the discovery." Mather thought that God had prevented the discovery of North America until the Protestant Reformation had taken place. This was what he meant by the fullness of time whose arrival meant that "the Church of God must no longer be wrapped up in Strabo's cloak; Geography must now find work for a Christiano-graphy in regions far enough beyond the bounds wherein the Church of God had, through all former times been circumscribed."[15]

As England engaged in economic and military conflict with Spain, its merchants were emboldened to interfere with Spanish trade routes. These merchants had been advocating raiding since the 1530s early on in the English Reformation. It, however, was not until the 1560s that piracy became an instrument of state policy.[16] In the 1560s, Sir John Hawkins produced extraordinary returns to investors by smuggling slaves to Haiti. Sir Francis Drake realized a return of more than 4,500 percent in his 1577–1580 voyage to the Americas.[17] The success of such raiding expeditions sparked interest in establishing colonies for the purpose of serving as bases for the expansion of similar expeditions. This was the purpose of Sir Walter Raleigh's royal charter and the failed Roanoke settlement.

Eventually, however, the model for English economic ventures in the Americas would be one of permanent settlement rather than raiding. Virginia was provided with an export crop when John Rolfe successfully cured tobacco around 1612–1613. This crop and cotton were also produced in England's Caribbean colonies. England's colonial strategy was also influenced by its colonization of Ireland. Indeed, its treatment of the Irish was patterned on Spain's treatment of the Indios. The British viewed the Irish in the same subhuman categories. Such persons as Sir Walter Raleigh and Humphrey Gilbert "used their Irish experiences to confirm their assumptions of savagism, paganism, and barbarism and applied these" to the peoples they encountered in the Americas.[18]

A sudden rise in demand for sugar in the 1640s led to a thorough reorganization of the economic focus in Barbados and the Leeward Island referred to as the Sugar Revolution. England's Caribbean islands became the "hub of empire."[19] The sugar trade was inextricably linked to the slave trade. Both the sugar trade and the slave trade were integral components of a wider set of trading patterns that became known in the eighteenth century as the triangular trade. The simple pattern was that New England merchants would sail to the coast of Africa with simple manufactured goods that were exchanged for slaves. The slaves would be transported to the Caribbean and traded for rum and molasses that was sold in North America. Another pattern was New Englanders would export flour, meat, and other staples to the Caribbean in exchange for sugar. They would then transport the sugar to England in exchange for manufactured goods. The triangular trade actually consisted of different combinations of these two basic patterns. At any event, the English relied more and more on slave labor to meet the labor shortage created by tobacco, cotton, and, especially, sugar production. By the 1700s, most British merchants and colonists regarded the trade in slaves to be the very life of the colonies.[20] The British mercantilist writing in defense of the Royal Africa Company's interests wrote, "the Negroe-Trade and the natural consequences resulting from it, may be justly esteemed an inexhaustible Fund of Wealth and Naval Power to this nation." According to him the slave trade was "the first principle and foundation of all the rest, the mainspring of the machine which sets every wheel in motion."[21] Such eminent a churchman as Evangelist George Whitefield shared this opinion. He commented, in opposing the section in Georgia's charter that prohibited slavery, that "it is plain to demonstration that hot countries cannot be cultivated without Negroes."[22]

About a quarter of Virginia's planters were slaveholders in 1720; by 1770 the percentage had increased to 50 percent. The south's slave population at the time of the American War of Independence was one-third of the overall population. Barbados had 5,680 slaves in 1645 when it was first shifting to sugar production; in 1698 it had 42,000 slaves! Jamaica had only 1,410 slaves in 1656; by 1698 it had 41,000 slaves![23] In the Caribbean climate and the intensity of sugar production reduced the slave's life expectancy to approximately seven years.[24] Planters needed therefore to import new supplies of slaves from Africa just to maintain existing levels. In 1688 the number of slaves that needed to be imported to maintain existing supplies was 10,000 for Jamaica, 6,000 for the Leewards, and 4,000 for Barbados.[25] *What this description indicates is that African people's first contact with Protestants was a purely accidental by-product of their incorporation into an expanding Euro-American economy through enslavement.*

Reformed Protestants had no theory or practice of foreign mission in the sixteenth century when their first contacts with Africans were being made. Thus, the political economy in which Reformed Christians were involved seriously interfered with their proper understanding of the Divine Economy. By the time Reformed Protestants began to introduce the Gospel to blacks the political structure in which they were situated had already constructed laws that limited the effect that the Gospel could have on black converts other than reinforcing their servile status. The Virginia colony passed a law as early as 1667 stipulating, "Baptisme doth not alter the condition of the person as to his bondage or freedom."[26] Other colonies rapidly followed suit. In New England the staunch Calvinist Cotton Mather asked rhetorically "What law is it that sets the baptized slave at liberty?" He answered that "the law of Christianity" does no such thing.[27] To insure that the slaves understood the limited scope of baptism, the Anglican missionary for the Society for the Propagation of the Gospel in Foreign Parts Francis Le Jau required blacks seeking baptism to answer affirmatively to the oath: "You declare in the presence of God and before this congregation that you do not ask for the Holy Baptism out of any desire to free yourself from the duty and obedience you owe your master while you live; but merely for the good of your soul and to partake of the grace and blessings promised to the members of the church of Christ."[28] Whether you were black and Reformed or black and Anglican or black and Roman Catholic you were still a slave. All of them offered the same enticement: continued bondage on earth and eternal life in heaven. Luckily the slaves were able to engage in independent theological reflection on their own condition and not rely on their master's heretical notions regarding their humanity and place in the social structure.

French Occupations and Missions

The French explored North America in search for a northwest passage. Giovanni da Verrazano (1485–1528) sailed under the French flag in 1524 along the coast of North America from Florida to New York. Jacques Cartier reached Newfoundland, the Bay of Fundy, Labrador, and La Chine Rapids via the St. Lawrence River. Samuel de Champlain (1567–1635) founded a trading post at Quebec in 1608 and became Canada's first governor. His explorations were followed up by the Jesuit missionary Jacques Marquette and Louis Joliet. Marquette and Joliet traveled the Great Lakes, the Wisconsin River valley, and as far south as the mouth of the Arkansas River. Robert Cavelier and Sieur de la Salle (1643–87) reached the Gulf of Mexico in 1682. France's territories thus extended from the St. Lawrence River through the Great Lakes Region then down the Mississippi River to the Gulf of Mexico. Quebec, Three Rivers, and Montreal served as major shipping ports where goods from France were imported and furs were exported to France and elsewhere in Europe. The French got along well with the Huron and other Indian politico with the exception of the Iroquois with whom the Dutch and later the British were in alliance. The most valuable of France's New World colonies was St. Dominique (formerly Hispaniola) which it acquired in 1697 by the Treaty of Ryswick.

The progress of Saint-Dominique from 1783 (the year of the independence of the United States of America) to 1789 (the year of the outbreak of the French Revolution) is one of the most astonishing phenomena in the history of imperialism. Its exports in 1788 amounted to 31,350 tons of clayed sugar, 41,607 tons of brown sugar, 2,806 tons of cotton, 30,425 tons of coffee, 415 tons of indigo; the value amounted to 193 million livres or nearly eighty million pounds of sterling. The colony contained 800 sugar plantations, 3,000 coffee, nearly 800 cotton, and 2,950 indigo. Saint-Dominique supplied half of Europe with tropical produce. Its exports were one-third more than those of all the British West Indies combined; its commerce employed 1,000 ships and 15,000 French sailors. Saint-Dominique was the world's premier sugar producer, the gem of the Caribbean.[29]

The Kongo

Dutch strength was founded upon three bases: its merchant fleet, its Bank of Amsterdam, and the Dutch East India Company formed in 1602. Of the total of 25,000 ships sailing between Europe and the Caribbean and other parts of the world in the mid-seventeenth century, 15,000 were owned by the Dutch. In 1614 the Dutch fleet employed more sailors than Spain, France, England, and Scotland's combined! Amsterdam served as the Wall Street of the world. It imported from the East 66 percent of all pepper and spices between 1648 and 1650 and 55 percent of all textiles between 1698 and 1700; developed sugar cane cultivation in Java; and traded slaves in Africa as well as the rest of Europe.

Holland became the intellectual and cultural capital of the world. Grotius in international law; Descartes...and Spinoza in philosophy; Christian Huygens in science; his father in poetry; Rembrandt, Hals, Vermeer, van Ruysdael and Steen in painting...The symbol of this intellectual hegemony over Europe was the University of Leyden; two of its prime bases were the triangular trade and the trade with the Caribbean sugar colonies.[30]

The disruptions and shocks inherent in the nature of the afore-mentioned contacts and exchanges had profound and far-reaching religious consequences for all parties. Apocalyptic forms of religion appeared throughout the Atlantic World. One of the most dramatic forms of apocalyptic religion was associated with a woman known as Dona Beatrice Kimpa in the Kongo Kingdom. She led a movement in 1704 aimed at expelling the Portuguese from the area. Thus, she is regarded by some Africanists as the mother of African Independence. However, we should not ignore the religious content of Dona Beatrice Kimpa's political movement. She could also very well be regarded as the mother of black theology. Christianity had become the official state cult in the early sixteenth century and had spread among the local populace through the encouragement of King Alphonse and subsequent Kongo rulers. The alliance between Kongo rulers and the Portuguese allowed Christianity to spread primarily through the missionary efforts of the Capuchins. The demise of native populations in the Americas and the transfer of techniques of sugar cultivation from San Tome made the transportation of Africans economically feasible. However, the intensification of slave trade increased the economic power and independence of the Afro-Portuguese traders operating on the coast and the Kongo interior. Attempts by Kongo rulers to suppress the slave trade exacerbated already existing social conflicts and resulted in the Portuguese arming Angola to the south to supply this demand. These developments eventuated in a civil war between two contenders for the throne in the mid-seventeenth century. *Mbanza Kongo*—the capitol and pivot of political power and social cohesion—was destroyed and abandoned. Kimpa urged the contending parties to unite, return to *Mbanza Kongo*, and anoint a king. One of the claimants followed her advice and returned to Mbanza Kongo where he was crowned by Kimpa. When that claimant's rival, Pedro II, got the upper hand, he had Kimpa burned as a heretic. Her movement, however, continued for several years after her death.

Kimpa is thought to have been a spiritual medium in the Kongo's indigenous cult before converting to Christianity. Subsequently she began to communicate with St. Anthony, Jesus's disciple. This is the reason her followers were known as *Antonians*. Kimpa demanded a thorough Africanization of Christianity and claimed that the Holy Family hailed from *Mbanza Kongo*—the Kingdom's capitol—and was black. Kimpa's career gives us a glimpse into the syncreticism in black religion on the African side of the Atlantic.

The religiously based royal ideology was called *nkisi. Nkisi* was under girded by three important cults: ancestor worship centered at the royal cemetery grove; ancestor spirits served by the *Mani Kabunga* (the name of the clergy assigned to worship the territorial spirits from the village level on up); the worship of royal charms or *nkisi.* The king was addressed as *Nzambi mpungu* (Supreme Creator). The sacredness of his person was confirmed by the ceremony of investiture and reinforced by court etiquette. The king was the most important and living *nkisi.* In other words, spiritual power was always associated with some material object. Europeans developed the notion of the fetish that will be discussed in the next chapter from the observations they made of this phenomenon.

> One of the most dramatic forms of West African revelations seems to have been speaking shrines, in which an otherworldly being possessed a physical item and spoke through it. When N'axera was living in Allada in 1660–2, he noted the presence of a shrine ("idol") there that spoke in the voice of a deity (which, of course, assumed was the Devil), which the king himself admitted to hearing
>
> Possession of material objects by beings from the other world lay at the root of the efficacy of magical charms whose use was widespread.
>
> Modern descriptions of *nkisi,* the Kongo charms, suggest that the priest might actually fix the being into the object, thus subjugating it to his will…Cavazzi did note that when preparing to make such a charm and give it efficacy, the priest would first sacrifice to the soul of the first person to make the charm. Apparently the soul of this "inventor of the art" provided the otherworldly power that made it possible for the entity to be captured.[31]

Christianity was assimilated through this cultural notion. *Nkisi* became a term that was applied to anything that was sacred. The church became the house of nkisi, the bible was the book of *nkisi,* the priest the *nganga* (religious expert) of *nkisi.* Thus, must we regard Kimpa's movement as a religious one that entailed a new way of imagining matter to address the disruptions in the exchange mechanisms brought about by the Portuguese presence. As discussed in the previous chapter, my point is that religion in Africa was already undergoing very rapid changes resulting from contact and exchange with Europeans.

> From the sixteenth century onwards there can be said to have been a single religion in which, at least among the nobles, features of Christianity and features of the old religion had merged. The main spread of this religion took place in the seventeenth century. This explains how Garcia II came to be defender both of Catholicism and of the *kitomi*. He was even nicknamed "the sorcerer." *This new religion was the source of Haitian voodoo.*[32] (my emphasis)

In the next chapter Long's concept of the imagination of matter will be discussed in greater detail as it applies to modernity and the study of black religion. The same exchanges implicated in the apocalyptic modes of religious imagination were exercised by black consciousness and carried out in practice on the other side of the Atlantic.

Conclusion

What I have tried to establish in this chapter is a framework for studying religion in the modern period that enables us to discern not only modernity's surface but its "underside" as well. Such a framework is one that will allow us to observe the nature of the contacts and exchanges from which modernity's epistemological categories and orientations ensued and through which its power inequities are legitimated as the inevitable consequences of progress seen as an inherent feature of Western exceptionalism.

> Millions of Africans were torn away from their countries and their lands through violence and barter. And millions of unpaid workers were used up, exhausted and consumed within a couple of years. We should never forget that this was the essential basis (though largely erased and ignored in Western thought) for the bourgeois enrichment of the sixteenth, seventeenth, and eighteenth centuries.

> Dominated Latin America "played a decisive role in the accumulation of wealth by the bourgeoisie of Western Europe," while black Africa functioned as "the periphery of the periphery" and "was reduced to the role of furnishing slave labor for the plantations." In effect, the forced labor of black slaves and populations of South America permitted the release of a huge mass of surplus value, which was appropriated in monetary form mainly by the traders, manufacturers, bankers, and financiers of England. But surplus value was also appropriated

by the North American colonies and by Europe, either directly or indirectly by the sale of manufactured products (fabrics, arms) or by provision of transport.

This forced labor gave rise on the one hand to the development of private enrichment in Europe and on the other hand to an increase in the purchasing power in the rest of the world, especially in Asia. The process trading companies extended their activities, making huge profits (the profit rate often reached 100 per cent, and sometimes 200 per cent).[33]

3

The Imagination of Matter in the Atlantic World's Political Economy

Both of these paradigms [Renee Descartes and Max Weber] locate a meaning of the "self" as a form of inwardness that must then negotiate with the world that is "out there." This "world out there" is necessary for the manifestation and showing of the self, but it does not partake of its inner constitution. This is one of the primary meanings of selfhood that has been evoked within the interstices of the Atlantic world economy of mercantilism and capitalism. What is clear here is that, however the self may be constituted, it is dependent on things, forms, modes, matter—stuff—that it does not create. In the case of the Atlantic world, one of those forms upon which a European American self depended was the bodies of Africans transported as chattel slaves into the New World as the basis for the accumulation of wealth and resources for the mercantile and capitalistic form of production. (*Significations*, p. 20)

Introduction

The above quotation from Long's *Significations* situates the modern "self" within the network of exchanges that constituted the "Atlantic world economy of mercantilism and capitalism." The network of exchanges constituting the Atlantic World determined how people involved in them would conceive the relationship between and among themselves and God and between themselves and nature. The break up of the medieval synthesis made it improbable that theologians could provide a comprehensive framework for merchants, monarchs, nation-states, ecclesiastical bodies, and so on to operate since Christendom was fractured between Roman Catholics and Protestants. What would emerge as a modern sensibility—a modern way of imagining matter—ensued from a number of factors rather than a single cause. Although it is convenient to periodize the transition from the medieval to modern period with the Renaissance/Reformation there is no way to prove this irrefutably. Some would prefer the Age of Reason and others the Industrial Revolution. For our purposes we are locating the transition to modernity in the long sixteenth century because this is when Europeans first began their Voyages of Exploration that connected Africa, the Americas, and Europe for the first time. As we began to discuss in the previous chapter, the nonreciprocal nature of the contacts and exchanges that resulted from these voyages was a key factor in bringing forth new ways of imagining matter characteristic of modernity (figure 3.1). Giambattista Vico was one of theorist to elaborate an epistemology of the imagination which he viewed as the founding moment for human consciousness and culture. Mircea Eliade understood this faculty as constitutive of religious experience. Charles H. Long looks regards the imagination of matter as a means of investigating the underlying religious meanings attributed to modern modes of interaction by various actors who underwent modernity. Most accounts discuss the transition from mercantilism to capitalism as if it was merely a practical matter that was destined to occur once people adjusted their thinking to actual reality. This understanding is a result of what we wish to describe. The triumph of modern way of imagining matter has made it—on this side of the long sixteenth century—seem normal. However, before it became such it had to be theorized to

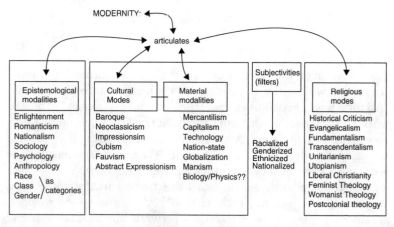

Figure 3.1   The articulation of modernity.

conform to and guide other practices that shaped various subjectivities under such categories as race. Yes, race also falls within the realm of materiality. A brief aside will illuminate this last point.

Through this process those who became white imagined their god as having the same attribute of whiteness. In her seminal article, "Whiteness as Property," Cheryl Harris demonstrates the interrelationship between white racial identity and property rights by explaining how "slavery linked the privilege of whites to the subordination of Blacks through a legal regime that attempted the conversion of Blacks into objects of property."

> Because the "presumption of freedom [arose] from color [white]" and the "black color of the race [raised] the presumption of slavery," whiteness became a shield from slavery, a highly volatile and unstable form of property…Because whites could not be enslaved or held as slaves, the racial line between white and Black was extremely critical; it became a line of protection and demarcation from the potential threat of commodification, and it determined the allocation of benefits and burdens of this form of property. White identity and whiteness were the sources of privilege and protection; their absence meant being the object of property.
>
> Slavery as a system of property facilitated the merger of white identity and property. Because the system of slavery was contingent on and conflated with racial identity, it became crucial to be "white," to be identified as white, to have the property of being white. Whiteness was the characteristic, the attribute, the property of free human beings.[1]

Harris also points out that within the construction of this white/black scheme the fundamental criteria for incorporation of various European ethnicities in an American white identity was not actually who the dominant system would consider white. As I will discuss in the chapter four, the "mulatto" posed a particular challenge to this scheme. Blackness, incarnated in the bodies of Africans transported into the New World, made its appearance through the imagination of matter in the structures and mentalities of modernity. Whiteness also made its appearance in this manner as a function of the subordinate reality signified in blackness. Thus, both white and black subjectivities were nonreciprocally constructed in relation to the imagined materiality of the Other. This chapter discusses the historical genesis of modernity in terms of the nonreciprocal contacts and exchanges that gave efficacy to black and white subjectivities. As stated in the first chapter: Black religion and black people appeared simultaneously in modernity. Black people made their appearance as what Long calls the "empirical Other" in the consciousness of those who constructed themselves as "white" through this perception. They also made their appearance through their perception of being apprehended by what Rudolph refers to as the "Holy Other." Through this process those who became white imagined their god as having the same attribute of whiteness. Because a white god served as the source of ultimate value whose entitlements accrued only to those who shared the attribute of whiteness, this attribute—whiteness—assumed materiality and functioned in the United States as a form of property.

Adam Smith

Although the two theorist Long quoted at the beginning of this chapter are Descartes and Weber, the reference to capitalism invokes another theorist of modernity—Adam Smith. As we no longer regard religion as being connected with our exchanges of matter, Adam Smith is not regarded as a religious theorist. However, his thinking is quite pertinent to our discussion of the way matter is imagined in modernity. Because religion entails the imagination of matter, Smith's thought can be also analyzed theologically. In our theological seminaries, Smith, if mentioned at all, is listed merely as the economist who provided the theoretical basis for the West's—more particularly, Britain's—transitioning from mercantilism to "laissez-faire" capitalism. Thus situated, theological students are not made to appreciate the degree to which Smith and other thinkers of the Scottish Enlightenment were at the forefront in tackling issues of theodicy within the framework of their discourse on "political economy." The title of Smith's first work—*Theory of Moral Sentiments*—should have provided the perceptive theology instructor or student with a clue to its theological importance. Not attending to the issues addressed by the Scottish Enlightenment thinkers resulted in the need for them to be tackled later by a separate discipline of Ethics or Social Ethics after the latter term was popularized by Walter Rauschenbusch with the publication of his book *Toward a Theology of Social Ethics*. In the late eighteenth century, in the wake of the French Revolution and the Napoleonic Wars, as inequality was becoming more glaringly obvious in the midst of Britain's increasing commercialization, debates about the disparity between want and abundance became more frequent and intense. A simplistic application of the Augustinian/Calvinist concept of predestination did not provide a satisfactory enough account of inequality to assuage troubled consciences and/or direct public policy. Thus, first and foremost (writes Istvan Hont and Michael Ignatieff in *Wealth and Virtue: The Shaping of Political Economy in the Scottish Enlightenment*), "*The Wealth of Nations* was centrally concerned with the issue of justice, with finding market mechanisms capable of reconciling inequality of property with adequate provision for the excluded."[2]

Smith occupied the chair of Moral Philosophy and Political Economy at Glasgow. In his analysis, Smith observed that poor people in Britain were materially better off than their counterparts in equalitarian primitive societies because the system of economic production in the commercial society of the former were based on the division of labor that, in turn, was depended upon inequality of property ownership. Since a nation's wealth depended on exports, wages needed to be kept low for its goods to be competitively priced on the international market. This basic formula, seemingly, relegated the worker to perpetual misery and exploitation. Smith argued, however, that in the context of a global economy richer nations could afford to increase wages while maintaining lower costs of productivity through the division of labor. Poor countries, in turn, could concentrate on exports of materials falling under the category of primary production to participate in the global economy.

Smith's formulation accorded well with the theodicy of moderate evangelicals. God operated not directly by active intervention in human affairs but, rather, remotely through the laws of nature that God had established at the beginning of creation. Human society, however, was not natural but by definition human. How were humans to see providence operating in exchanges occurring in their society? For Smith it could be observed in the "invisible hand" of the market that in absolute terms was benevolent toward everyone but in relative terms made the worker bear the burden of providing luxury and comfort for the rich. In Calvin's theology one was never certain if one was numbered among the elect or the damned. Smith's theodicy gave no assurances in the ultimate sense on this issue while, at the same time, providing the rational for why some were assigned to the lot of workers and other to the lot of owners in this present life. No other scheme was possible. One alternative of the "classical civic humanist ideal of a virtuous republic which delegated productive labor to slaves" was repugnant to Christian scruples. The other alternative based on "the Christian ideal of a society as a positive community of goods" would not be wealth producing. Evangelical—the moderate, postmillennial, laissez-faire, Clapham group—MPs argued for non-government intervention on behalf of the poor but for the abolition of the slave trade and slavery because, in their minds, it was consistent with God's design.

With the publication of *Wealth of Nations* (1776), Smith did not create global capitalism; rather, he identified the laws and principles of what was already becoming the case and through their articulation in secular language provided global capitalism with a theological rational. How did this happen? It happened because Smith's political-economy set the limit upon the modern Protestant theological imagination with the exception of the utopians. With rare exceptions, no Protestant thinkers after Smith have been able to address the aforementioned megaquestion from outside his framework of political-economy: What are the possibilities and limits of human freedom in the world in relation to their ultimate source who is God? In having convinced all but a very few skeptics that the system of exchanges constituting global capitalism is the best of all possible worlds, the pragmatic possibilities conceivable to the Protestant theological imagination have already been foreclosed before its theoretical activity is even initiated.

Vico, Eliade, Long, and Pietz

As I stated already, the beginning of the modern period is traced either to the Renaissance, Protestant Reformation, or Enlightenment. The Atlantic Slave Trade proceeded throughout the development of theses three aforementioned "eras" in the West's history and accordingly played a crucial role in the new subjectivities characterizing modernity. We can comprehend how this was so by describing the way subjectivities occur through the imagination of matter. The self is constructed through involvement in materiality. One form of materiality constituting the West's non-self was the black body it had reduced to commodity form. Giambattista Vico, Mircea Eliade, and Charles H. Long have shown that invisible religious realities are imagined through material forms. The way the black body was imagined, described, painted, and forgotten allowed Europeans to imagine the valorized category of "whiteness" as the basis of their modern identity. How is human consciousness able to accomplish this?

In trying to understand the nature of human consciousness, Vico posited the concept of "imaginative universals." The first human beings, he speculated, were incapable of knowledge because their consciousness was hopelessly trapped within the ceaseless flux of sensations. Each new sensation canceled out the preceding one. What ordered experience—or, we should say, what made experience possible—were the imaginative universals. These were something like metaphorical, mythic-poetical, mental-linguistic formations of the forces of nature which had, heretofore, been experienced only as immediacy—which is to say, they were not experienced because they were not imagined, remembered, and contemplated. Vico privileged Jove as the primal "imaginative universal" that established a cardinal point of orientation amidst the total flux of sensations. Donald Phillip Verene wrote, in *Vico's Science of Imagination*, "Thunder is the first thought...The divine is the first name. Vico regards the first men as beginning to think by becoming aware of the sky." Jove, the sky, was imagined by early humans as another body looming over and above their bodies. Humans thought through their bodies. Says Verene:

> The first of these forms of bodily thought is a process in which the world is embodied by the first men by apprehension of their own bodies; and they see the forms of nature and their bodily activities, their work and life, as alter bodies. Because the largest dimensions of nature are apprehended as bodies—sky, earth, and water as the divine bodies of Jove, Cybele, and Neptune—the more specific embodiment of the world by the same metaphorical process is possible.[3]

This is remarkably similar to what Charles H. Long had to say about the thought of his former colleague at the University of Chicago's School of Religion, Mircea Eliade's in his paper "Mircea Eliade and the Imagination of Matter." In commenting on Eliade's description of the symbolism of the Sky, Moon, Water, and Stone, Long wrote:

> In all of these statements Eliade is speaking of a primary and primordial intuition of matter...The specific intuition of the human consciousness is always correlated with an a priori form of the world. It is the universality of matter itself in all its several forms, rather than simply the inner working of the human consciousness epistemologically or psychologically which is the source of religiousness. Mind and phenomena go together.[4]

Long's understanding of how religious consciousness is constituted is very similar to Eliade's. Long's interest, however, is not in some primal phase of human evolution, that is, humans in their original, natural state. He focuses his attention on the contacts, exchanges, and new understandings of materiality that emerged within the structures of colonialism. Here speculation about the constitution of religious conscious in humanity's primitive natural state is unnecessary because all the data is available if we know where to look. Melanesia is one of the places Long looks. This is where we encounter the phenomenon of the Cargo Cult. For Long, the Cargo Cult is the paradigm for a new approach to the Study of Religion not only because it has a direct comparison with other millennial movements such as those found among Native Americans and blacks in the Americas, but also because the phenomenon occurs within the context of the relationship between the colonizer and the colonized that is mediated by European manufactured goods. The Cargo Cult forms an interpretation and critique, from the side of the colonized, of the lack of reciprocity in the exchange between the colonizer and the colonized. The Cargo Cult and, in a certain sense, all religious movements of the oppressed are attempts at reestablishing reciprocity in the exchanges that were disrupted by colonialism. The phenomenon, however, is not a utopian attempt to move backward in time. "Cargo cultist through their rituals," writes Long, "attempt to bring about new modes of human constitution (to make new beings who are neither Melanesian or European)."[5]

The Cargo Cult, like the Father Divine Movement and Daddy Grace Movement—and, to some degree, the Nation of Islam—among African Americans, can be seen posing a very serious question to the West: Where is the cargo? You gave us your Christianity but you deprived us from learning all its magic. It is the magic that produces the cargo and we have been deprived of that. The West, at least since the publication of Adam Smith's *Wealth of Nations*, has relegated the cargo not to the religious sphere but to economics. Was this a slight of hand trick,—as Karl Marx thought—whereby the West hides its own idolatry from itself? Long wrote:

> I think that the revolution in anthropology and in all the human sciences arises around the issue of the cargo cults because this phenomenon points not only to an acentric and seemingly anomic situation in other cultures but equally to an acentric and anomic situation in the sciences of humankind. That is to say that in the attempt to understand

human life, the prestige of the Western scientific apparatus is no longer an adequate tool. In some way the objects of the study, other cultures, must be participants in the study as subjects and objects. The methodological problem of cultural contact is itself an aspect of a cargo cult.[6]

But we are getting ahead of ourselves. Regarding the rationale for taking serious stock of the Cargo Cult phenomenon, Long writes:

It is through a juxtaposition of this meaning of human constitution with that of its meaning in the tradition stylized in Europe from Descartes through Kant that I hope to establish a new theory of the study of religion and a new religious epistemology. The modern period has for the most part been incapable of showing how materiality enters into epistemological constitution. This has in part been due to the fact that the "disenchantment of the world" that took place within Europe beginning with mercantilism could find no way of religiously valorizing the manufactured commodity. Any meaning of materiality as far as religion was concerned was relegated to "other" cultures or to nature or occurred in theological ethical studies concerned with the proper relationship between a religious ethical orientation *and* materiality.[7]

As we apply these categories to the study of black religion, we are also aware of their application to the religion of whites. One place to where we can focus our attention in studying the relationship between the West's understanding of spirit and matter. We begin with the history of the ideas and practices pertaining to Roman Catholicism's penitential system. I will first discuss Max Weber's theory regarding the rise of Western Europe to preeminence before discussing how the Reformation's new view of grace implicated materiality as it was experienced in the West. A number of scholars have attempted to account for the rise of the West over the rest of the world's population. The racist view is that it is due to some special genius in western people themselves that accounts for their dominance over everyone else. In modern times a more social-historical approach has been offered. Max Weber explanation is worth paying to because he tries to avoid the Marxist tendency to reduce everything to economic causality by accounting for the role of ideas and ideals in history. Ideas and ideals don't merely reflect but also affect their material contexts. One of the things Weber studied, therefore, was the relationship between religious ideas and economic behavior in historical context. The reason the Protestant Reformation caught Weber's attention was because it represented the most decisive change in the West's religious thought and signaled, for many, the transition from the medieval to the modern period. This view is challenged by many medieval historians but our purpose here is not that of testing Weber's thesis. Whether the Protestant Reformation was causal or not, it is possible to discuss an increase of "rationalization" in western society during the long sixteenth century. According to Daniel Chirot,

> The rationalization of law and religion in Western Europe, combined with the increasing protection given to townsmen who embodied market and economic rationality, ultimately led to the creation of capitalist economic relations in northwest Europe. It was then that the slowly accumulated wealth and relative geographic advantages of this part of the world were translated into decisive economic advantages.[8]

Rationality means predictability achieved through agreed upon laws, procedures, and enforcement mechanisms that make the merchant less vulnerable to the capriciousness of the ruler. Chirot points out that cultural rationality—"a drive to turn the human and nonhuman universe around each of us into a set of clearly understood calculable objects and relations that behave according to a set of understood 'natural' laws"—is something that accompanies economic rationality.[9]

> The preservation of a distinct church hierarchy and a professional priesthood was also an important element in strengthening the rational component of medieval Christianity, but would not have resulted in such a strong push in that direction without the church-state split which characterized Western Christianity.

> The tension and lack of concordance between a religious promise and secular political events will drive religious thinkers to seek more logical and objective proofs of the meaning of the world, just as, at the opposite end, it will drive many ordinary people to escape into mysticism. But for the intellectual and rational element to thrive, it is necessary for it to retain a material base capable of supporting abstract speculative activity.[10]

There was supernatural legitimization of the material base that supported the church's abstract speculative activities. The church initially faced some serious obstacles to its acquisition of this base. With the decline of the Western Empire, and the emergence of a number of

Germanic successor states, one of the affinities to develop between Christianity and Germanic culture was the confusion between private and public office and institutions. The term "dominium" or ownership came to signify office and proprietary right and, also, private rather than public law. This confusion manifested itself not only in the conflict between the notion of service and the reality of "benefice." As early as the First General Council of Nicea (325), for example, we find clerics being admonished against engaging in usury. At the Second General Council of Nicea, bishops are prohibited from making gifts to relatives of "things of God." What these aforementioned canons indicate is the church's effort to combat simony within the proprietary church system that treated the tithe as just another feudal due that could be disposed of an one would any other item of personal property. All of this was inimical to the church's exercise of authority and discipline and the one component of the church's concerted effort for autonomy from lay control was the monopoly it had on Grace. By the mid fourteenth century Pope Clement VI could claim to a believing audience that

> One drop of Christ's blood would have sufficed for the redemption of the whole human race. Out of the abundant superfluity of Christ's sacrifice there has come a treasure which is not to be hidden in a napkin or buried in a field, but to be used. This treasure has been committed by God to his vicars on earth, to St. Peter and his successors, to be used for the full or partial remission of the temporal punishments of the sins of the faithful who have repented and confessed.[11]

As Grace was of such a high premium in the medieval political economy, it became a quantity of exchange through the mechanisms of the church's penitential system. Through its receipt of tithes, endowments, and other wealth obtained from the sale of indulgences we get the impression that Grace was thought of almost as a kind of spiritual substance with monetary equivalents. As early as the eleventh century, Peter Damian would describe how:

> When priests impose a penance of many years on certain sinners, they sometimes indicate the sum of money necessary for remission of the annual stint so that those who dread long fasts may redeem their misdeeds by alms. This money payment is not found in the ancient canons of the Fathers, but it is not, therefore, to be judged absurd or frivolous.[12]

This development in the church's penitential system occurred within a broader framework of change within the West's political economy during the Middle Ages. Important features of this process were the possibility of calculating the precise weight of a sin, the growth of towns, and the development of a money economy. Such equivalencies were spelled out in confessors' handbooks. Thus we can appreciate how Martin Luther's theological breakthrough in terms of his understanding of "justification" would be concomitant with his attack on the church's sale of indulgences. We might speculate that the secularization of church properties in those areas that embraced the doctrines of the Reformers facilitated and helped legitimize a new sensibility about matter.

The whole theological debate about the nature of the Eucharist can be viewed as a debate about the nature of the Divine-human exchange and the material substance mediating this exchange. Some Protestants such as Zwingli argued that the Eucharist's material substance does not become Christ's body and blood although he is somehow present for the believer through faith. We note that as the nature of the Divine-human exchange in the Eucharist was being debated in Europe, other exchanges were taking place in the world as a result of Europe's voyages of discovery that brought it into contact with Africans, Americans, and Asians. Eric Williams periodizes the modern period as beginning with the voyages of the Portuguese down the coast of Africa. Through the Portuguese the term "fetish" is introduced into the discourse of Europeans about African religions and cultures around the same time that the debate about the Eucharist is taking place.

After the Reformation era and during the Age of Reason matter became despiritualized in the modern psyche. Keith Thomas in his *Religion and the Decline of Magic*, Robert K. Merton in his "Science and Technology in seventeenth Century England," Max Weber in his *The Protestant Ethic and the Spirit of Capitalism*, have, respectively, posited a relationship or "elective affinity" between the Protestant Reformation and the decline of witchcraft and magic, the growth of science, and the rise of capitalism. What this thesis suggests, as we have already been pointing out, is that the new religious sensibility brought about by the Protestant Reformation was associated with a new form of materiality. Here, we must be extremely cautious so as to not imply causality in one direction or the other. What Long noted earlier was that the West had difficulty developing a linguistic syntax for the new materialities resulting from the contacts and exchanges effected by Europe's global expansion.

As we pointed out earlier, all of this is occurring in Europe as the slave trade is taking off and gathering momentum in the Atlantic World. With the dawn of mercantilism, a number of new materialities suddenly appear on the horizon. There arose the notions of "whiteness" and "blackness" as racial categories along with mulattos, mestizos, and other names used to identify and isolate the offspring of Europeans and their enslaved and colonized subjects. There was the commodity. There were the people, whose subjectivity we will discuss in the next chapter, were turned into commodities. There was the notion of the fetish.

In his study, "The Problem of the Fetish," William Pietz has shown that this term, used to characterize primitive African religious practices, was invented to bridge the gap between the way "radically heterogeneous social systems" established value.

> This novel situation began with the formation of inhabited intercultural spaces along the West African coast...whose function was to translate and transvalue objects between radically different social systems...these spaces...were triangulated among Christian feudal, African lineage, and merchant capitalist social systems. It was within this situation that there emerged a new problematic concerning the capacity of the material object to embody—simultaneously and sequentially—religious, commercial, aesthetic, and sexual values. *My argument, then, is that the fetish could originate only in conjunction with the emergent articulation of the ideology of the commodity form that defined itself within and against the social values and religious ideologies of two radically different types of noncapitalist society as they encountered each other in an ongoing cross-cultural situation.*[13] (my emphasis)

In other words, the fetish became a way of explaining why Africans valued objects differently than the European mercantilists who were developing a notion of material value based purely on objective criteria, that is, use-value. The explanation was that Africans were superstitious, lacking in reason, and, consequently, could not determine the proper value of material objects. Africans simply failed to realize that material objects are just that, material objects and nothing more. In the early seventeenth century, we find Dutch Calvinist traders making the comparison between African fetishes and religious objects associated with Roman Catholicism. The Roman Catholic Mass, we will recall, was a constant object of Protestant ridicule—particularly, the Roman Catholic celebration of the Eucharist that Protestants derided as superstitious magic. Added to the early accounts of African fetishism made by traders were those of the missionaries and anthropologists who came later. These accounts were read by theorists in Europe and through them the term "fetish" entered into the currency of western discourse.

In coming across some of the descriptions of how Africans arbitrarily posited value to material objects, Karl Marx was provided with the key for unlocking the mysteries of capitalism. To unlock the secret Marx says, in the first volume of *Capital: A Critique of Political Economy*, that because the commodity is "a very queer thing, abounding in metaphysical subtleties and theological niceties"

> We must have recourse to the mist-enveloped regions of the religious world. In that world the productions of the human brain appear as independent beings endowed with life and entering into relation with one another and the human race. So it is in the world of commodities with the products of men's hands. This I call Fetishism which attaches itself to the products of labor, so soon as they are produced as commodities, and which is therefore inseparable from the production of commodities.[14]

Throughout *Capital*, Marx draws upon material from the History of Religions and terminology from Christian Theology and Paul's letters to discuss the political economy's inner logic. A commodity such as iron has a natural body or substance but this natural body is put off and transubstantiated into another substance, gold, when the iron is converted into money. Notwithstanding the church's assertion that Christ is The Mediator; Marx saw money is the new god because of the role it plays as the mediator of all human exchanges and its role as the measure of all value. Because of its seeming sovereign power over human exchanges, "this instrument has now become the real God, since the intermediary is the real authority over that which it reconciles me. Its cult becomes an end in itself. Objects, divorced from this instrument, lose their value."[15] Marx challenges the view that modern secularism banished religion. Capitalism is the religion of modernity and its idol is the commodity—hence the redundancy: commodity fetishism.

Marx never offered a substantive analysis of the slave as a commodity form. Hence Marx's analysis, while identifying class as the new mode of human materiality, is inadequate in its treatment of race. What Marx said about the commodity being "a very queer thing, abounding in metaphysical subtleties and theological niceties" whose understanding requires us to "have recourse to the mist-enveloped regions of the religious world," applies also to the being of persons whose slavery relegated them to the commodity form. Nell Irvin Painter gets to the heart of the matter when she states that the slaves in being: "Fetishized as commodities...embodied their owners social prestige."[16] Here we want to recall Long's discussion of Peitz's study of the fetish. We learned that one of the fetish's characteristics is that humans attribute some divine or supernatural quality to something material that is their own invention. Furthermore, once this mode of materiality is arbitrarily created it becomes the locus for determining and assigning value to other objects. Since the commodity serves this function in modern society and its value is measured by money, Marx used the term "commodity fetishism" to signify the social phenomenon that replicates and valorizes this new form of materiality. In other words Marx's critique of modernity is not that its deity is an illusion but that its so-called secularization or disenchantment masks its valorization of a new god—the commodity and, also, money. But let us recall that the slave was reduced to the form of materiality of the commodity. The slave, therefore, is also one of modernity's fetishes. While devaluating human beings by reducing then to chattel Europeans created the category of "race." The category black served as the negative signification through which the opposite category "white" received its value. The Bible was interpreted to show how God had authored these categories and the exchanges through which they were sustained. Thus a theologically undergirded world view rationalized the enslavement and colonization of peoples on a global scale.

Immanuel Wallerstein

Who do we need to include in our conversation? Immanuel Wallerstein authored a two-volume book titled *The Modern World System: Capitalist Agriculture and the Origins of the European World Economy in the Sixteenth Century* that was published in 1974. In 1980 he published the second volume that was titled *The Modern*

World System II: Mercantilism and the Consolidation of the European World Economy, 1600–1750. In 1944 Eric Williams posited an equally provocative thesis that connected modern slavery with capitalism in *Capitalism and Slavery*. When these books are read together a certain picture, which we can only sketch in the broadest of strokes, emerges regarding the relationship between Reformation Europe and people of color, or, more particularly, Africans. (Note the dates in the title of G. R. Elton's book on the Reformation; *Reformation Europe 1517–1559*) I will not be arguing that the Reformation caused certain behaviors; rather, my argument is that when Europeans made contacts with Africans the outcome was the same regardless of whether the Europeans were Roman Catholic or Reformed.

The modern world that appears through Wallerstein's description is one divided economically into three societies: core, semiperipheral, and peripheral. Core societies export raw materials from peripheral societies that are transformed into manufactured products that are, in turn, exported to peripheral and semiperipheral societies. The core societies that emerged during and after the sixteenth century turn out to be precisely those societies in Western Europe that established overseas colonies. These are the nations that were able to participate in the slave trade—that's where William's "capitalism and slavery thesis" fits in. These nations are also those that became Protestant—that's where Weber's "Protestant Ethic Thesis" fits in. Of course, it is a known fact that Spain and Portugal—as the first European nations to establish New World colonies—were heavily involved in the demise of Native American peoples in the Americas and the enslavement of Africans. The Iberians, for a number of reasons, were not able to translate the wealth extracted from the Americas into the infrastructure that was prerequisite for the kind of Industrial Revolution that occurred in England. Max Weber observed that these nations that were able to industrialize happen to be the places where Calvinism took root. (But we must exercise extreme caution in positing causal relationships here since many of Weber's critics see only accidental connections between Calvinism and capitalism.) His thesis does not establish a causal relationship between Calvinism and capitalism—it is much more sophisticated that most people assume. What Weber argues is that there is an "elective affinity" between Calvinism and the new capitalist mode of production that we associate—along with other things—with modernity. Weber's argument is that Protestantism in its Puritan variety helped foster the kind of punctilious character structure that was required by emerging northern European capitalist economies. As Christendom fragmented the nation state arose to fill the power vacuum along with a class of entrepreneurs who freed from burdensome tithes, and so on were able to put capital to productive uses.

Thus, we can appreciate how the Reformation helped liberate Western Europe from Roman Catholic political, economic, and intellectual domination by situating it within the global framework of Wallerstein's *Modern World System*.[17] Political theories, such as John Locke's, that grounded political freedom and individual liberties in the ownership of private property went hand in hand with these historical and economic developments. Adam Smith's wrote *The Wealth of Nations* as a moral philosopher because the lines were still blurred then between Christian Ethics and Political Economy. His "invisible hand" seems to be a direct application of Augustin, Luther, and Calvin's notions of Divine Providence to the distribution of goods and services. The freedom to pursue wealth and its justifications were made possible by the revolution Luther started when he nailed his Ninety-five Theses protesting indulgences to the door of Wittenburg in 1517. Of course it was not his intent to facilitate the emergence of this new mode of production that indeed was already in the works in embryonic form in some parts of Europe. By the accidental conjunction of forces, certain "elective affinities" were brought about through the play of historical forces that profoundly implicate the Protestant Reformation in modernity.

Conclusion

What I have tried to present in this chapter is an analysis of the historical structures and processes that imposed modernity on Africans via the imagination of matter and the way they resisted dehumanization through the same means although with a difference. Modernity for Africans entailed being defined as material objects rather than as subjects. When we view things from this perspective, we can see the truth in the observation of one of my students that Africans were formed in Africa, deformed by their first contacts with Europeans, and reformed through their liberation struggle. Their praxis is a commentary on the debate about the possibility of matter being transubstantiated.

For them transubstantiation was an urgent necessity—not transubstantiation of the bread but of their own being that was becoming objectified. They had to enter into a modality that would counter that negative process and turn their objectified existence into flesh. What I have done in a round about way, in the above remarks, is talk about modernity. I have sketched it as something other than progress—the movement through time from the Dark Ages into the Age of Reason. What I have been signifying is slavery and colonization. These two radically different and distinct ways of viewing modernity represent difference between what I might term the historical conscious and the historical unconscious.

> Blacks have undergone the rise of the West, in the most intense manner, and their every subjection to the hegemony of the modern West has been affirmative and critical. In many respects, the West has been severely criticized by this community for not being the West, for not living up to its cultural ideals, and this critique could not have taken place if the black traditions had not themselves internalized the meanings and possible meanings of this cultural formation. But there were other moments. The situation of the cultures of black peoples in the United States afforded a religious experience of radical otherness, a resourceful and critical moment that allowed these communities to undertake radical internal criticisms of themselves, their situation, and the situation of the majority culture.[18]

The repressed, in other words, is the psychoanalytic analogue to the oppressed. As Long puts it: "Through academic and popular discourses, the extra-European cultures of the world were relegated to a different temporal sphere, thus isolating and inoculating them the very contacts and relationships that played so great a role in the rise of the modern West."[19] Robert J. C. Young is a little more inclusive and explicit regarding the nature of the exchanges we are talking about.

> It is clear that the forms of sexual exchange brought about by colonialism were themselves both mirrors and consequences of the modes of economic exchange that constituted the basis of colonial relations; the extended exchanges of property which began with small trading-posts and the visiting slave ships originated, indeed, as much as an exchange of bodies as of goods, or as goods...economic and sexual exchange were intimately bound up, coupled with each other...The history of the meanings of the word "commerce" includes the exchange both

of merchandise and of bodies in sexual intercourse. It was therefore wholly appropriate that sexual exchange, and its miscegenated product, which captures the violent, antagonistic power relations of sexual and cultural diffusion, should become the dominant paradigm through which the passionate economic and political trafficking of colonialism was conceived.[20]

4

Being, Nothingness, and the "Signification of Silence" in African American Religious Consciousness

We are so finite that we are not able by our own decision and will to bring ourselves originally face to face with the Nothing.

—*Martin Heidegger*

Ontology—once it is finally admitted as leaving existence by the wayside—does not permit us to understand the being of the black man.

—*Frantz Fanon*

The fact that silence presupposes words is what gives it this ironic twist. Without words there can be no silence, yet the sheer absence of words is not silence. Silence forces us to realize that our words, the units of our naming and recognition of the world, presupposes a reality which is prior to our naming and doing.

—*Charles H. Long* (Significations, pp. 60–61)

Introduction

In this chapter, I explore the meaning of the category of nothingness in the African American experience as something that occurs through their ontological encounter with Non-Being. I am using Long's description of silence not as an equivalent of nothingness but as its phenomenological companion. In this chapter, I am also pressing Long's notion of contact and exchange to its farthest limits not as a metaphysical exercise but to properly grasp the ineffable nature of the historical experience that blacks underwent. This notion of nothingness that I discuss has its analogue in Long's thought in his discussion of silence where he explains: "It is difficult to get at the meaning of silence, for, though a kind of power is signified through its quality, the power of silence is so unlike the power of words that we have no words to express it." Nothingness, while not necessarily synonymous with silence, is that about which nothing can be said or thought—hence, its ineffability. The irony, however, is that this ineffability does not contradict the fact that "the power of silence can only be expressed through words—words that are able to move beyond and back through their own creative intent to the intentionality of the silence." Longs reflections are enriched by his reading of Ludwig Wittgenstein's *Tractatus* whose most profound statement Longs regards as the aphorism "what can be shown cannot be said." The black encounter with Non-Being cannot be said. On the other hand, this encounter must be said because just as "silence does not mean absence; rather, it refers to the manner in which reality has its existence," so to does the encounter with Non-Being become the occasion for apprehending Being.

So what have such concepts as Being and Nothingness to do with African Americans? One answer to this question is to observe that African Americans are a part of the modern world. An essential component of their entrance into modernity was the experience of Non-Being that formed the basis for their apprehension of Being. Therefore, African Americans have a particular take on the twin concepts of Being and Non-Being. This places African Americans in the center of the conversation about modernity because Being lies at the center of the modern world's problematic. At least, this is the view of some Philosophers such as Martin Heidegger regarding Being's significance. What I assert in this chapter is that there has always been an urgent existential concern with Being among the Africans that were brought to the New World. I will attempt to demonstrate that black folk's concern for Being is something that has been hidden in the silence of the black experience. I will try to show how this silence might be entered and linguistically bridged by drawing an analogy between its phenomenology and discourse drawn from Christian mysticism-particularly, that of the author of St John of the Cross who introduced the notion of *The Dark Night of the Soul* and the unknown author who introduced concept of *The Cloud of Unknowing* into Christian spiritual discourse.

Heidegger and the Forgetfulness of Being

According to Heidegger, the West suffers from a forgetfulness of Being.[1] Even though he was indebted to the Christian Mystic Meister Eckhart for certain insights, Being was not synonymous with God in Heidegger's thought. I am using the term in much more religious sense than Heidegger intended but don't wish to get bogged down in elaborating upon all the distinctions and qualifications that have to be made in distinguishing Heidegger's from Eckhart's use of the term Being. There is a thorough discussion along these lines in John D. Caputo's *The Mystical Element in Heidegger's Thought*. This forgetfulness of Being to which we alluded has brought Western Philosophy to its present impasse. Epistemologically speaking, the West lacks a transcendent frame of reference to evaluate its truth claims or gauge its own experience. Empirical data and experience no longer lead to a sense of the truth or a certainty of the self but only serve to contribute to the already acute sense of fragmentation. In *An Introduction to Metaphysics* Heidegger points out that "being as such is precisely hidden from metaphysics, and remains forgotten."[2] Philosophy has lost its ability to contemplate the nature of Being. Western rationalism has placed the Decartian "cogito" outside the empirical object. Moderns no longer enjoy a mode of knowing and speaking that enables them to participate in the object of consciousness and, thus, overcome the subject-object split. According to Levy-Bruhl, in his *How Natives Think*, this is not true for all cultures. The thought patterns of some cultures follow the rule of participation and function to establish an identity between the subject and object. Western thought is characterized by a concern for objective and causal explanations of phenomena.[3] Louis Dupre, discusses the breakdown of the West's "ontotheological synthesis" in *Passage to Modernity: An Essay in the Hermeneutics of Nature and Culture*. He credits nominalist theology with having "effectively removed God from creation." Mental life was no longer organically connected and interwoven with the cosmos. "Thus reality split into two separate spheres: that of the mind, which contained all intellectual determinations, and that of all other being, which received them."[4]

We might account for this forgetfulness of Being solely in terms of developments internal to Europe's intellectual history but this would provide an incomplete picture. Among the important things characterizing the Modern Period in Europe's story are the contacts and exchanges that occurred between Europeans and Africans, Native

Americans and Asians. These contacts and exchanges also helped determine how Being would be perceived in the West. The notion of freedom as constituting the fundamental meaning of the human is something that occurred during the aforementioned exchanges. This notion arose within the larger context of an emerging political economy in the Atlantic World that condemned a particular class of people to the status of unfreedom and functioned to transform them into commodities. When humans are denied the exercise of their rights as humans, it must affect the way Being can be apprehended by all parties in a given culture. For example, in The *Ideological Origins of the American Revolution*, Bernard Bailyn shows how the existence of slaves in the British colonies gave clarity to the colonist's valuation of freedom.[5] In their pamphlets, direct reference was made to slavery as the antithesis of freedom. What I am wondering is whether the near dehumanization of Africans and other Third World peoples through slavery and colonialism was somehow refracted in the reflections of Western Philosophy on the problem of Being. Historical events may not only change the way Being is conceptualized, they may also change the nature of Being. This is suggested in Dupre's observation that "Cultural changes, such as the one that gave birth to the modern age, have a definitive and irreversible impact that transforms the very essence of reality. Not merely our thinking about the real changes: reality itself changes as we think about it differently. History carries an ontic significance that excludes any reversal of the present. Nor is it possible to capture that changing reality in an ahistorical system."[6]

The philosopher's historical location affects his/her conceptualization and historical location comprises not the events of which the philosopher is consciously aware but, in addition, everything that gives distinction to his/her epoch. Therefore, it is almost possible to read philosophy as one mode through which historical reality becomes conscious-this conscious layer of historical reality that is philosophy has an unconscious in the form of the repressed. The repressed, in terms of our discussion, are black people and the perception of Being that lies hidden in their historical memory.

Non-Being in the Middle Passage Experience

Only when Being—as it either discloses or veils itself in modernity—is accounted for exclusively from the myopic perspective of Western cultural history and philosophy can it be thought of as confined or conformed solely to the European experience. When modernity is accounted for in terms of the contacts and exchanges that occurred during the period of the West's global expansion, we are forced to consider the epistemological experiences of nonwestern peoples during these encounters. Africans were one such group. In *The Black Atlantic Modernity and Double Consciousness*, Paul Gilroy *proposes* that we undertake a "reassessment of the relationship between modernity and slavery." Gilroy is particularly interested in the "master/slave dialectic" Hegel constructs in his *Phenomenology of Spirit*:

> It points directly to an approach which sees the intimate association of modernity and slavery as a fundamental conceptual issue...A return to Hegel's account...foregrounds the issues of brutality and terror which are too frequently ignored. Taken together, these problems offer an opportunity to transcend the unproductive debate between a Eurocentric rationalism which banishes the slave experience from its accounts of modernity while arguing that the crises of modernity can be resolved from within, and an equally occidental anti-humanism which locates the origins of modernity's current crises in the shortcomings of the Enlightenment project.[7]

The nature of the contacts and exchanges that occurred between Africans and Europeans beginning in the sixteenth century of our era destined the former to embark upon a quest for Being albeit quite different than their white counterparts in the modern world. This is not to say that this quest was initiated by those encounters. Africans had a concept of Being before their contacts with Europeans. Father Placid Temples has attempted to demonstrate this in his study of how the notion of "muntu" functions in Bantu language and consciousness in his book *Bantu Philosophy*. We can say, in terms of Heidegger's prognosis, that Being has always been the foci of black people's existential aspiration. Being for the Bantu mentality is vitality, life in the most dynamic understanding of the term. "Force is the nature of being, force is being, being is force."[8] In other words, even before African's contacts with Europeans of Being in terms of power. What this chapter seeks to emphasize, however, is the disjunctive nature of what African's experienced during their contacts and exchanges with Europeans.

The apprehension of Being in the African consciousness will be discussed within the historical and phenomenological context of the above-mentioned disjunction. The Atlantic Slave Trade was what created this disjunction. In this disjunctive phenomenological space Africans had to apprehend Being from the predicament of a powerlessness that was experienced as absolute. Never in its history had the people of the African continent been so thoroughly ravished and threatened by the ferocious and relentless forces of death and destruction that were unleashed on them through the mechanisms of the Atlantic slave trade. By conservative estimates approximately 12 million African were forcibly transported across the Atlantic to the Americas. Several times that number died en route to the coast from the interior or aboard ship during the Middle Passage. However, statistical data is a weak indicator of the collective horror and terror connected with this collective experience. Only in reading Olaudah Equiano's account do we gain some understanding of the Middle Passage experience:

> The first object which saluted my eyes when I arrived on the coast was the sea, and a slave ship, which was then riding at anchor, and waiting for its cargo. These filled me with astonishment, which was soon connected with terror, when I was carried on board. I was immediately handled, and tossed up to see if I were sound, by some of the crew; and I was persuaded that I had gotten into a world of bad spirits, and that they were going to kill me...

> Indeed such were the horrors of my views and fears at the moment, that, if ten thousand worlds had been my own, I would have freely parted with them all to have exchanged my condition for that of the meanest slave in my own country. When I looked round the ship too and saw a large furnace or cooper boiling, and a multitude of black people of every description chained together, every one of their countenances expressing dejection and sorrow, I no longer doubted my fate: and quite overpowered with horror and anguish, I fell motionless on the deck and fainted...

> In a little time...I found some of my own nation...I inquired of these what was to be done with us? They gave me to understand we were to be carried to these white people's country to work for them. I was then a little relieved...

> But I still feared I should be put to death, the white people looked and acted, as I thought, in so savage a manner; for I had never seen among my people such instances of brutal cruelty; and this was not only shown toward us blacks, but also to some of the whites themselves.

Once under deck the slave's situation worsened considerably.

> The closeness of the place, and the heat of the climate added to the number of the ship, which was so crowded that each had scarcely

room to turn himself, almost suffocated us. This produced copious perspirations, so that the air soon became unfit for respiration, from a variety of loathsome smells, and brought on a sickness among the slaves, of which many died, thus falling victim of the improvident avarice, as I might call it, of their purchasers. This wretched situation was again aggravated by the galling of the chains, now become insupportable; and the filth of the necessary tubs, into which the children often fell, and were almost suffocated. The shrieks of the women, and the groans of the dying, rendered the whole a scene of horror almost inconceivable.[9]

Note the adjectives Equiano uses in trying to describe what he was experiencing: astonishment, terror, fear, and horror.[10] What strikes us in Equiano's account is the degree to which unfamiliarity added intensity to these emotions. Unfamiliarity with the layout of the deck and the European's white complexion leads him to draw the false conclusion that he is going to cannibalized by evil spirits. Equiano is somewhat relieved upon discovering that he is only destined to work for his captors in a foreign land across the waters. However, what he then experiences beneath the deck is worse than the death he had previously mistaken as his fate. He would have preferred a cruel death as long as he could have died as a human; but the life underneath the deck was subhuman. Many slaves, therefore, sought to end their lives through starvation or by throwing themselves overboard into the sea. Some captives died by a different means. Nathan Huggins reports in *Black Odyssey: The African American Ordeal in Slavery* that "Many captives simply retreated, thus, into death-from no disease and no apparently conscious act. Europeans were baffled for an explanation. Some claimed these captives wanted death so badly that they had held their breath. Rather, it would seem that these captives died of shock. Almost in a void of will, the biology had perhaps ceased functioning, and life extinguished itself-an involuntary suicide."[11]

However, most of them were thwarted in exercising this desperate option for ending their suffering by forced feedings and beatings. In being denied death they were forced to undergo, nevertheless, not a death that ended their suffering but one that was the inauguration of their suffering. "Affliction" was what Simone Weil termed this experience. She described it as "an uprooting of life, a more or less attenuated equivalent of death, made irresistibly present to the soul by the attack or immediate apprehension of physical pain." In *The Body in Pain: The Making And Unmaking of the World*, Elaine Scarry analyzes the relationship between physical pain and death. She points out that "pain is the equivalent in felt-experience of what is unfeelable in death." The body is what makes both pain and death possible. She says: "In each, the contents of consciousness are destroyed. The two are the most intense forms of negation, the purest expressions of the anti-human, of annihilation, of total aversiveness, though one is in absence and the other a felt presence."[12]

The experience defies linguistic expression. Equiano can only use such adjectives as horror, terror, anguish, and fear. The captives had "been transported beyond the bounds of known or imagined sensibility." Accordingly, black people did not give objective linguistic expression to their direct encounter with terror. Anthony Pinn was correct in making the experience of terror central to his analysis of black religion in *Terror and Triumph*. Terror is something that could not be named. It lied outside the realm of anything heretofore experienced or imagined. There not only were no linguistic categories adequate for capturing and giving meaning and sense to the horror, there were no thought categories as well. Terror is never experienced voluntarily and when it is experienced it is ineffable because it has no comparison with anything contained in the individual or collective memory. It arrests thought but it does not obliterate awareness. The terror of the black experience is vaguely analogous to what Heidegger was trying to get at in his analysis of the mood he termed "anxiety." In my view, terror is much more tangible than anxiety. Terror, as will be discussed in the next section, is related to the sublime. What terror and anxiety have in common is that neither are mental states that we can enter by our own volition. The apprehension of Non-Being or Nothing is what gives rise to the moods of terror and anxiety. These moods are not willfully invoked or rarely so because, according to Heidegger, "we are so finite that we are not able by our own decision and will to bring ourselves originally face to face with the Nothing." The experience of Nothing is not something that can normally be willfully approached. It entails an acute perception of the "withdrawal" of Being that cannot be stopped. What Heidegger meant by the term "withdrawal of Being" was that there is not particular entity on which Being can be founded—Being is, therefore, always contingent and contained within the possibility of Non-Being. This awareness allows for the condition of possibility wherein Being can disclose itself in the particularity of a single being whose uniqueness is grounded in the possibility of its not being. What African captives were confronted with in the Middle passage was this Nothing.

John D. Caputo remarks in *The Mystical Element in Heidegger's Thought* that: "In the Nothing, Dasein experiences its own lack and finitude in the face of that which is "simply other" than every being. This is the same realization which affects every religious, and particularly every mystical, consciousness."[13]

Nothing is not, as some would argue, merely a concept that occurs to the mind through the logical process of negation. Nothing as something "experienced," "encountered," "run into," at the most fundamental level of one's self. It was run into not as an abstraction but as a living hell on earth. Huggins reconstructs the collective experience of the Middle passage in the following:

> For when the mind dared to accept its consciousness and the dim light of reality pierced through, one would hum remembered chants. The heart and soul would want to be propelled by the voice through the void and darkness to familiar spirits...Here in this darkness, rocking, the voice could only awaken the most feeble echo, and nothing would come back on the ear save the hiss and roar of the sea, the whine and whir of the wind, the moans and whimperings of desolation. It was as if all the spirits that had made life whole were deaf and dead, or perhaps they did not inhabit the domain of the sea. Sometimes, the eye would discern another, more familiar than the rest...But as his eyes opened and as one looked into them, there was the same hollowness and emptiness that one saw all around. Better to retreat behind one's own eyes than look into the void of others.[14]

The only appropriate existential category that can be correlated with what Africans were forced to undergo is Non-Being. Non-Being confronted the captives on every side; it was suffocating. Non-Being was different than the death preferred by the captives. Death in the African experience provided continuity between the past, present, and the future. There was an inherited tradition and numerous rituals that helped one make the transition from life to death. But the Non-Being that menaced the captives in the Middle Passage was totalizing in its discontinuity with anything previously known or imagined. Nothing in the cultural memory provided coping mechanisms for dealing with this Nothingness. There was no naming it. In this disjunctive space what Africans experienced was not Presence or Being but the totalizing Nothingness of Non-Being. Non-Being constitutes, therefore, the primal experience of black identity and black religion. But since the experience of Non-Being is ineffable what language can we employ in describing black religion's origin?

The Signification of the Sublime in the Black Experience

The language of some of the Spirituals is what slaves used to describe their religious conscious. Certain of these songs describe their first apprehension of Being but not the actual experience of Non-Being preceding that apprehension. The actual experience was and continues to be enveloped in silence. Charles H. Long discussed the methodological problems that ensue from this linguistic situation in *Significations* where he states that: "Silence forces us to realize that our words, the units of our naming and recognition in the world, presuppose a reality which is prior to our naming and doing."[15] In this same discussion Long invokes an aphorism from Ludwig Wittgenstein's *Tractatus* "What we cannot speak about we must pass over in silence."[16] Could we also say that what is experienced in this silence cannot be spoken? Here we are not just referring to silence as the absence of speech but a profound silence that stems from the absence of thought because what was experienced was unthinkable. Does this silence function similarly to Ernst Troeltsch's "religious a priori" in the black religious experience?

When we think of black religion we immediately think of the bodily movements and vocal sounds associated with this phenomenon. There rarely, however, is any discussion of the deafening silence that preceded and is insinuated in black religion's objective manifestation. The deafening silence of which I refer arises out of the ineffability of the terrifying encounter with Non-Being. The a priori does not lie in its being a naturally structured aspect of the universal human condition. This may or may not be the case. The "religious a priori" in black consciousness has an historical genesis—it is a priori in relation to what this consciousness presently has accessible to its awareness. For Troeltsch the religious a priori was the ontological and epistemological foundation of all religious experience. It was a universal part of the human constitution; he does not attempt to historicize it. Troeltsch's argument is with Kant who, in *The Critique of Practical Reason,* made religion depended upon the intuition of good and evil in practical reason. Troeltsch's move gave religion an independent sphere of operation and an ultimate validation for its idea of God. A similar move is made by Rudolph Otto in *The Idea of the Holy.* In discussing the numinous he states:

> We find, that is, involved in the numinous experience, beliefs and feelings qualitatively different from anything that natural

sense-perception is capable of giving us...And they are not them-selves sense perceptions, so neither are they any sort of "transmuta-tion" of sense-perceptions...The facts of the numinous consciousness point therefore-as likewise do also the "pure concepts of the under-standing" of Kant and the ideas and value judgments of ethics and aesthetics to a hidden substantive source, from which the religious ideas and feelings are formed, which lies in the mind independently of sense-experience; a pure reason in the profoundest sense, which must be distinguished from both the pure theoretical and the practi-cal reason of Kant, as something yet higher and deeper than they.[17]

But how does the religious a priori in black consciousness become insinuated in the phenomenon of black religion? In *Being and Time* Heidegger asserts that Being appears when one comes face-to-face with the possibility and inevitability of one's own death "In the Being of beings, the negating of the Nothing comes to pass."[18] This brings to mind the dialectical relationship Hegel establishes in *The Phenomenology of Spirit* between Being and Non-Being. Neither concept, Hegel insists, can be imagined without its dialectical oppo-site. What this suggests, in light of our present discussion, is that black consciousness apprehended Being during its terrifying encounter with Non-Being. From the experience of Non-Being—an experience for which there was hardly any corresponding utterance and certainly no concept—the notion of Being was intuited. The experience of Non-Being and the apprehension of Being gave rise to black religion and black consciousness.

When we listen to the lyrics of the Spiritual that says: "My Lord he calls me, he calls me by the thunder" we are being put in touch with the way the "sublime" was articulated in black religion and black consciousness. In Kant's aesthetic the sublime was an idea or concept "that cannot be unfolded." Thus, like the numinous and, as well, Non-Being the sublime is beyond explication. Edmund Burke emphasized the aspects of greatness and terror in his discussion of the sublime. In *The Sublime and Beautiful*, he wrote that "terror is in all cases whatsoever, either more openly or latently, the ruling principle of the sublime."[19] Otto had a need to coordinate a discus-sion of the sublime with his treatment of the numinous. He explains that nothing comes as close to being equivalent in the religious con-sciousness of the numinous as the incomprehensible thing. "This will be all the more true," according to Otto, when it is simultaneously "mighty and fearful." With this conjunction "there is a twofold anal-ogy with the numinous—that is to say, an analogy not only with the mysterium aspect of it, but with the tremendum aspect, and the latter again in the two directions already suggested of fearfulness proper and sublimity."[20]

The Dark Night of the Soul and the Cloud of Unknowing in Black Consciousness

What I would like to propose is that the states of consciousness referred to as "dark night of the soul" and "cloud of unknowing" can be invested with new meaning when seen from and appropriated into the black religious experience. I am in no way trying to make the author of *Cloud of Unknowing* and Saint John of the Cross's descriptions in *Dark Night of the Soul* equivalent to what African's underwent during the Middle Passage. Nevertheless, can see an analogy to the Middle Passage experience in John's argument that ordinary experience is unable to provide any comparison to the soul's journey through the dark night. St. John of the Cross advocates a rejection of images (Dark Night of the Sense) and then a rejection of concepts (Dark Night of the Soul). These mystical categories can enrich our understanding of the black religious experience because, heretofore, most descriptions have been limited to sociological categories or those of black theologians. The later have drawn almost exclusively from a Protestant theological framework.

The descriptions of black religion that black theologians provided for us are ones that emphasize its political dimension. The title of the first book authored by James Cone, the father of black theology, was *A Black Theology of Black Power*. His second book was titled *A Black Theology of Liberation*. Around the same time that these two books were published Gayraud Wilmore published *Black Religion and Black Radicalism*. What the works of both these scholars served to do was to refute the charge from certain quarters in the African American community that Christianity was "the white man's religion" and only served to make blacks passive and complacent. According to Wilmore, the black religion was radical during slavery. It was only after emancipation that the black church became "deradicalized." From then on the radical impulse in black religion flowed into other institutional and organizational channels such as Garveyism and the Nation of Islam. Wilmore provided the documentation and interpretation of black religion that black theologians needed to posit theological norms modeled on their reconstructions of what Albert

Rabateau called *Slave Religion*. Thus, black theologians have revised the earlier negative evaluation of black religion that had been the consensus of sociological studies and replaced that with a positive evaluation. Black religion was not seen as being inextricably linked with the quest for liberation and black protest. The Slave narratives and Spirituals have served as primary source material for documenting African American beliefs and attitudes regarding God's relevance to their suffering. Black Theology has helped us see the belief structure that undergirded and oriented the agency blacks assumed in resisting the dehumanization of slavery.

Black Theology has tended, therefore to have a strong ethical orientation and be more concerned with praxis than what we might identify as more the concern of Philosophical Theology—the issue of ontology. We note that James Cone did not build upon the foundation that had been developed from Howard Thurman's studies of black religion such as *Jesus and the Disinherited* and, also, *The Negro Sneaks of life and Death*. Thurman uses categories to describe the black religious experience that allows the reader to imagine the ontological condition that made protest a possibility—before protest there was the issue of sheer survival that had to be addressed and solved. What one had to master was the ability to undergo the unthinkable and endure it without completely losing a sense of one's humanity. Black theology never entered that level of description because its level of interpretation was focused on the speech acts and political acts of blacks during slavery.

Black theology did not discern the silence toward which black speech also points. It failed to produce any radically new categories for analyzing the experience that served as its theological reflection's object. In North America the religious language to which slaves were exposed was predominately Protestant and of the most rudimentary nature in terms of theological depth and complexity. The slave thus had to invest surplus meaning into the vocabulary available to him through the language of the master. He knew all along however that what had undergone was unspeakable and at best could only be abbreviated in any language. Black theology, however, never produced a category to signify the ineffable in the black religious experience. Charles H. Long, was trying to correct this methodological and conceptual failing of black theology by introducing the notion of "the opaque." He began to employ this term to talk about religious symbols in the History of Religions discipline. Unfortunately, there are few second or third generation black theologians who have properly understood Long's critique and been able to adopt his method. "Dark night of the soul" and "cloud of unknowing" are terms that black people themselves could easily adopt to describe what they had to undergo during the Middle Passage and Slavery.

Protestant discourse, for reasons that are too lengthy to summarize in this chapter, is not good at accounting for the ineffable in religious experience. It has no highly developed negative theology. Such would have had to grown out of a "via negativia" contemplative tradition that encouraged the mystical state of emptiness. Protestantism has, however, has always been suspicious of mysticism. One reason for this that we do have to mention has to do with the way Protestantism understands grace. If human asceticism can sanctify the individual then, according to the Protestant sensibility, Christ's objective work on the cross is not totally sufficient for our salvation.

In the black religious experience, we are not dealing with the voluntary assumption of religious exercises. We are, quite to the contrary, dealing with a mode of oppression that was meant to be anything but religious. This mode was designed to turn human beings into commodities. In other words, they were to be transformed into things. This is equivalent to the complete loss of being. This is equivalent to entering into a state of Non-Being. I cannot overemphasize the fact that this state was entered into involuntarily, unwillingly, against their will. There is a poverty of images in Protestant discourse to signify the involuntary movement into and out of this state other than the symbolism of death and resurrection. Black slaves duly noted this symbolism along with that of water baptism signifying death and rebirth. The element of water was concrete in its materiality as well as symbolic. It was the vehicle that transported the slave to the Americas. The new birth of the soul out of the waters of chaos was historical experience as well as symbol. There was no language, however, to describe what it was like to be submerged in those waters—what it was like, physically and spiritually, to be chained underneath the deck. What I have been saying is that the experience defies description because what was experienced was Non-Being or Nothingness. This has no representation. The reason I am drawn to the imagery of "dark night of the soul" and "cloud of unknowing" is these images are understood to point to the ineffable in religious experience. In *The Cloud of Unknowing*, we are told also that one has to enter into "a darkness, and as it were a cloud of unknowing, thou knowest not what, saying that thou feelest in thy will naked intent unto God."[21] Humans are unable to see God by the light of reason or to feel him by their own affections. All that is possible is for the soul to remain in the darkness and the cloud of unknowing. Heidegger, as I stated earlier, avoided giving a Christian interpretation to his use of the term Being even though he was heavily indebted to the Christian mystic, Meister Eckhart for certain aspects of his use of the concept. I would like to follow Heidegger's attempt to discover Being in time and history. It seems to me, however, that for Being to disclose itself to human consciousness—and, therefore, in time and history—it must will to do so. If we imagine Being having a will we can also imagine that will being motivated. For Meister Eckhart, Being was synonymous with God. In his thought no particular being or concept could qualify as God because anything particular could not be the totality. Accordingly, if one wanted to reach God one had to empty the mind of all thoughts because even thoughts of God's attributes were not equivalent to God in and of him/herself. Mystical theology regarded the mind as something in need of purging before the soul could become united to God. But how the mind could empty itself of itself was a problem for mystical theology. How was one to reach a state wherein ones consciousness was unperturbed by sense impressions and those produced from memory? Then, how was the mind itself to be extinguished. In deep contemplation the sense of a self is last hindrance to absorption in God.

> If you are willing to make serious trial of this, you will find, after you have forgotten all other creatures and all their works, yes indeed and your own works as well, what remains between you and your God is a simple knowing and feeling of your own being. This knowing and feeling must always be destroyed, before it is possible for you to experience in truth the perfection of this exercise.[22]

The "I" that seeks and aspires after God must disappear for God to become present or else the awareness will be of the self and not God. This is something that the self is unable to accomplish on its own. The author of *The Cloud of Unknowing* asks rhetorically, "Next you will ask me how you can destroy this simple awareness and experience of your own being." He goes on to explain that it can only be accomplished with a "special grace" without which "this simple awareness and experience of your being can in no way be destroyed." The special grace is the soul's capacity to experience a "strong and profound spiritual sorrow." This sorrow is born from the acute awareness of one's own ungodliness before Holy one with whom one seeks to unite. But as long as one remains unclean on will be unable to fulfill one's spiritual desire. Hence, one despairs and longs to be annihilated rather than remain in this state of separation from the Divine. One's desire is really not to cease to be but to cease to have an awareness of one's being. "He desires without seeking to lose the awareness and experience of his being."[23] So too can we recognize the applicability to the black religious experience of John's assertion that one's spiritual awakening is initiated by a profound awareness of one's own misery. For John the Dark Night's misery was caused, in part, by a heightened sense of one's sin. The soul comes to "recognize its own lowliness and misery." This leads the soul further into the dark night wherein it is purged of sense and desire. The more purified the soul becomes the more excruciating the darkness. Andrew Louth points out in *The Origins of the Christian Mystical Tradition* that what is often missed in St. John of the Cross's description of the dark night is that the soul is experiencing the purifying love of God while enveloped in this state of obscurity.[24] How is this to be explained? Perhaps we might reason that the absence or separation is one that is experiential but not actual. God's presence must be experienced as absence for God's absence to provide the condition for the soul to apprehend the actuality of God's presence. In the darkness the soul is stripped bare and emptied. What is experienced is a void containing only profound longing. St. John refers to the void and emptiness in terms of "deep caverns of feeling." In *Living Flame of Love* he wrote:

> Since this transformation and union is something that falls beyond the reach of the senses and of human capability, the soul must empty itself perfectly and voluntarily—I mean in its affection and will—of all the earthly and heavenly things it can grasp. It must through its own efforts empty itself insofar as it can. As for God, who will stop Him from accomplishing His desires in the soul that is resigned, annihilated, and despoiled?

> Insofar as they are capable, people must void themselves of all, so that however many supernatural communications they receive they will continually live as though denuded of them and in darkness. Like the blind, they must lean on dark faith, accept it for their guide and light, and rest on nothing of what they understand, taste, feel, or imagine. All these perceptions are a darkness that will lead them astray. Faith lies beyond all this understanding, taste, feeling, and imagining.[25]

There are clearly stark differences between the dark night and the cloud of unknowing and what African experienced during the Middle passage and Slavery. However, there are enough analogies to commend these categories to our use. For example, the suffering and misery experienced by captives during the Middle Passage caused many of them to opt for death over life not but for different reasons than identified in *The Cloud of Unknowing*.

What I have been suggesting throughout this chapter is that in the black religious experience God was not apprehended as presence but as absence. This absence was unlike anything heretofore experienced in African history and culture. This absence was something African captives perceived during their descent into the realm of Nothingness and Non-Being. The miracle that occurred during this descent was that the captives' being was not obliterated and swallowed up by Non-Being. In that darkness, where horror and terror banished all images and concepts of God from consciousness, the African captive intuited the Being that supported and affirmed his/her existence. We identified this precognitive intuition as the African American religious a priori. We may also want to relate this phenomenology to the notion of the "feeling of absolute dependence" elaborated on by Friedrich Schleiermacher in *The Christian Faith*. Religious consciousness is determined by this religious affection and this religious affection determines every other religious affection. Many theologians regard *The Christian Faith* as marking the beginning of modern theology. The religious affection I attempted to describe in this chapter is what gave rise to black consciousness and black religion. African Americans can identify the historical origin of their primal religious sentiment in the Middle Passage.

What I have argued is that certain discourse found in the literature of Christian Mysticism enables us to probe the meaning and phenomenology of that primal religious condition that gave rise to black religion. What we cannot be underemphasized is the involuntary nature of this primal black religious experience. The involuntariness of this experience is what makes it unlike anything else. Heidegger's philosophical discourse and that of St. John of the Cross and the author of *The Cloud of Unknowing* assume a freely acting subject. The Christian mystics advise the aspirant on the spiritual path to assume an attitude of passivity before the pursued religious object. Heidegger seems to have failed in specifying the condition wherein Being might disclose itself to modern consciousness. He doses say that we cannot voluntarily apprehend Being. From the aesthetic standpoint Being is intuited in one's perception of the sublime. For Burke the sublime was connected with the feeling Rudolph Otto associated with religious experience—the "mysterium tremendum." The paradoxical aspect of the experience of Being at this level of depth is that it contains a profound perception of Nothingness, Non Being, or let us say, the absence of God.

This does not have to be evaluated negatively. The experienced absence of God in the black religious experience provided a foundationless ground from which arose an assurance of God's presence. Heidegger introduced the idea in *Introduction to Metaphysics* that

> Nothing, in its various senses, is a legitimate topic of thinking: far from leading to nihilism, such thinking is necessary in order to revive the question of Being...Any sense of the Being of beings involves a sense of what it means not to be; for instance, Being of beings as presence implies not-Being as absence. Second, we may find that, within a certain sense of the Being of beings, what "is" requires what "is not": for instance, what is present may depend on what is absent.[26]

The presupposition of nothingness and darkness as supports for the transcendental experience of God's presence and light is captured by James Baldwin in his account of the conversion of one of his characters in *Go Tell It on the Mountain*. At the beginning of the event of John's conversion he experienced himself sinking into the abyss whose depths could not phantom. "There is, his soul cried out again, no bottom to the darkness." But at the end of the ordeal of John's conversion he "saw the Lord—for a moment only; and the darkness for a moment only, was filled with a light he could not bear." Finally, "the light and the darkness had kissed each other, and were married now forever, in the life and vision of John's soul."[27]

Conclusion

I have attempted to describe the way Nothingness was apprehended in the primal mood of the black consciousness and black religion. Nothingness is an important analytical category for exploring the primal moment of black religion and black consciousness. Visually, nothingness can only be imagined as darkness. Hence, the above quote from Baldwin and those from the Christian mystical tradition. Vocally, it is invoked in the "moan" that I will discuss later. It defies thought categories. Nothingness certainly defies Descartean epistemology. It can be experienced as terror but not objectified empirically. Long wrote: "For the sake of thought, blacks must now freely accept for themselves that which in a previous history they were forced to undergo. This critical recursus is a vital resource for critical thinking. But this time the return is in the form of a critique." I am positing "Nothingness" as the phenomenological ground for black religion's critical stance. What has been implied in the above analysis is that the West must now search for Being among the peoples whose being it sought to obliterate. What has been implied is that the West forgetfulness of Being is connected with its forgetfulness of temporality—the West's temporality as it relates to those it captured and conquered. Modern contacts between Europeans and their "Others" that resulted in the dichotomies of primitive/civilized, black/white, and the like created a world devoid of Being. The West will never recapture Being in isolation to the Other whom it still holds captive. This is what Hegel almost intuited in his Master/Slave dialectic.

5

Epistemologies Opaque: Conjuring, Conjecture, and the Problematic of Nat Turner's Biblical Hermeneutic

Even when slaves, ex-slaves, or colonized persons become aware of the autonomy and independence of their consciousness, they find that, because of the economic, political, and linguistic hegemony of the master, there is no space for the legitimate expression for such human form. The desire for an authentic place for the expression of this reality is the source of the revolutionary tendencies of these religions. But on the level of human consciousness, religions of the oppressed create in another manner. The hegemony of the oppressors is understood as a myth—myth in the two major senses, as true and as fictive. It is true as a structure with which one must deal in a day-by-day manner if one is to persevere, but it is fictive as far as any ontological significance is concerned.

....

The oppressed must deal with both the fictive truth of their status as expressed by the oppressors, that is, their second creation, and the discovery of their own autonomy and truth—their first creation. The locus for this structure is the mythic consciousness, which dehistorizes the relationship for the sake of creating a new form of humanity—a form of humanity that is no longer based on the master-slave dialectic. The utopian and eschatological dimensions of the religions of the oppressed stem from this modality.

The oppressive element in the religions of the oppressed is the negation of the image of the oppressor and the discovery of the first creation. It is thus the negation that is found in community and seeks its expression in more authentic forms of community, those forms of community which are based upon the first creation, the original authenticity of all persons which precedes the master-slave dichotomy. There is thus a primordial structure to this consciousness, for in seeking a new beginning in the future, it must perforce imagine an original beginning. (*Significations*, p. 170)

Recapitulation and Preliminary Considerations

I pointed out in chapter two that whites constructed themselves over and against blacks who appeared in the consciousness of the former as the "empirical Other." In chapter six I discussed Du Bois's description of how blacks experienced the distinction between their own subjectivity and the externally imposed empirical self as "double consciousness." What I wish to assert at this point is that since whites are never aware of their own identity as dependent upon the one they created over against the black empirical Other, they never fully comprehend the true nature of their own social construction. Furthermore, since whiteness has been such an integral part of their religious identity, they never fully comprehend the relationship between their religious with their racial sensibility. The curious thing is that this is maintained and reproduced through the positing and presupposition of white religion as normative. *Thus whites can never pierce beneath the veil to encounter the "mysterium tremendum" of black religion because in so doing they would necessarily have to overcome the epistemological divide that always constitutes the Other in their consciousness as an empirical object rather than as a subject.* Therefore, we must remind ourselves that throughout this study we are never looking at black religion in and of itself or in isolation to its white counterpart. To say this in another way: whites must see themselves in the emergence of blackness and black religion because they themselves have no a priori existence relative to blackness. However, they think otherwise and this false notion undergirded their fiction of "discovery" during their conquest, colonization, and enslavement of others.

Let us return again to what was discussed in chapter one. It is important to remember in constructing this account of African Americans colonies in the Caribbean. This was due to at least three causes: the lack of interest in converting the slaves, the lack of missionaries even when there was interest in instructing slaves in the faith, and active opposition by whites. In the late eighteenth century at St. Vincent's whites vandalized the chapel of a Rev. Clark was and displayed its Bible on the public gallows. In 1792 St. Vincent's Assembly passed laws making it difficult to obtain a preacher's license. Those found guilty of preaching without a license were to be fined 18 pounds for the first offence or face imprisonment; the second offence made the culprit liable to whatever corporal punishment the court deemed appropriate; the third offence could result in expulsion from the island. By no means, however, did being unchurched mean African Americans were irreligious. The modalities of African American religiousness were very similar to those practiced in Africa but with a different task in view. Imposing this task on African American religion uniformly throughout the Americas was the constant of racial exploitation.

African American religion's task was to oppose the process of objectification to which slavery tended to reduce slaves. As a product of human creativity, African American religion was the only product produced by slaves that could not be alienated from them by their masters. It was also the only product that gave full expression to their humanity. Saying this is almost tautological because things are not capable of worship—hence, religious practice presupposes the exercise of one' humanity. Religion involves feeling, cognition, and the ecstatic mood that provides a sense of distance and autonomy from "the troubles of this world." Whether the slave cognized the ecstatic moment as the coming of the "Holy Ghost" or as being ridden by an "orisha," the end result of this experience of transcendence was empowerment and the overcoming of fragmentation.

Religion is an activity that makes itself in positing a separation that it then endeavors to bridge in the maintenance of the separation originally posited. Religion seeks to establish an exchange between humans with some ultimate from which they have been separated. This separation occurring in human consciousness is the distinction between the sacred and the profane. This distinction between the sacred and the profane has its correlates in the time-space dimensions in terms of other distinctions occurring in consciousness between; spirit and matter, heaven and earth, chaos and cosmos. As alluded to earlier, the separation African American religion was concerned with was geographical as well as metaphysical and ontological. It was concerned not only with the separation of the soul from God; and of the soul from the body, which is rendered soulless in becoming another's property; but, also, the separation of the body from its original home—Africa. Even during the Middle Passage, slaves developed the myth that if they happened to lose their lives in a revolt they would be reborn in Africa. In North

America this remembrance and longing for Africa is expressed—at least as one of its multivalent meanings—in the Spiritual "Swing Low Sweet Chariot." African American folklore contains tales of slaves who upon reaching the North America either flew or walked back to Africa. Thousands of African Americans returned to the Angola-Congo area and Hausaland from Brazil throughout the period of the Atlantic Slave Trade and to Liberia and Sierra Leone from Jamaica, the United States and Nova Scotia in the early nineteenth century. Indeed, the mass appeal Marcus Garvey's Back to Africa Movement among blacks in the United States, Caribbean, and Central America during the 1920s through 1930s demonstrates the persistence of this idea in the African American psyche.

The meaning of this striving after Africa was an attempt on African American's part to locate the basis of "somebodiness" without which there can be no freedom. In other words, by holding on to the religious meaning of Africa they were saying to themselves, "I am not just a body; I am somebody." It was a strategy aimed at situating the self outside the context of an hostile space into the realm of sacred space via the reference to a specific place of origin and eventual return. The Africanisms and survivals, Herskovits and others have demonstrated, as present in varying degrees in the Americas can be interpreted in terms of this structure of meaning being explicated here. The regard among Brazilian Candomblists for African ancestry, the organization of religious confraternities along the lines of African nationality, and the ritualistic exactitude of cultic practices wherein specific African orishas are invited to possess devotees are consistent with the above explanation. The orishas were believed to reside in Africa when they were not manifesting themselves by taking possession of their devotees in the Americas. In becoming possessed the devotee was transported to a sacred sphere of existence and the religious ceremony and its space became sacred and holy because the orisha was among his or her people. Thus, the community traversed time and space to be in Africa by bringing Africa to the community. Since, in actuality, the community remained in the Americas, the invocation of this memory through ritual formed the community as a hyphenated entity—in other words, an African American community.

Comprising the ontological structure of this formation was the materiality of sound in African American music whose percussive polyrhythms resonated with the primal vibrations that transformed chaos into cosmos. The drum was the instrument for beating out the

"mantra" of African American's spiritual contemplation. Its sounds
are heard in Rumba, Bomba, Samba, Salsa, Marengue, Raggae,
Calipso, Spirituals, Blues, and Jazz. Sound is the African means by
which the body's latent energies are awakened and joined in collective
participation of life. Thus, dance is necessitated by the nature and
potency of rhythm. It is the underlying basis of speech, language, and
matter. Hence, the phenomenon of "the talking drum" that could
produce sounds which can heal and sounds which can harm. Each of
the orishas has his or her corresponding rhythms by which they can
be invoked. Therefore, the rhythm is a recollection. Black music is
the improvisation of memory, the vehicle of return. That memory is
not just lodged in the mind, but, in the body, also. Therefore, black
dance is an improvisation of memory. We shall look at this again in
chapter nine.

   This improvisation of memory was a mode of traversing time and
space and for resisting the cultural hegemony of religiously sanctioned
definitions and prohibitions. The fact of syncretism, therefore, was
more than a case of cultural blending but represented—especially,
in voodoo, candomble, and macumba—"important competitors of
formal Catholicism." (Harris, p. 50) The same symbols took on a
different significance in the mind of the slave than what they meant
for European-American lay and clergy. Slaves put up crosses in New
Spain during the first slave revolt to occur there in 1523 (Davidson,
p. 89). In 1585 soldiers discovered a runaway slave at a maroon society in the vicinity of Lake Maracaibo, Brazil who said mass and performed baptisms. Another runaway slave performing priestly rites
was reported about the same time in Venezuela at Ring Bayano's
settlement. In 1622 a slave named Leonor de Isla was tried by the
Mexican Inquisition and accused of having invoked the spirit of the
sea and communicating with the spirits of the deceased. The records
indicate that she began her prayers by calling on "Jesus Christ, Son
of God, Savior of the World" before invoking other saints.[1] In the
United States, Nat Turner's narrative is replete with apocalyptic
biblical imagery. His denial of being a conjurer and insistence that
the influence he had over his fellow slaves was "not by the means
of conjuring and other such tricks...but by the communion of the
Spirit" is somewhat suspect. His fellow slaves may placed Turner in
the role of a conjurer early in his life. During his childhood Turner
once described events that had taken place before his birth. This
confirmed the belief among the slaves that Turner's special abilities
which they already had formed from observing the marks on his

head and chest. (Turner, pp. 64–66) In *Conjuring Culture: Biblical Formations of Black America*, Theophus H. Smith studied the use of biblical imagery in black identity formation. He viewed conjuring as a cultural and hermeneutical mode of interpretation and community formation. He said that he was using the concept of "conjuring culture" as the vehicle for analyzing some of those representations, and the role they play in the historical projects and cultural strategies by black North Americans.[2]

In Turner's narrative we observe the ecstatic-mystical mode that African American religion assumes in continuity with its African antecedent. It authenticates itself in, making contact with its object in the trances and visions of its adherents, the collective ravishment by the "Wholly Other," and the experienced dread of that "pythian madness, demonic possession" described by Du Bois.[3] Joseph Washington's assessment of black religion in the United States is applicable as well to its counterparts in the Caribbean and Latin America:

> Born in slavery, weaned in segregation and reared in discrimination, the religion of Negro folk was chosen to bear roles of both protest and relief. Thus, the uniqueness of black religion is the racial bond which seeks to risk its life for the elusive but ultimate goal of freedom and equality by means of protest and action. It does so through the only avenues to which its members have always been permitted a measure of access, religious convocations in the fields or in houses of worship.[4]

Nat Turner's Opacity

Now let us deal more directly with Nat Turner. He led one of the most violent slave insurrections in U.S. history in Southhampton County, Virginia in 1831 in which ten men, thirty-five children, and fourteen women were killed. The details of his insurrection were narrated to a lawyer named T. R. Gray in what is now known as *The Confession of Nat Turner*. Turner begins his narrative by addressing Gray, "Sir, you have asked me to give a history of the motives which induced me to undertake the late *insurrection, as.* you call it. To do so I must go back to the days of my infancy, and even before I was born." He goes on to explain that as early as three or four years of age while playing with other children, he began to relate incidents that occurred on the plantation before his birth when these things were verified by the older slaves it so impressed them that they remarked: "He surely would be a prophet," as "the Lord had shown me things that had happened before my birth." In addition, the way Nat Turner learned to read and write was equally remarkable. He says, "It not only had a great influence on my mind, (as I had acquired it with the most perfect ease, so much so, that I have no recollection whatever of learning the alphabet), but to the astonishment of the family, one day when a book was shown me to keep me from crying, I began spelling the names of the different objects." Turner says that after this incident his learning constantly improved. Whenever he was not working he spent his time in prayer "or in making experiments in casting differing things in molds made of earth; in attempting to make paper, gunpowder, and many other experiments."

After reaching adulthood, while listening to a sermon, Turner was struck by the passage saying, "Seek ye the Kingdom of Heaven and all things shall be added unto you." After praying daily for the interpretation of this passage, one day at his plough, the Spirit spoke to him and quoted this same passage. When asked by Gray what he meant by the Spirit, Turner said, "The Spirit that spoke to the prophets in former days." After this occurrence Turner prayed consistently for two years and then had the same revelation. More years passed during which he was given additional revelations and confirmations that he was ordained for a special task. At one time Turner says:

> I saw white spirits and black spirits engaged in battle, and the sun was darkened—the thunder rolled in the Heavens, and blood flowed in streams—and I heard a voice saying, "Such is your luck, such you are called to see, and let it come rough or smooth, you must surely bear it."

After this vision he stopped interacting with his fellow slaves as much as the plantation schedule would allow to devote himself more fully to the Spirit—

> and it appeared to me and reminded me of the things it had already shown me, and that it would then reveal to me the knowledge of the elements, the revolution of the planets, the operation of the tides, and the change of the seasons.... The knowledge of the elements being made known to me, I sought more than ever to obtain true holiness before the great day of judgment should appear; and then I began to receive the true knowledge of faith.[5]

The reason, we can assume, that Turner was instructed in the knowledge of the elements, revolution of the planets, and operation of the tides was connected with what we learn elsewhere in his narrative, the precise timing of his revolt. This explanation, though, in no way exhausts the meaning of this. What we notice, however, is that the way nature was constantly being transfigured before his vision into the Bible's apocalyptic imagery collapses the neat yet, apparently, artificial dichotomy in Christian theology between revealed and natural religion. This dichotomy gets involved in debates about biblical authority that concerns the exploration of this chapter. Was the Bible the source of Nat Turner's authority? This can only be answered by first discussing not only the issue of what it is that makes the Bible authoritative but, of equal importance, which reading strategy best lends itself to locating its message. This is because the Bible is not authoritative merely by being read, but by virtue of being accurately understood and, of course, put into practice. This fact partly explains why in the church arguments over what the Bible is saying are inextricably linked to those over methodology and *vice versa*, and why those whose reading strategy yields unwelcomed social practices will so often be indicted as unbiblical. Nat Turner seems to have intuited that he would encounter the same difficulty at the point in his narrative where he, while in the midst of saying "knowing the influence I had obtained over the minds of my fellow-servants," interjects the parenthetical caveat (*not by the means of conjuring and such like tricks*, for to them I always spoke of such things with contempt), but by the communion of the Spirit, whose revelation I often communicated to them, and they believed and said my wisdom came from God.

Since religious visions were what motivated Nat Turner's insurrection, visions which provided him with interpretations of nature and biblical passages that in turn, needed to be interpreted through subsequent visions; his disclaimer of any connection or similarity between his methodology and conjuring is intriguing. The African practices of conjuring, divination, witchcraft, and so on are things that would not have come to the mind of the contemporary reader had Nat Turner not mentioned it. Thus, the brief reference he makes to "conjuring and such like tricks" would indicate that he wants to set himself apart from slaves who were engaged in these practices and that there at least were some who must have suspected that this was the secret behind his method. It is interesting to note here that Turner was refused baptism at the local white church and so he and a white man whom he had healed of boils and converted to Christianity "went down into the water together; in the sight of many who reviled us, and were baptized by the Spirit." This shows that the source of Turner's inspiration and the methodology behind his interpretive scheme was suspect among some in and near his plantation. In defending himself against the accusation that he was a conjurer, Turner is telling the truth but it is a truth that is not unmixed with error. This becomes clear when we ask ourselves the question of what similarity there might be between conjuring (and its related practice of divination) and any act of discursive interpretation. The content of Turner's visions, as reported by him, is quite bizarre and impervious to our understanding; that they occurred to him does not provide us a clue as to the hermeneutic principle he used in their interpretation. Turner only tells us that he did not employ the method of conjuring. Yet for the practitioner of divination cowrie shells thrown on the ground elicit from him the same complex task as words written on the page for the modern biblical scholar—that of discerning a pattern from some visual configuration of signs that is restructured by the interpreter in terms of meaning.

Hermeneutical Implications

From Raymond Brown's informative article "Hermeneutics" in the *Jerome Biblical Commentary*, we learn that during the Patristic Era when thought was heavily influenced by Neo-Platonic and Stoic philosophy the two major schools of biblical interpretation were located at Alexandria and Antioch. At Alexandria exegetes such as Origen and Clement engaged in an allegorical method of biblical interpretation aimed at achieving a Christian form of gnosis. Persons such as Clement and Origen have been criticized for overlooking the literal historical *meaning* of the Bible in favor of more arbitrary and allegorical interpretations. This characterization has been used to contrast the Alexandrian method with the one that later developed at Antioch. Such an overly simplistic contrast has been shown to be inaccurate. The controlling category of Antiochene exegesis was the concept of "Theoria" that was the vision through which the prophet intuited the future by the medium of his/her present situation. This being understood as the process account for the biblical text, it was the task of the Antiochene exegete to discern these dual meanings. Both the Alexandrian and the Antiochene approaches sought to penetrate the negative nature of the text.[6]

By the time of Augustine allegorical exegesis reigned dominant in the West guided by the conceptual distinction of four levels of interpretation: (1) the historical or literal, (2) the allegorical or Christological, (3) the moral or tropological, and (4) the anagogical or eschatalogical. The word Jerusalem, for example, would have the sense of a city at the literal level of exegesis, the church at the allegorical or Christological level, the soul at the moral or tropological level, and the Heavenly City at the anagogical or eschatological level. The ability of a word or passage to convey all these levels of meaning can only be explained in terms of an organizational or interpretative scheme transcending the signs printed on a page. Augustine advised the exegete in "On Christian Doctrine" to "carefully turn over in our minds and meditate upon what we read till an interpretation be found that tends to establish the reign of love."[7] The guarantee against heresy was that Augustine's method carefully operated within the parameter of the church's teaching and doctrine as well as its characteristic Neo-Platonic philosophical assumptions.

Despite Luther and Calvin's attempt during the Reformation to overcome the allegorical method of biblical interpretation by putting emphasis on the literal historical sense of scripture, they both frequently resorted to the method they disapproved of especially in their Christological isogesis of the Old Testament. Contemporary biblical interpretation is in no way free from allegorization even though language functions differently in our post-Enlightenment context than it did during the patritic and medieval eras. Fredric Jameson explains that

> The system of the four levels or senses is particularly suggestive in the solution it provides for an interpretative dilemma which in a privatized world we must live far more intensely than did its Alexandrian and Medieval recipients: namely that incommensurability...between the private and the public, the psychological and the social, the poetic and the political.[8]

The incommensurability that Jameson speaks of above is something that Turner's visions functioned to overcome and as allegories that were at the same time interpretations that facilitated his movement from the literal to the allegorical, moral, and anagogical levels of meaning. When Turner related that during one of his visions he saw "on the leaves in the woods hieroglyphic characters and numbers, with the forms of men in different attitudes, portrayed in blood...." the images of the hieroglyphs possibly adumbrates that with him language operated metynomically. The means by which the gap between the symbol or text and its meaning(s) is overcome constitutes interpretation. When the observed process for arriving at an interpretation seem to us to be based on ritualized and arbitrary gestures on the part of the interpreter—somatic or cerebral—it is regarded as divination. On the other hand, when an interpretation appears in a seemingly supernatural fashion as the result of such a process, it can be regarded as due to conjuration. Thus the terms are being used somewhat interchangeably in this chapter. According to the preceding definitions what would distinguish "modern" interpretative practices from those which we would apply the pejorative term "primitive" becomes, as we shall see, difficult to justify through the binary opposition of such labels.

If divination is "primitive" this description should not be mistaken for a lack of sophistication. Joseph M. Murphy, who investigated divination as practiced among the Yorirba-derived Santeria cults in New York, reports that only after years of intense and arduous study can any degree of proficiency be gained in learning to read the palm nuts or cowrie shells used in divination. The principle underlying the practice is based on

> the linked concepts of order, creation and destiny, the number sixteen
> represents the variables of the human condition, the sixteen possible
> situations of human life...from each of which are drawn sixteen sub-
> ordinate signs....This means 256 possible combinations....The goal
> of the calalawo [priest] is to arrive at the appropriate order for the sit-
> uation of the querent.[9]

From this account we might be warranted in our view that "divination" is the negative label moderns use for the practices engaged in by "primitive" religions in interpreting meaning. In literate societies, the interpretive practices though different are no less esoteric and closed to the noninitiated. Instead of cowrie shells, texts or, we should say, words become the objects of interpretation—words whose meanings remain ever hidden from anyone who attempts to grasp them without the mediation of a scheme whose necessity contradicts any claim of direct access. Turner claimed to have received his meanings of particular biblical passages through direct communication with the Spirit. When, however, we examine his narrative we discover that the interpretations communicated to him of the biblical passages he was contemplating obliged him in turn to interpret the interpretation since its imagery, though vivid, remained ambiguous as to significance. Thus, if Nat Turner's hermeneutics did not, as he stated, involve conjuring what distinguished it from that practice was not its greater claim to rationality, since Murphy has shown that conjuring and divination are performed according to an inherent set of rules. Turner's disclaimer does not explicate the procedures of his own hermeneutic and what he asserted about interpretations having been communicated to him directly from the Spirit invites us to question exactly what this entails. The ambiguity of Turner's visions, their multivariant meanings and their discontinuity with both the texts they purport to interpret, and the praxis they inspired all reinforce the presupposition of one modern approach to literary criticism that all reading is nonneutral, ideologically conditioned and mediated by pre- and misconceptions. As Fredric Jameson says in the Preface to his *The Political Unconscious*:

> we never really confront a text immediately, in all its freshness as a thing-in-itself. Rather, texts come before us as the always-already-read; we apprehend them through sedimented layers of previous interpretations, or—if the text is brand-new-through the sedimented reading habits and categories developed by those inherited interpretative traditions. This presupposition then dictates the use of a method (which I have elsewhere termed the "meta commentary") according to which our object of study is less the text itself than the interpretations through which we attempt to confront and to appropriate it. Interpretation is here construed as an essentially allegorical act, which consists in requiting a given text in terms of a particular interpretative master code.[10]

The preceding quote from Jameson says it all and what we will want to do in the following discussion is to draw out its implications for the church's contemporary problematic of biblical authority. What we will postulate is that the opposing protagonist in this issue represent two distinct yet related approaches to biblical interpretation that we will characterize as the Materialist and Authoritist readings or interpretive strategies. The way these reading strategies differ can be appreciated by detailing the presuppositions of the Materialist strategy so as to identify what it is that causes others, whom we are calling Authoritists, to mount a defensive counter-maneuver to defend the authority of the Bible they perceive the Materialist readings threaten.

The foundation for the Materialist reading strategy was established in the writings of such figures as Karl Marx, Georg Lukacs, Theodor Adorno, Walter Benjamin, Mikhail Bakhtin, and Karl Mannheim, to name a few. Mannheim termed his project a sociology of knowledge that held among its principle theses that while thinking is recognized as a possibility only for individuals, the source of an individual's ideas do not originate in the individual isolated from his/her wider context. In *Ideology and Utopia* he states that "the sociology of knowledge seeks to comprehend thought in the concrete setting of an historical-social situation out of which individually differentiated thought only gradually emerges.[11]

Presently one of the main literary theorists working along these lines is Terry Eagleton who differentiates six interrelated categories explicated in Materialist reading strategies which are the: General Mode of Production (GMP), Literary Mode of Production (LMP), General Ideology (GI), Authorial Ideology (AuI), Aesthetic Ideology (AI) and Text. Concerning the GMP, Eagleton says that it

> always produces a dominant ideological formation...[which] is constituted by a relatively coherent set of "discourses" of values, representations and beliefs....A literary text is related to GI not only by how it deploys language but by the particular language it deploys. The linguistic is always at base the politico-linguistic....Literature is an agent as well as effect of such struggles, a crucial mechanism by which the language and ideology of an imperialist class establishes its hegemony, or by which a subordinated state, class or region preserves and perpetuates at the ideological level an historical identity shattered or eroded at the political (level).[12]

Materialist critics while disagreeing among themselves as to how and through what intermediary structures the GI becomes embodied in a text, all share the type of orientation that comes across quite powerfully in the earlier quote from Eagleton. The relevance of this quote to the present discussion is clear when we take a look at Robert and Mary Coote's *Power, Politics and the Making of the Bible.*

Contradicting the popular view of the Old Testament being written initially to record the faith history of the Hebrews escape from Egypt whose journey involved the receiving of the Law that evolved after their conquest of Canaan, the Coote's penetrate beneath the biblical text to give a slightly different version of what really happened. Their version causes us to question whether Israel was ever really in Egypt. Rather, we are persuaded that Egypt was in Israel and during the decline of its hegemony over Canaan, David took advantage of the political vacuum, to usurp power for himself and, later, legitimate it through the commissioning of sacred texts written by "J," the Yahwist, for use in his court. The same process was recapitulated with the rewrite of the "J" strand by "E" on behalf of Jeroboam, "D's" rewrite of "J" and "E" under Josiah, and "P's" final rewrite and additions during the Babylonian captivity.

The Coote's discussion of the New Testament is equally provocative. Whereas Jesus shared the Pharisees' Cynical evaluation of recorded oral law preferring a more open-ended situation ethic bent to the needs of the poor and therefore had, also, the "pharisaic aversion to recorded wisdom [and thus] left his teaching open to various interpretation" (p. 103). Church politics compelled the bishops who were vying for power with Rabbis, Marcionites, Gnostics, Montanists to develop a doctrine of biblical authority. Though many Christians had been willing to dispense with the Old Testament, or more properly speaking "temple scriptures," and concede jurisdiction to the rabbis over temple institutions, "scriptures survived once again on their gift for legitimating authority in contest for power" (p. 128). The chief theorists for this were Diognetus, Justin, Irenaeus, and Clement. Some of the components of their argument were that

> The right understanding of Christian prophecy depended on the right interpretation of the scriptures and not on direct access. For Justin, the churches that retained the temple scriptures were the true successors of the people of God described in them....
>
> Irenaeus...defended the unity of the Christian scriptures, old and new, and through them the unity of the church under the bishops....He emphasized the apostolic authority and the authority, of Christian writing the bishops defined as apostolic....Against the Gnostics' unrestrained claim to authority he advanced the authority, of the scriptures, whose interpretation the bishops as the churches' heads controlled.[13]

As can be seen in the above is that the Coote's Materialist reading strategy, like Eagleton's, regards the political-economic context of a text's production as the major key to its interpretation. The implications of this assumption are far reaching—the context displaces the individual author particularly with regard to the concept of intent. As a psychoanalytic issue, this question of intent palls beside the more compelling one of how the text functions politically through time and in changing social settings. Thus, text production originates not within the individual consciousness of the author but from the intersection of complex sociopolitical forces expressed and addressed by the text. The particular author's significance is a function of his/her mediation of Eagleton's General Ideology, Authorial Ideology within the arena of the Aesthetic Ideology producing the particular genres of the text

The results of Materialist biblical interpretation have been appropriated by Liberation Theologians in a biblical hermeneutic that interrogates the consequent social practices ensuing from particular readings of the Bible and previous formulations of Christian doctrines. This is motivated by their commitment to doing theology and interpreting the Bible in a way that facilitates liberation. Such a project entails critiquing antagonistic theologies and reading strategies functioning to legitimate the status quo by obfuscating the issues of power and domination hidden in particular theological modes of discourse. The problem encountered in pursuing this strategy is that the Bible and Christian Theology have for so long been drawn into the service of European and Anglo-American hegemony that theological perspectives subservient to the ideological (disguised as theological) reinforcement of this hegemony are neutralized. This is accomplished through outright rejection by labeling them unbiblical or untheological or, when this fails, through pseudo-appropriation.

Furthermore, Liberation Theologians are confronted by the fact that, on face value, there is much in the Bible that condones slavery, racism, sexism, homophobia, anti-Semitism, and so on—at least to those reading it without the political commitment of the Liberation Theologian or method of the Materialist critic. This is a formidable problem because the unconverted can be persuaded only after having accepted Materialist assumptions concerning the text. Threatened by such presuppositions, having intuition where such presuppositions are leading, the unconverted reject the very basis upon which the Liberation Theologian and Materialist critic build their case: a certain conception of what the Bible is.

Rather than labeling the Authoritist position reactionary, it is high time to be straight forward in getting at the heart of the matter. This is something few Materialist Biblical Scholars have been willing to do and even fewer Liberation Theologians. Part of their hesitancy in doing so is due to the fact that stating clearly what a Materialist reading says about the Bible undermines the goal of wresting jurisdiction over the enterprise of biblical interpretation from the Authoritists. To question God as author and subject of the Bible seems to delegitimate the ability of one who does so to advocate social change with an appeal to scripture. If the Materialist position assumes all texts, the Bible notwithstanding, are products of an identical process then it is hard put to define any inherent quality distinguishing the Bible from any other text. Talking about God does not constitute or qualify a text as the Word of God. Indeed, Materialist readings result in interpretations in which God can only be discussed as an ideological construct, or as a component of the religious belief system of the texts human protagonists. Hence as the political-economic forces underlying the biblical text become more specified God becomes less so. The more startling conclusion we reach is that it is not the text per se that we seek to know in bothering to read it but the manner in which the social systems is replicated in the text—but any text will do and the possibility of all text yielding results of equal value is at least implied in the maxim of Liberation Theology that all history is the arena of God's activity.

Yet we sense at this point that we have pushed this line of reasoning too far. After all, to say that God acts in and, even, through history by no means identifies God with history. If this were the case, we could dispense with the Bible and develop Calvin's idea of providence into a philosophy of history. Suddenly, as far as knowledge of God goes, our Materialist strategy has rendered us like one who sits gazing at cowrie shells strewn on the table in what, to our eyes, are only a random pattern because we lack training in the practice of divination. The canon of the Bible whose boundaries are unfixed though a Materialist reading is one whose God has become veiled by the very arena in which God's revelation is anticipated—that of historical activity. We are almost willing to withdrawn any possibility of vindication for the Materialist and scold them for the mischief they have caused in seeming to have undermined the Bible's authority through their method. But before carrying out this verdict, we should clarify for ourselves what we mean by the notion of biblical authority.

Schubert M. Ogden engages in a very in-depth study of this question in his book *On Theology*. There Ogden argues that the Roman Catholic principle of tradition plus scripture, is preferable to the principle sola scripture of the Reformers. One of the reasons for him saying so has to do with the formation of the canon that "expresses a decision or more exactly, a whole history of decisions, on the part of the Church." In its final form "it emerged only in the course of the Church's continuing attempts to control all putative authorities in relation to the primal source of all authority in Christ himself." Thus, from the standpoint of chronology, a tradition was before the Church's canon and determinative in its formation.[14] One of the criteria used in guiding the selection of what would be included in the canon was a theological one of how faithfully it conformed with what the church regarded as the original witness to Christ In that the early church may not have been correct in its judgment "the canon that thus emerged from the early Church's experience and decisions is and must be open to revision." The authority of the New Testament is not derived from it directly, but from that which establishes its own norm "the message that its various writings more or less adequately express.... In other word, 'the canon within the canon' " From this line of reasoning, Ogden asserts that "given our present historical methods and knowledge, the locus of the canon—in the early church's own sense of the apostolic witness—cannot be the writings of the New Testament as such but can only be the earliest traditions of Christian witness accessible to us today by historical-critical analysis of these writings...this means that the first essential procedure involved in the actual use of scripture as a theological authority is not so much hermeneutical as historical"[15] (p. 64).

Thus we can infer from Ogden's study that the biblical Authoritist when pressed to elucidate exactly how the Bible becomes authoritative are required to employ the same historical critical methods as their Materialist counterparts. Where we may want to differ with Ogden is with the apparent optimism he has over the possibility of a successful outcome in this undertaking. In addition, what is problematic for a number of reasons that cannot be gone into here is his view that it is the historic, apostolic Christ rather than the historical Jesus that is to be uncovered as both the norm of theology and the canon within the biblical canon Coote and Coote make us skeptical about this. Such a view places us in the same position as that which Materialist reading puts us: that of reconstructing the religious views of the earliest believers in Jesus as a means of indirect encounter with his person. This indirection and the uncertainty as to whether the apostolic witness corresponds to the one being witnessed is then overcome by abandoning historical critical methods to assume that in such witness Jesus is articulated. On what basis is one who engages in a Materialist or biblical Authoritationist reading justified in claiming that his/her ability to say anything about God or Jesus does not involve divination and conjuring? Paul de Man can perhaps assist us out of this impasse. In *Blindness and*

Insight he—relying on Rousseau's Theory of Rhetoric characterizes the cognitive structure of interpretation as something inescapably entailing the polarity of blindness/insight. Discussing Rousseau's *Discourse on the Origin of Inequality* and *Essay on the Origin of Languages*, de Man points out that their rhetoric is accounted for in their discursive assertions:

> What is being said about the nature of language makes it unavoidable that the texts should be written in the form of a fictionally diachronic narrative or if one prefers to c4ll it so, of an allegory.... Accounting for the rhetoricity of its own mode, the text also postulates the necessity of its own misreading. It knows and asserts that it will be misunderstood. It tells the story, the allegory of its misunderstanding: the necessary degradation of melody into harmony, of language into painting, of the language of passion into the language of need, of metaphor into literal meaning.[16]

The relationship between truth and error does exist in any literary text and can never be severed through the act of interpretation. This is what is presumed in the interpretation of any text that, as de Man points out, narrates the allegory of its own misreading. Paul de Man's theory is supported when we try to determine how accurately it describes what goes on when we read/misread the Bible; it narrates the allegory of its own understanding/misunderstanding. We can easily illustrate de Man's theory by arbitrarily focusing upon the story of Bartimaeus in *"He is blind and while sitting at the roadside he hears Jesus and the crowd passing by for the destination of Jerusalem."* Bartimaeus calls out for mercy addressing Jesus by the Messianic title "Son of David' and not by his proper name that would have been Jesus bar (son of) Joseph. Bartimaeus's blindness through some unexplained process has been transformed into insight. On the other hand, Bartimaeus's insight is not unaccompanied by blindness because he, like everyone else does not understand the way this messianic title has been completely redefined by Jesus's self-understanding. This as with any number of other passages we could choose at random demonstrates the coexistence of truth and error that the Bible posits as a condition of its own interpretation. Therefore, de Man's consolation to us is that "critics' moments of greatest blindness with regard to their own critical assumptions are also the moments at which they achieve their greatest insight." Yet it should always be borne in mind that we never completely overcome the "constitutive discrepancy, in critical discourse, between the blindness of the statement and the insight of the meaning."[17] We are in, what Jonathan Culler describes in his discussion of de Man, one of those "impossible situations where there is no happy issue but only the possibility of playing out roles dramatized in text."[18]

But which roles do we by virtue of our reading practices assign ourselves? Which roles are we committed to playing and what motivates that commitment? If anyone thinks the preceding discussion has avoided the possibility of a Reader Response strategy that misconception should have been dispelled with the quote from Culler. But to show how a reading of the text in which we play out the roles it dramatizes makes reading an ethical act we only need turn to the person we introduced at the beginning of this chapter, Nat Turner. He narrated that

> on the 12th day of May, 1828, I heard a loud noise in the Heavens, and the Spirit instantly appeared to me and said the Serpent was loosened, and Christ had laid down the yoke he had borne for the sins of man, and that I should take it on and fight against the Serpent, for the time was fast approaching when the first should be last and the last first. Question. Do you not find yourself mistaken now? Answer. Was not Christ crucified?[19]

Conclusion

Nat Turner's hermeneutic discovered something about Jesus's teaching that his white contemporaries avoided which is the same thing the Coote's point out about Jesus when they remark:

> His teaching also lent itself to apocalyptic interpretation, as under prevailing circumstances there could be no doubt to anyone who knew the scriptures that God would crate the new order through war. Teachings by and about Jesus soon were called Vishara, "war report" (Greek: evangelion, translated "gospel").[20]

Whether Turner reading strategy was Materialist, Authoritative, or one involving conjuring and divination remains an open question. While we may conjecture about Turners hermeneutical method, the result it yielded was more than conjecture but a visionary liberation process through which—notwithstanding the coexistence of truth and error—he located and followed even unto death, the canon within the canon who is Jesus. His final remark to Gray was "I am here loaded with chains and willing to suffer the fate that awaits me."

The meaning of his deed would be fulfilled and revealed in his execution. Turner's execution would, in turn, serve as a sign of indictment upon the system that provoked his rebellion. Therefore, whites would have to search their own souls to discover the meaning of Turner's rebellion. Turner's opacity is directly related to white's incapacity and unwillingness to encounter the Other through a radical self-critique.

6

The Mulatto as Material/Sexual Site of Modernity's Contacts and Exchanges

"Why, you'se a nigger, too."

—W. E. B. Du Bois, *"Jesus Christ in Georgia"*

[I]n the case of the modern meaning and reception of the Bible in the world of the Atlantic after 1492, a world coincidental with the slave trade, the issue of the trade in human beings who were from Africa, injected the meaning of fundamental distinctions based on physical appearance into the interpretations and meaning of the Biblical text…they explicitly and tacitly assumed that all the important personages in the Biblical text were assumed to be white persons…The place and role of color in the Biblical text during the modern period of the massive introduction and enslavement of peoples of African descent thus took on a metaphysical structure—a structure not limited to the Biblical text but one finding a wide range of verification and justification in the apology for slavery from all European nations. (Charles H. Long, pro., pp. 2–3)

Corporeal properties have also furnished the metaphorical media for distinguishing the pure from the impure, the diseased from the clean and acceptable, the included from the excluded.

—David TheoGoldberg, Racist Culture

Introduction

I briefly mentioned the "mulatto" in chapter two in relation to Cheryl Harris's article "Whiteness as Property." Both whiteness and blackness are forms of materiality that appear in modernity through the imagination of matter. It is through the imagination that black-ness and whiteness assume ontological status. The mulatto category, however, poses a problem for this scheme of allotting entitlements based upon the opposition of these two materialities because of the porous nature of its boundaries. Although this category would seems to reflect some biological reality, it can just as well operate through cultural, linguistic, or religious markers since any such marker can be employed in the service of racialization. The question this category poses for us is that of determining the ultimate source of human value. This is the question that became acute when the West entered into the modern period that it comprehended as "sec-ular." We were discussing this matter in chapter two—how matter was valorized while Africans were dehumanized during the mercan-tilist exchanges occurring at modernity's inception. For W. E. B. Du Bois the mulatto was a sight for reflecting on "the problem of the color line" that he had identified in *Souls of Black Folks* as *the* prob-lem of the twentieth century.[1] Du Bois's selection of this peculiar site should not surprise us since we know that he disciplined him-self not to think in binaries. The notion of "double-consciousness" that Du Bois describes also in *Souls of Black Folks* is one example of the way Du Bois saw the need to think in the liminal spaces of America's racial construct to resist and critique its foundations. In this chapter, I wish to first provide some biographical data about Du Bois and next discuss the significance of *Souls* in the creation of an African American folk tradition. Black religion was at the core of this phenomenon. However, the porous nature of blackness in relation to American culture's broader cultural spectrum and indeed modernity itself is indicated in the porous nature of race as a so-called ontological category. I will then discuss Du Bois's use of the mulatto as a site for critiquing America's racial consciousness and the hypocrisy of American Christianity. For Du Bois, America's god was the idol "whiteness."[2] According to Edward Blum, Du Bois viewed Christianity in America as something that had been turned into "a religion of belligerent and jingoistic whiteness."[3] The final point I will discuss are the implications of Du Bois's treatment of the mulatto for the notion of the imagination of matter.

Du Bois's Phenomenology

W. E. B. Du Bois's *Souls of Black Folks* can be viewed not only as a phenomenology of blackness, but also as a literary invocation of the subjectivity it elucidates. Du Bois's black consciousness, which he termed "double-consciousness," was the dialectical product not only of his encounter with whites but also of his encounter with southern rural blacks whom he posits as "folk." This was a literary move wherein Du Bois engages in self-fashioning while laying the groundwork for a positive African American identity. I will first situate Du Bois's "double-consciousness" notion within the broad context of modern intellectual history. Next I will trace the development of Du Bois's black consciousness as the prelude to his double-consciousness notion. I will then describe more fully this chapter assertion that Du Bois's double consciousness notion emerged from his location vis-à-vis not only the white other but also the black other whom, in identification with, he posits as the folk. Finally I will identify several ways that the projects of black theology and the study of black religion are implicated in this discussion.

W. E. B. Du Bois's *Souls of Black Folks* was first published in 1903—this was around the same time that the German Philosopher Edmund Husserl, as the founder of the phenomenological discipline/method, was entering what is called his mature period. Husserl had been impressed and influenced by William James who taught Du Bois at Harvard University. Initially Husserl understood his method to have affinity with James's radical empiricism and the depiction of interior life as a "stream of consciousness." He later began to see an affinity between his phenomenology and Descartes's earlier project that grounded apodictic certainty in the doubting subject—the "cogito." Then, still later, Husserl would revisit Kant's epistemological notions about the transcendental subject. But it was not until as late as 1923 that Husserl came to the realization, in his *First Philosophical Lecture*, that his phenomenology suffered from its failure to account for the being of others. Later, Husserl was able to frame the problem as being not how the other is constituted for consciousness but how the other actually enters into consciousness.[4] (M, p. 176) Had Husserl read Du Bois's *Souls* he would have observed a provocative move that may have indicated the solution required him to account for the subject in his phenomenology.

What distinguished Husserl and Du Bois was, among other things, where they situated themselves in the world of perceivable entities. Husserl's began his phenomenological investigations by situating human consciousness before nature and the imagined objects of mathematics. Du Bois began his phenomenology by situating consciousness in the social realm where the consciousness of blacks encountered that of whites. After so doing Du Bois was able to make the observation that

> After the Egyptian and Indian, the Greek and Roman, the Teuton and Mongolian, the Negro is a sort of seventh son, born with a veil and gifted with second-sight in the American world, a world which would yield him no true self-consciousness, but only lets him see himself through the revelation of the other world. It is a peculiar sensation, this double-consciousness, this sense of always looking at one's self through the eyes of the others, of measuring one's soul by the tape of a world that looks on in amused contempt and pity. One ever feels his two-ness,—an American, a Negro, two souls, two thoughts, two unreconciled strivings; two warring ideals in one dark body, whose dogged strength alone keeps it from being torn asunder.[5]

Du Bois's notion of "double-consciousness" anticipated by twenty years the move Husserl would make in accounting for how the other appears in consciousness. But Husserl's description attempts to be universal and, as such, fails to illuminate the existential dimension of what Du Bois—again in *Souls*—defined as the issue confronting us in modernity when he said: "The problem of the twentieth century is the problem of the color-line,—the relation of the darker to the lighter races of men [*sic*] in Asia and in Africa, in America and the islands of the sea."[6] Beginning at about the first quarter of the twentieth century, such figures as Martin Buber (1878–1965) and Martin Heidegger (1889–1976) developed independent treatments of the role of the other in consciousness. An irreducible priority is imputed to the Other (which now is capitalized) in the phenomenologies of Emmanuel Levinas (1906–1995) and Jean-Paul Sartre (1905–1980). Nevertheless, neither Levinas nor Sartre provided us with an actual phenomenological description of what happens in encounters between blacks and whites. This occurred in 1952 when the Martiniquean psychiatrist Frantz Fanon published his *Peau Noir, Masques Blancs* in Paris, France that appeared in English in 1967 under the title *Black Skin, White Masks*. In that book where Fanon applied Sartre's phenomenological analysis to the mentalities of colonized blacks, we hear distinct echoes of Du Bois's analysis in *Souls*. Fanon wrote:

> Ontology—once it has finally admitted as leaving existence by the way side—does not permit us to understand the being of the black man [*sic*]. For not only must the black man be black; he must be black in relation to the white man [*sic*]...Overnight the Negro has

been given two frames of reference within which he has to place himself.[7]

Here Fanon, without using the term double-consciousness directly, is describing the phenomenon of double-consciousness. What I have said thus far, hopefully, speaks to the importance of Du Bois's notion of double-consciousness not only for black thought but also within the wider spectrum of Western Intellectual History. Nevertheless, these observations have not spoken directly to the issue of Du Bois's relevance to black theology and the study of black religion. Nor have my observations indicated how Du Bois came to formulate his notion of "double-consciousness." I shall address this later question—how Du Bois came to formulate his notion of double consciousness—as a means to answering the former question regarding Du Bois's relevance to black theology and the study of black religion. To do so I will utilize material from Du Bois's autobiographical writings to serve as commentaries on *Souls*.

Childhood and Early Adulthood

Du Bois's childhood in Great Barrington was relatively free of racial tension and oppression. He developed a sense of his intellectual prowess early in life and seems never to have suffered from feelings of racial inadequacy. Strange as it may seem, Du Bois seems to have lived during his early childhood years almost oblivious to his racial identity. We might accurately say Du Bois lack a racial identity during these early years. One of the first occasions that Du Bois had reason to contemplate what his race signified in the perception of others was in high school when students were exchanging visiting cards. Du Bois wondered if his skin color was what caused a white girl who was new to the community to refuse his card. Another incident that records the emergence of a racial identity in Du Bois's consciousness was more positive. This took place during his first trip away from Great Barrington when he was in high school. Du Bois stopped in Providence to visit his grandmother's friend on his return from visiting his paternal grandfather in New Bedford. While in Providence he attended an annual picnic attended by blacks from three states. Du Bois had never seen that many African Americans. He wrote in his autobiography that he witnessed "The whole gorgeous gamut of the American Negro world; the swaggering men, the beautiful girls, the laughter and gaiety, the unhampered self-expression. I was astonished and inspired. I apparently noted nothing of poverty or degradation, but only extraordinary beauty of skin-color and utter equality of mien, with absence so far as I could see of even the shadow of the line of race."[8]

Du Bois wanted to attend Harvard University[9] immediately after he graduated from high school. Lack of finances prevented this. His mother had died the same year of his high school graduation. Some local clergy and the high school principal came to Du Bois's aid by providing a scholarship for him to attend Fisk University in Nashville, Tennessee. Recalling his first impressions of the South and Fisk University, Du Bois wrote:

> I was thrilled to be for the first time among so many people of my own color or rather of such various and such extraordinary colors, which I had only glimpsed before, but who it seemed were bound to me by new and exciting and eternal ties. Never before had I seen young men so self-assured...above all for the first time I saw beautiful girls...

> So I came to a region where the world was split into white and black halves, and where the darker half was held back by race prejudice and legal bonds, as well as by deep ignorance and dire poverty. But facing this was not a lost group, but at Fisk a microcosm of a world and a civilization in potentiality. Into this world I leapt with enthusiasm. A new loyalty and allegiance replaced my Americanism: henceforward I was a Negro.[10]

At Fisk Du Bois became black and developed a sense of racial vocation.

> The excellent and earnest teaching, the small college classes, the absence of distractions, either in athletics or society, enabled me to arrange and build my program for freedom and progress among Negroes. I replaced my hitherto egocentric world by a world centering and whirling about my race in America.

> For this group I built my plan of study and accomplishment. Through the leadership of men like myself and my fellows, we were going to have these enslaved Israelites out of the still enduring bondage in short order...I could think of it mainly as a battle of wits; of knowledge and deed, which by sheer reason and desert, must eventually overwhelm the forces of hate, ignorance and reaction.[11]

We may want to qualify Du Bois's claim that he became a Negro at Fisk. Du Bois became aware of being a Negro for sure. Indeed, this awareness was accompanied by a sense of pride. However, by Du Bois' own admission he still lack a full and profound existential understanding of what it meant to be black. Thus, Du Bois had come to problematize himself during this early period in intellectual formation. In a certain sense, we can see this search for self-definition, clarification, and formation in all of Du Bois's articles, books, and essays. Du Bois assumed a teaching assignment in rural East Tennessee during his summer vacation because: "I determined to know something of the Negro in the country districts...I had heard about the country in the South as the real seat of slavery. I wanted to know it. Needless to say the experience was invaluable. I traveled not only in space but in time. I touched the very shadow of slavery."[12]

In Tennessee's back country, Du Bois not only made contact with folk who were still emerging from slavery, he encountered the religion that was born in the crucible of that experience. This left an indelible impression on his mind and is recounted some years later in the *Souls*. One night while attending a revival, Du Bois beheld the God of African Americans. I believe this was a transformative experience but more at the unconscious spiritual level than at the level of conscious existential awareness. Du Bois did not quite know what had happened to him. What we notice is that Du Bois was feeling an urge—sense of call—to go into the wide world and liberate his people from bondage just as Moses did when he advocated for the Hebrews before Pharoah. But before Du Bois could have the faintest chance of accomplishing this he would need to journey into the heart of darkness and encounter the Negro's God. Hence, when we read Du Bois's *Autobiography* he seems to have willed himself into courageous action. Reading with a theological sense, however, allows us to see—or, at least, imagine—how Du Bois is being called and then sent into his vocation. It was the God whose heirophany occurred in the funkiness of black communal gathering that called Du Bois to himself and then commissioned him for his great work. Du Bois wrote in *Souls*:

> It was out in the country, far from my foster home, on a dark Sunday night...we could hear dimly across the fields a rhythmic cadence of song—soft, thrilling, powerful, that swelled and died sorrowfully in our ears. I was a country schoolteacher then, fresh from the East, and had never seen a Southern Negro revival...And so most striking to me as I approached the village and the little plain church perched aloft, was the air of intense excitement that possessed that mass of black folk. A sort of suppressed terror hung in the air and seemed to seize us,—a pythian madness, a demonic possession, that lent terrible reality to song and

word. The black and massive form of the preacher swayed and quivered as the words crowded to his lips and flew at us in singular eloquence.[13]

From this mystical experience of the Negro world, Du Bois entered the white world of Harvard University. Du Bois acquired a black consciousness at Fisk University. He acknowledged this transformation when he wrote: "I went to Harvard as a Negro not simply by birth but recognizing myself as a member of a segregated caste whose situation I accepted but was determined to work from within that caste to find my way out." After studying at Harvard, he spent a year at the University of Berlin. Du Bois experience an epiphany while in Europe where, under the spell of Europe's more liberal racial attitudes and the atmosphere of the German Romantic Movement, he wrote:

Night—grand and wonderful. I am glad I am living. I rejoice as a strong man to win a race, and I am strong—is it egotism—is it assurance—or is it the silent call of the world spirit that makes me feel that I am royal and that beneath my scepter a world of kings shall bow. The hot dark blood of a black forefather is beating at my heart, and I know that I am either a genius or a fool. O I wonder what I am—I wonder what the world is—I wonder if life is worth the Strum...If I strive, shall I live to strive again? I do not know and in spite of the wild yearning for Eternity that makes my heart-sick now and then—I shut my teeth and say I do not care. Carpe Diem! [Seize the day!—that is, enjoy the present.]...I am striving to make my life all that life may be—and I am limiting that strife only in so far as that strife is incompatible with others of my brothers and sisters making their lives similar.

What we note in the above is this notion of striving. Ten years after penning those lines in his journal, Du Bois would be using the same term to describe the social psychology of African Americans in general in the chapter in *Souls* titled "Of Our Spiritual Strivings."

Du Bois's Construction of African American Folk

Martin Favor authored a book with the interesting title *Authentic Blackness: The Folk in the New Negro Renaissance*. In this book, Favor focuses on several African American intellectuals associated with the Harlem Renaissance to explore the issue of black identity in America. Relying heavily on literary theory, Favor explored the issue of who defined black identity and how it was defined. Favor found that during the 1920s, black identity was largely a literary product of the black intellectuals located in Harlem who wrote about the "New Negro." The interesting thing in Favors study is that he shows how most of the writings about the New Negro by the middle-class black bourgeoisie intellectuals were based on their representations of the "folk" who were seen to embody authenticity. Thus, Du Bois's notion of "double-consciousness"—about which more will be said later—contains more complexities than he was able to express in his description. The black consciousness that Du Bois posits as a double-consciousness is indeed something that the individual and group fashion for themselves—and, as such, this black consciousness incorporates and masks other factors such as class, geography, sexuality, and gender.

In making this observation we must reconsider Frantz Fanon's statement about the phenomenon of double-consciousness in *Black Skin, White Masks* when he wrote that:

> As long as the black man [*sic*] is among his own, he will have no occasion except in minor internal conflicts to experience his being through others. There is of course the moment of "being for others" of which Hegel speaks, but every ontology is made unattainable in a colonized and civilized society.[14]

This statement taken along with Du Bois's description of double-consciousness in *Souls* masks the fact that the notion of the "folk" in "black folk" was a result of Du Bois's sense of separation not only from white society but also from the social group he invokes as the "folk." I used the work 'invoke" quite deliberately to indicate that although they existed before Du Bois wrote about them, they had no literary presence and certainly not one wherein they represented and embodied the essence of black culture. Du Bois, like the German Romantics with whom he was well familiar at the time of his authorship of *Souls*, had to identify who was to represent the real essence of the nation so to speak. Du Bois pointed not to his own class but to one to whom he did not belong and initially knew nothing about. *Souls* being a phenomenological description of black life or, we could even say, blackness represents also Du Bois's achievement of self-fashioning. Double-consciousness, therefore, is not structured by a simple binary opposition ensuing from the way African Americans internalize the signification of blackness in the white psyche. Double-consciousness has other levels wherein class and geographic location and, perhaps, gender are implicated in the alienation experienced by the certain African American from the black masses whom they signify in the minds of the white other.

What we observe through reading Du Bois's autobiographical works is that in becoming a Negro Du Bois had to do several things. One of the things he had to do was make a change of geographic location. He had to go to the South where most blacks were living. He also had to move away from his own privileged social-class background into that of rural blacks. According to Favor:

> Du Bois feels the necessity to write himself into the folk through *Souls* in an effort to prove himself as a legitimate critic and theorizer of black culture and identity...he willingly submerges aspects of his status as a "brilliant yankee Negro from Harvard and Europe" in an effort to draw on—indeed, to make central to his arguments about culture—the African American fold tradition. In a series of conscious moves, Du Bois writes himself into a folk positionality that lends authority to his explication of blackness in America. Yet "race" must be, at least in some respects, performative rather than essential to make such transformation possible.[15]

What we should bear in mind is that the debate that ensued among black intellectuals and cultural critics during the 1920s was how to depict the true black experience. Langston Hughes was taken to task for depicting lower-class Negroes in his novels who were an embarrassment to the black bourgeoisie. So too was Zora Neale Hurston taken to task for her writings documenting Negro folklore. For Du Bois the rural blacks who were just emerging from slavery embodied authentic blackness. Their consciousness was not one structured solely by racial oppression—it was a religious consciousness; its strength was drawn from a connection with life's primal depths. Du Bois observed that during his brief sojourn in the south's backwoods—but as an outsider who still had not entered into the experience whose observation filled him with dread. Du Bois, however, was close enough to that world to intuit its genius. In other words, when Du Bois talks in *Souls* of having to simultaneously assume two frames of reference—the way the world appears to him and the way he appears to the world—the white world, he is leaving the reciprocal gaze of the black folk world out of his analysis. He is able to do this because he has positioned himself in this world, and it is from this vantage point that he lodges his description of black folk culture. This description is at the same time a critique of American culture. Du Bois did not wish to provide a ceiling of black achievement—his own accomplishments prove this point; he did, however, wish to provide it with a foundation.

Contemplating the Mulatto

"Why you'se a nigger, too," is a quotation taken from short story W. E. B. Du Bois published in 1911 titled, "Jesus Christ in Georgia." So as to feel the full weight of the signifier, I have chosen deliberately to retain Du Bois's original language and not translate the objectionable term "nigger" into some politically correct equivalent. In this story Jesus, described as the stranger, appears in Georgia. The stranger has somehow hitched a ride with the colonel who had been engaged in conversation with a promoter about using convict labor on the construction of a railway line. The stranger has seemingly appeared out of nowhere and joined in the conversation. The colonel found himself asking the stranger if he needed a lift into town. When they approached the colonel's mansion, he invited the stranger into his home. The colonel and his wife talk for some time with the stranger in the dimly lit parlor. The parlor lights are brightened when it was time for tea.

> With one accord they all looked at the stranger, for they had hardly seen him well in the glooming twilight. The woman started in amazement and the colonel half rose in anger. Why, the man was a mulatto, surely—even if he did not own the Negro blood, their practiced eyes knew it.[16]

During the commotion the black butler entered the room. "The old man paused in bewilderment, tottered and then, with sudden gladness in his eyes, dropped to his knees as the tray crashed to the floor. 'My Lord!' he whispered, 'and my God!'"

> Later in the tale the stranger's path crosses that of an escaped convict. "The stranger made a cup of his hands and gave the man water to drink, bathed his hot head, and gently took the chains and irons from his feet. By and by the convict stood up. Day was dawning above the tree tops. He looked into the stranger's face, and for a moment a gladness swept over the stains of his face. "Why you'se a nigger, too," he said.[17]

In this story Du Bois has brilliantly coupled the issue of race in America with the Christological issue that lies at the heart of the

Christian faith and is found in the definition of Christ's nature in what is called the Chalcedon Creed. Some have said that the controversy centered on a single Greek letter. One party understood Christ to be one person out of (the Greek "*ek*") two natures while another party understood him to be one person in (the Greek "*en*") two natures. The final wording represented an attempt to find a formula that would be acceptable or at least a middle way between the *Monophysite* and *dyophysite* propositions. Christ was defined as consubstantial (*homoousios*) with God with regard to his divinity and, at the same time, consubstantial (*homoousios*) with us with regard to his humanity the only difference being, Christ was without sin.

Du Bois's story bears upon this doctrine in its critique of the complicity of American Christianity with racism. The story illustrates that the failure of the church to develop a nonracist Christian Anthropology has had dire consequences for its Christology. Du Bois's critique, to state the matter in stronger terms, is that a racist society will always err in its Christology and even wind up murdering the Christ. The Christ always appears in the guise of the most despised in society and not among those who have elevated themselves to the status of gods. A racist society can never recognize and pay appropriate homage to Christ because its gaze cannot perceive beyond his external appearance and reach the depths of his humanity where his divinity also is revealed. What is the identity of the stranger? According to the colonel he is a mulatto. According to the black butler he is the Christ. According to the convict he is "a nigger too."

Du Bois's Christology is a radical critique of America and the church's Anthropology. The two natures of Christ are understood to exist in such a way that allowed Christ to be fully human and fully Divine. Christ's double-consciousness is resolved by his complete identification with humanity—even slaves. America and its churches, however, divided humanity into inferiors and superiors, whites and blacks. In so doing they did violence to their own Christology. The colonel was outraged because he has mistaken the stranger for a white man but where and how do we draw the line of demarcation separating a white person from a black person. Supposed the individual has one white and one black parent? Such an individual was termed a mulatto. But at what point does the person cease to be a mulatto and become white and able to enjoy all the privileges reserved for persons enjoying that status? A society based on race oppression must have an answer to this question or else be plagued by such embarrassing incidents as described in Du Bois's short story. Discerning physical differences among persons allowed a system based on distinct privileges and entitlements to function. But this system could not define the offspring of a black and white parent in the manner that the church fathers resolved the Christological issue at Chalcedon when they pronounced Christ as both fully human and fully divine. At what point does white society recognize the non-white person as being essentially "consubstantial" with its own identity?

Whiteness and blackness—as mutually dependent social constructs—have always been contested category in the United States. Few people have taken the time to read the Supreme Court decision that provided the basis for segregation by constructing the "separate but equal" doctrine. The wording of this decision indicates that to maintain an apartheid type social system the powers that be had to legally define the operational racial categories signifying the distinctions being made. Thus, the issue in the Plessy v. Ferguson[18] decision was "whether, under the laws of Louisiana, the petitioner belongs to the white or colored race." Plessy v. Ferguson was decided during a time when according to Joel Williamson:

> Southerners came to fear hidden blackness, the blackness within seeming whiteness. They began to look with great suspicion upon mulattoes who looked white, white people who behaved as black, and a whole congeries of alien insidious in their midst who would destroy their whole moral universe. The continuous search for invisible blackness, the steady distrust of the alien, and the ready belief in the existence of the enemy hidden within gave rise to a distinctly paranoid style in Southern white culture in the twentieth century.[19]

In *Racechanges: White Skin, Black Face in American Culture*, Susan Gubar documents the preoccupation with this theme in a number of novels published between the late nineteenth and mid twentieth centuries. Mark Twain's 1894 story *The Tragedy of Pudd'nhead Wilson* expressed the need for eternal vigilance. In this story the slave mother places her light-skinned infant in the clothes and cradle of her master's son to prevent him from being sold down river. The master's son is placed in her own infant's clothes and cradle. William Faulkner provides another example of what we are discussing in the 1942 story "Delta Autumn" in *Go Down Moses*. At a certain point the protagonist, as in Du Bois's short story, is identified as not white but "a nigger." Isaac McCaslin recognizes the black identity of a woman who has born a child by his distant relative Roth Edmonds. "Though she sounds like 'a Northerner,' the mysterious mother mentions an aunt taking in washing, thereby providing a clue that leads Ike to look at 'the pale lips, the skin pallid and dead-looking yet not ill, the dark and tragic and foreknowing eyes' and proclaim her 'a nigger.'"[20] Williamson wrote:

> Southern whites of the Radical persuasion became very fearful of mulattoes passing for white…Southern whites became deeply suspicious of dark strangers, sometimes even expelling such persons from their community on the ground that he was attempting to pass for white. Prospective brides and grooms, applicants to schools, fraternities, and sororities, and people in general with whom one's children might come in general contact came to have their ancestries closely scrutinized.[21]

Plessy v. Ferguson must be understood within the framework of this psycho-cultural context. The argument made by Plessy's attorneys was not that he should have been afforded the right to sit wherever he liked on the railway train as an African American enjoying the equal protection clauses of the amended U.S. Constitution. Their argument was that because Plessy looked white he should have been able to afford himself of the rights of other people from whom he was physically indistinguishable. Plessy belonged to a group of Creoles who named themselves *Comite des Citoyens*. They were proud of their mixed racial ancestry and thought of themselves as neither black nor white. They referred to themselves as *gens de couleur* or people of color and sought to carve out a space for themselves beyond the black-white dialectic of racial segregation.[22]

Plessy's attorneys argued that there was no legal definition of who was white or black. Plessy was the material embodiment of their appeal that race was a porous category. Albion Tourgee argued:

> There is no law of the United States, or of the state of Louisiana defining the limits of race—who are white and who are colored? By what rule then shall any tribunal be guided in determining racial character? It may be said that all those should be classed as colored in whom appears a visible admixture of colored blood. By what law? With what justice? Why not count everyone as white in whom is visible any trace of white blood? There is but one reason to wit, the domination of the white race.[23]

Plessy's attorneys also argued he was deprived of the value of being phenotypically white.

> How much would it be *worth* to a young man entering upon the practice of law, to be regarded as a *white* man rather than a colored one?...Probably most white persons if given the choice, would prefer death to life in the United States as a *colored persons*. Under these conditions, is it possible to conclude that *the reputation of being* white is not property? Indeed it is the most valuable sort of property, being the master-key that unlocks the golden door of opportunity?[24]

Plessy's defense strategy challenging whether it was possible to legally categorize him as either white or black backfired terribly. Justice Henry Billings Brown had nothing but contempt for Tourgee's assertion that race was legally indefinable and arbitrary. He found nothing illegal or strange in Louisiana's segregation practices. According to Justice Brown Louisiana's segregation practices conformed to "the established usages, customs and traditions of the people." Indeed, segregation laws were reasonable, necessary, and "must always exist so long as white men are distinguished from the other race by color." In his opinion whether Plessy was white or black was not the issue before the court. It was for Louisiana's courts to determine "whether under the laws of Louisiana...[he] belongs to the white or colored race."[25] In the Supreme Courts decision was a tacit admission of the property function of whiteness. The Court admitted if the plaintiff had been white he would have been entitled to "damages against the company for being deprived of his property." However, "if he be a colored man and be so assigned, he has been deprived of no property, since he is not lawfully entitled to the reputation of being a white man."[26] This opinion begged the issue of whom and by what criteria people are assigned to one or another racial category.

This confusion has a legislative history going back to slavery. What we see in various statutes are legal definitions of the slave associated with the concept of race that was emerging in the imagination of the colonies. I use the word association because slavery was never based solely on race in colonial law. One reason that slavery could not be legally based on race was because there were people being held in bondage who were phenotypically white. There also were people who were recognizably Negro who were free. But since there was an association between slave status and race, there was a need eventually to devise a legal definition for deciding who was white and who was Negro. Generally whites were not held in perpetual bondage.

However, since people who looked white—people who were pheno-typically white but were known to have a black ancestor—could be slaves the necessity arose to distinguish whites from mulattos. All of these classifications were driven by economic consideration. If, for example, a male slave fathered a child by a free white female, the child would inherit the father's status. The child did not, however, inherit the father's status if it was the other way around—if the father was free and the mother was a slave. Maryland passed a statute in 1664 stipulating that

> all Negroes or other slaves already within the Province and all Negroes and other slaves to be hereafter imported into the Province shall serve Durante Vita [for life]. And all children born of any Negro or other slave shall be slaves as their fathers were for the term of their lives. And forasmuch as divers freeborn English women forgetful of their free condition and to the disgrace of our Nation does intermarry with Negro Slaves…shall serve the master of such slave during the life of her husband. And the Issue of such freeborn women so married shall be slaves as their fathers were.[27]

Other colonies passed similar statutes. Numerous such statutes were originally generated to address specific legal problems arising from interracial unions and then, in the course of composing the statute, stretched to cover as many scenarios that were conceivable at the time. In 1692 Maryland enacted another statute pertaining to inter-racial unions. This was the first statute that imposed the penalty of life-time bondage on any free Negro for a particular crime. That statute stated that

> Any free born English or white woman be she free or servant shall hereafter intermarry with any Negro or other slave or to any Negro made free shall immediately upon such marriage forfeit her freedom and become a servant during the term of seven years…and if he be a free Negro or slave to whom she intermarried, he shall thereby also forfeit his freedom and become a servant to be used aforesaid during his natural life.[28]

These statutes represent legal attempts to settle the vexing question was how to distinguish a mulatto from a white person. The mulatto's existence made the surveillance of black bodies difficult since these blacks looked white. Furthermore, if some blacks looked white, how could black subordination be based upon white superiority?

Defining Race and Determining Value

The confusion and phobia around racial purity was connected with the parallel and connected issue of money. Race and money entail the imagination of matter. Imagining money as either an arbitrary sign or as consisting of something endowed with intrinsic value has always been an item of contention. In "The Anthropology of Money" Bill Maurer observes that money functions as a "metaphor for and exemplar of the problem of the relationship between sign and substance, thought and matter, abstract value and its instantiation in physical and mental labors and products."[29] Michael O'Malley has shown in his article, "Specie and Species: Race and the Money Question in Nineteenth-Century America," that debates in Congress during the mid- nineteenth century about specie, and the gold standard were coupled with the debate over the status of blacks in the Union. That these debates were also about purity should not come as surprise to anyone acquainted with psychoanalytic theory. Without going into the reason these two things become linked, suffice it to say that money was at one time somehow subconsciously associated with feces and even the devil in both western and nonwestern societies. This is documented in Keith's *The Decline of Magic* and Tussag's *The Devil and Commodity Fetishism in Latin America* respectively. What O'Malley's article is about is how the fetishization of both intrinsic value and racial purity took place in American society. According to O'Malley "the freer a market society becomes, the more it would imagine differences—such as racial or sexual differences—that resist negotiation because of their 'intrinsic' character." He concluded his study by pointing out that "facing the possibility that men such as Plessy could renegotiate racial value—facing the 'staring sign' of Plessy's mixed heritage—the court responded with irrational theories of intrinsic racial difference."[30]

In discussing O'Malley's article, Nell Irvine Painter points out that the connection between black people and money in mid-nineteenth-century Congressional debates was more than just metaphorical—blacks were indeed property that "served simultaneously as an embodied currency and a labor force...they were a kind of money...slaves were collateral for commercial, speculative, and personal loans. Enslaved persons, along with real estate, were subject to exchange, and as such, they undergirded the economies of eighteenth-century New York City as well as that of nineteenth-century southern states."[31] Chief Justice Taney testified to the slave's exchange value in his opinion in the Dred Scott case when he wrote that Negroes

> had for more than a century before been regarded as beings of an inferior order, and altogether unfit to associate with the white race, either in social or political relations; and so far inferior, that they had no rights which the white man was bound to respect; and that the negro might justly and lawfully be reduced to slavery for his benefit. He was bought and sold, and treated as an ordinary article of merchandise and traffic, whenever a profit could be made by it. This opinion was at the time fixed and universal in the civilized portion of the white race. It was regarded as an axiom in morals as well as in politics.[32]

The underlying issue connecting race and money in O'Malley's study is that of value. What is the locus of value per se and what is the locus of human value? Was value a convention of society or the state or was it based on something intrinsic to the material being valued? August Merrimon of North Carolina is quoted in the Congressional Record, 43rd Congress, 1st session (January 21, 1874) as saying that "money implies essential value. It is of the essence that money shall have essential value in it; and the experience of the world from the earliest periods down to the present time is that nothing constitutes the medium of exchange like gold or silver...it would seem that the Almighty had provided these substances to answer for this very purpose." Several months later in speaking in opposition to the civil rights Merrimon asked, "Why did God make our skins white? Why did he make the negro's skin black?...I ask the Senators, where do they get the authority to change the color God has blessed us with? Where can any authority be found to make my skin black and corrupt my blood?" Lincoln Stephens regarded the Fifteenth Amendment as "exactly analogous to the prohibition on the States in the original Constitution—that no State shall coin money; emit bills of credit; make anything but gold or silver a legal tender. His argument was that the Fifteenth Amendment coined counterfeit citizens."[33] Or perhaps we should say, the fear was that the Fifteenth Amendment, in giving blacks civil rights transformed everyone into a mulatto. The argument for money essentialism was related to the preoccupation with racial purity. According to O'Malley:

> The intrinsic value claims associated with silver and gold bear a close resemblance to the era's essentialist notions of identity—that is, its theories of racial character. Both use often identical metaphors and both

establish their claims on the authority of what they regard as natural law. In the work of those political economists who argued most strenuously for specie money and who opposed immigration, essentialist ideas about gold and silver and about identity come together, and it was this conjunction of "specie" and "species" that gave gold standard arguments their popular force.[34]

This fear is dramatized in Kate Chopin's 1892 story "Desiree's Baby." A white man, Armand, discerns black traits in the infant he has fathered by Desiree. This revelation causes him to immediately suspect Desiree's racial purity and to accordingly reject and banish her. At first he "read the baby's dark complexion as a sign of Desiree's race" and "he assumed the baby's materiality was maternal while its symbolic place in society was paternal...Armand saw visible links between Desiree and the baby, not between the infant and himself." However, later in the story Armand happens upon a letter from his mother written to his father stating: "I thank God for having so arranged our lives that our dear Armand will never know that his mother, who adores him, belongs to the race that is cursed with the brand of slavery."[35]

Black Religion and Ultimate Value

In understanding religion as the ideological replica of the political economy, Marx saw modern capitalism's chief components modeled in the theological doctrines concerning the Trinity, the two natures of Christ (Chalcedon), and the transubstantiation of the elements of the Eucharist into Christ's matter. The analogy Marx makes could be summarized as follows: Through the mystical processes of incarnation and transubstantiation, Jesus was both fully human and fully Divine; the Eucharist is both bread and Christ; the fetish is both a manufactured object and a god; the commodity exists as both a natural form in terms of its use value and an ideal form in terms of its exchange value; and the slave is both a thing and a person.

When it comes to the slave, however, this analogue does not quite work because, in the slave's case, his/her materiality is despiritualized to assign the slave an equivalent quantitative value whereas in the other cases—for example, those of Jesus humanity, the Eucharistic bread, the Fetishistic object, and the commodity as use value—the actual material form is being endowed with surplus value.

Slave religion can be seen, in this light, as expressing the slave's perception of the ultimate source of human value, as in the Spiritual: "O Freedom...before I'd be a slave I'll be buried in my grave and go home to my Lord and be free." African American Spirituality was a means by which its adherents made contact with the source of human value and thereby acquired value. Now as former chattel, African Americans must still probe the question of value from a very different material and existential location than their white counterparts—from within the veil of blackness and with a double consciousness. Du Bois coined this term at the turn of the century in his *Souls of Black folks*. That this term is still a relevant description of how African Americans adjudicate the spiritual problematic of blackness is evident in what John Edgar Wideman writes in *Fatheralong: A Meditation on Fathers and Sons, Race and Society*, published recently in 1995, which I will quote at length.

> If a certain kind of camera, yet to be invented, achieved the capacity to record the instantaneous give-and-take between two black people meeting on the street, looking at the artifact this "camera" produces you would see the shared sense of identity, the bloody secrets linking us and setting us apart, the names flapping in the air—black, negro, African American, colored, etc., etc.—we sometimes answer to but never internalize completely because they are inadequate to describe the sense of common ground we exchange at this moment. We acknowledge the miracle and disgrace of our history in the twinkling of an eye, many, many times a day as we meet each other, nodding or speaking or touching or just passing by, seemingly without a glance.[36]

It is interesting that, in the subtitle, Wideman calls his book a meditation. This brings to mind another *Meditation* authored at a much earlier moment in modernity, 1641—that of the celebrated founder of modern philosophy, Renee Decartes. Decartes's "cogito" was not depended for its apprehension on bodily awareness or the perception of nature. Indeed, his procedure was to doubt the existence of everything until the only thing remaining was the activity of doubting. From this arose the insight "I think therefore I am" that gave the "I" or "cogito" epistemological priority. According to Richard Kennington, Decartes's "cogito is...prior to, and independent of, any determination of the materiality or immateriality of the human mind."

David Theo Goldberg has observed that racist discourse always entails significations about the body. Certain bodies must be distinguished from others for the purposes of classification that justify those labeled for exploitation.[37] The exploitation was a form of commodification aimed at relegating certain human bodies to the realm of thinghood and thus depriving them of soul. We have seen in this chapter how the negative signification of black bodies as chattel and later as second-class citizens provides the constant or referent for the positive signification of everything and everyone associated with "whiteness." This last materiality has come to function as a form of property according to Cheryl Harris who was discussed at the beginning of chapter two in this volume. We have also seen how the mulatto problematized the logic of racist discourse in the United States by making the boundary between exploitable and nonexploitable bodies ambiguous. Indeed, the ambiguity itself undermined the very rationale for the distinction that was made between two kinds of bodies—white and black. The souls of black folks have a material locus. This locus is in their bodies. Their bodies form the locus for spiritual reflection because it was through the sale of their bodies that they became black and were relegated to the realm of pure materiality. The revelations that occurred during and after the terrors of the Middle Passage and slavery produced the somatic and oral syntax of the moans and shouts of the Spirituals, the Blues, work songs, jazz, and so on. These revelations were experienced through the bodies of black slaves—bodies that were beaten, castrated, raped, and rendered invisible developed a spirituality that would reverse the process of transfiguration that was reducing them to sheer matter. What African American slaves developed were covert practices of reverse transubstantiation whereby they were recreated and reconstituted as human beings. Among the most common of these reverse transubstantiation practices was "spirit-possession." The Spirit—whether that of the Holy Ghost, an *Orisha*, or an Ancestor—was one of the few things African Americans could possess that could not be alienated by the Master. What kept slave bodies from being reduced to sheer matter was the succor and guidance they received both through their exchanges with each other and, as well, the gods who inhabited their world. In being reduced to chattel, Africans represented a new form of materiality; but through their intercourse with the gods, that materiality was creatively transubstantiated to assert a new mode of modern consciousness. It was not a consciousness that emerged, like Decartes's "cogito," through isolation from its locus in the body; rather, it was a consciousness of the body—a suffering body—in its interaction with other bodies. The gods who appeared to help the slave transcend the immediacy

of his/her suffering was said to "ride" the bodies of the spirit possessed. This was a new mode of materiality and consciousness was
neither African, European, nor Amerindian—hence Du Bois's term,
"double-consciousness." This consciousness derived its value from
making contact with a mode of ultimacy lying beyond the empirical
dimension of those exchanges associated with its oppression. Rather
than being a consciousness devoid of content and reflection that
is unconsciousness, Du Bois describes black existence, feeling, and
thinking at its depth as "soul." Black souls are situated critically in
the West vis-a-vis the souls of those who derived their value from
property in things and persons through the enslavement and colonization of others. Their gaze has not pierced the veil or discerned
meaning in the opacity of blackness. However, it is otherwise with
the reflective souls of black folks. Du Bois call blacks into a recognition of themselves within the equation of modernity when he
writes of "The Souls of White Folks" in *Darkwater: Voices from
Within the Veil*. In this piece is recalled Du Bois's earlier formulated
sense of black folks embodying a collective "striving" connected
with the memory and presence of "strife." And this piece indicates
Du Bois's intuition of the black soul not as an ontological substance
absorbed in the contemplation of its own essence. Rather the black
soul is a critical mode of dynamic being and knowing whose epistemological frame of reference encompasses self, Other, and the ultimate source of its own value.

> High in the tower, where I sit above the loud complaining of the human
> sea, I know many souls that toss and whirl and pass, but none there are
> that intrigue me more than the Souls of White Folk.

> Of them I am singularly clairvoyant. I see in and through them. I
> view them from unusual points of vantage. Not as a foreigner do I
> come, for I am native, not foreign, bone of their thought and flesh of
> their language. Mine is not the knowledge of the traveler or the colo-
> nial composite of dear memories, words, and wonder. Nor yet is my
> knowledge that which servants have of their masters...Rather I see
> these souls undressed and from the back and side. I see the working of
> their entrails. I know their thoughts and they know that I know. This
> knowledge makes them embarrassed, now furious! They deny my right
> to live and be and call me misbirth! My word is to them mere bitterness
> and my soul, pessimism. And yet as they preach and strut and shout
> and threaten, crouching as they clutch at rags of facts and fancies to
> hide their nakedness, they go twisting, flying by my tired eyes and I see
> them ever stripped,—ugly, human.

The discovery of personal whiteness among the world's peoples is a very modern thing—a nineteenth and twentieth century matter, indeed.

Du Bois's mountain top experience is one wherein seems to be aware of God but he is not preoccupied with contemplating the Divine. He directs his gaze outward from the depths of the black soul to peer into the soulless souls of those who helped fashion him through slavery, racial discrimination, and its legitimating significations maintaining the white-black binary.

My poor, un-white thing! Weep not nor rage. I know, too well, that the curse of God lies heavy on you. Why? That is not for me to say, but be brave! Do your work in your lowly sphere, praying the good Lord that into heaven above, where all is love, you may, one day, be born—white!

I do not laugh. I am quite straight-faced as I ask soberly

"But what on earth is whiteness that one should so desire it?" Then always, somehow, some way, silently but clearly, I am given to understand that whiteness is the ownership of the earth forever and ever, Amen![38]

Conclusion

Du Bois reveals what those within the veil see. What they see is the soul of the civilization whose exploitation created the veil. This suggests that the only way for those outside the veil to see beyond its barrier is to apprehend themselves as they are apprehended by the oppressed in a mode similar to what Paul speaks of in his 1 Corinthians when he says "we shall know even as we have been known." Du Bois implies this knowing full well it is nearly impossible for a people who have sealed themselves off into the category "whiteness" so as to enjoy its entitlements. The process involved in this resulted in it being impossible for those enjoying the entitlements of whiteness to empathize with anyone not white. As we have seen in the mulatto's example, the not-white category—like the category of race itself—was not based on any inherent quality of human materiality but the imagined dehumanization of those destined for exploitation. The collective social-psychological mode that rendered whites, who are Christian unable, to empathize with non-whites is particularly problematic. Paul presents Christ's humanity as identified with all human kind in his Letter to the Philippians when he states Jesus assumed the form of a *doulos* or slave. In sealing themselves off from the rest of humanity through the construction of the category of race, whites have alienated themselves from Christ and replace the worship of God with the worship of whiteness. The mulatto, rather than providing a bridge for whites into blackness became a signification of shame, immorality, and uncleanliness. Both race and religion are implicated in Du Bois's treatment of the mulatto in his short story, "Jesus Christ in Georgia." By situating this story within Du Bois's entire oeuvre, we can envision black religion and the religions of the oppressed shedding their opacity and silence to the extent that whiteness can see the Other not in terms of an empirical object but as the occasion of self-revelation. This is what Hegel intimated as resolution in his master-slave dialectic. As we shall see in the next chapter, the other side of the veil is not only the space from which blacks apprehend an external reality of people, things, and their ultimate source or God, it is also the space where apprehension and meaning are articulated symbolically through cultural expression. By way of anticipation of what will be discussed in the next chapter: In Romare Bearden's series of collages titled "The Prevalence of Ritual," the viewer finds "it difficult but not impossible to interpret the fractured and displaced photographic image in relation to the sociological images which had their own kind of prevalence in the mid-1960s: 'accusing eyes,' 'anguished faces,' 'tales of horror.'"[39]

7

"The Signification of Silence" Revisited: African American Art and Hermeneutics

Historical memory is aided by a hermeneutic of the archaic in two ways. In the first instance, a hermeneutic of the archaic raises the problem of the constitution of the subject in the process of knowing. If it is the aim of historical knowledge to understand behavior and objects as well as ideas, the interpreting subject must be pushed back to a level of consciousness commensurate with the forms that the subject wishes to understand. This is the radical empirical level of meaning which is expressed in the forms of history. I understand, for example, Eliade's notion of religious symbolism as an expression of this primary pre-reflective experience.

The technical character of modern cultural life tends to dim this level of experience. We are able to be authentically and legitimately concerned with experience on this level as it is obscured in the "languages" of modernity—history, ethnology, linguistics, psychoanalysis, and so on. To prevent this level of experience from being subjected too quickly to the dogmatic categories of contemporaneity, we should try to understand it in culture and history where it is expressed as great cultural symbols. It is here that the history of religions plays an important part. In the premodern cultures, this symbolism has received a definitive expression. (Charles H. Long, *Significations*, p. 49)

Introduction

In this chapter I argue that African American art is one of the most productive sites for excavating the "archaic" in African American consciousness. It is only in this sense that African American art can function as "text." Perhaps we should substitute the term "site" instead. "Archaism," according to Long, "is predicated on the priority of something already there, something given. This 'something' may be the bodily perceptions, as it is for Alfred North Whitehead and Maurice Merleau-Ponty, or *a primal vision of aesthetic form*, as it is for the artist" (my emphasis).[1]

Numerous problems are associated with the archaic. The epistemological problem has to do with the possibility of even grasping what is primary in thought and experience—we might push it further to think in terms of the stuff that makes thought and experience possible and therefore is before thought and experience. If this level of reality is grasped at all, it will be done through the activity of interpretation. Thus the epistemological problem is related to the problem of hermeneutics. The interpreter will then discover the inadequacy of the language of interpretation or, we should say, the inadequacy of language per se.

Language is an inadequate interpretation and expression of the archaic because the archaic first take shape and form as symbol. The way Long suggests for bridging the gap between the archaic and its interpretation is by entering into a participatory mode of conscious whereby, according to Long, "the interpreting subject [is] pushed back to a level of consciousness commensurate with the forms that the subject wishes to understand." The problem with language in this modern period is that it obscures this level of experience. Long sees the History of Religions as offering a possibility for overcoming the dogmatic categories of what he terms the discourses of contemporaniety—"history, ethnology, linguistics, psychoanalysis, and so on." Even though it invites thought, the symbol can never be reduced or equated with a rational category.[2]

This is extremely provocative when we consider that blackness has served as a potent symbol in the semiotics of Western racism. This fact imposes on black persons the task of deciphering the symbolism of their own materiality. However, since the negative symbolism of blackness was achieved through linguistic means among others, becoming freed of this symbolism is difficult to achieve through the use of language. Perhaps this is why Africans in the New World are still determining what to call ourselves. Identity is archaic and the transformation of identity, therefore, must occur at the same level—at the level of the symbolic and where they make their appearance.

Besides the black preacher in sermons, it is the African American artist who operates at the level of the symbolic. I am dealing with visual artists in this chapter, but this statement is not just limited to them. In producing a work the black artist must reflect on himself or herself in the process of creating. At the same time it is also true that the artist must be able to lose his or her self in the process of creating only to rediscover the self in the completed work. However, the self's redefinition is ongoing because the work is open to constant reinterpretation even by the artist.

The work is rooted in the primal symbols, intuitions, and images that constitute the artistic urge. The artist, with the language of the archaic, interprets the archaic, and this interpretative language produces—in the case of genius—a fresh archaic strata. As I write it occurs to me that this is one way of interpreting Nat Turner's *Confession* that was discussed in the previous chapter. It also occurs to me that this is also what the novelist does but at the level of myth. Ralph Ellison said: "Beneath the surface of seemingly rational human relationships there seethed a chaos before which I was helpless. People rationalize what they shun or are incapable of dealing with; these superstitions and their rationalizations become ritual as they govern behavior. The rituals become social forms, and it is one of the functions of the artist to recognize them and raise them to the level of art."[3]

It is surprising to find hardly any mention made of African American art in the numerous studies of black religion. This is very peculiar since as far back as the late 60s and early 70s scholars such as Charles H. Long, James H. Cone, and Gayraud S. Wilmore had established the need and necessity of including a close examination of black culture within the methodology of black religious studies and black theology. Subsequent to the foundation established by these scholars, a younger generation has emerged—among whom are Womanist scholars—seeking to make more inclusive and deepen black religion's self-understanding pioneered by the first generation of African American scholars. Among us, nevertheless, African American art has, heretofore, escaped our focus for exploration into the realms of black religion and black theology. This chapter, in making a tentative attempt at remedying this oversight, will discuss primarily the works of Aaron Douglas (1899–1979), William H. Johnson (1901–1970), and Romare Bearden (1912–1988) as texts bearing profound relevance to the ongoing projects of black religious studies and black theology.

Context of African American Artistic Texts

Some may find the term text being applied to African American art somewhat odd. This perspective is partially due to the narrowing of this term to written records. This also accounts for the subordinate role performance aspects of black folk culture have played in our investigations of black religion. The absence of African American art in black theology and black religious studies can be seen as an unfortunate consequence of the fact that the black experience does not conform to the boundaries of academic disciplines, that is, anthropology, sociology, art history, theology, and so on. This explanation is not entirely satisfactory, however, because ever since the work of Aby Warburg, E. H. Gombrich, and Erwin Panopfsky in Christian iconography, Western art and architecture have served as texts for white history and theological reflection. Indeed, the term "religious art" or "Christian art" is generally associated with Italian Renaissance art to the point where those terms are nearly synonymous in the popular mentality. Today's teachers and writers who seek to illuminate the religious dimension of modern art—even those whose focus is North America—are unanimous in their exclusion of African American art from their canon. In those few rare instances where an African American artist is mentioned, his or her work is misappropriated and lifted outside of the cultural context of his or her artistic performance. This reflects the dichotomy, with obvious racist overtones, in the Euro-American aesthetic between high and low culture.

Subconsciously, African American and "artist" signify two mutually exclusive ontologies that cannot be joined, even dialectically. In addition to the above explanations of why African American art received little attention, we must mention the black artist's marginality within his or her own community as a factor.

In light of the above, African Americans artistic production is quite a feat. In the poem "Yet Do I Marvel" Harlem Renaissance writer Countee Cullen (1903–1946) wrote: "Yet do I marvel at this curious thing: To make a poet black, and bid him sing." Cullen finds it curious that with all the oppressive vicissitudes with which African Americans must cope some would be compelled by their Creator to make poetry in the midst of their suffering. Implied in Cullen's poem is a mysterious link between the object of black folk's devotion and the poetic act. He could just as well have marveled that God had made some men and women black in America and inspired them to paint. While to some painting and other artistic endeavors may appear superfluous to the black struggle for liberation and survival, Cullen's poem suggests their integral connection to that struggle and, moreover, that it is a Divine calling. African American art is not reducible to logical necessity but seeks to signify the presence of the Spirit or spiritual forces inspiring black life. How could a black Sisyphus doomed to meaningless toil or meaningless unemployment assert his or her own self-definition and sense of meaning, purpose, and beauty in life and life after life except through the aid of a black aesthetic?

The moment when the kind of self-assertion seen in slave rebellions, the invisible church, the underground railroad, black Abolitionist activities, Womanist quilt-making expresses itself self-consciously in painting is during and following the Harlem Renaissance in the 1920s and early 1930s. Of course, the Harlem Renaissance had its individual forbearers in anonymous black quilt-makers, craftpersons, and painters such as Joshua Johnston (1789–1825), Julian Hudson (active 1830–40), William Simpson (active 1854–72), Robert Stuart Duncanson (1817–1872), Edward Bannister (1828–1901), Mary Edmonia Lewis, sculptor, (1843–1911), Henry Ossawa Tanner (1859–1937), and Meta Vaux Warrick (Fuller) (1877–1968); but only beginning with the 1920s do we have a corpus of works with a common enough theme and intent justifying its designation as African American art.

During the turn of the century, Harlem was the black Mecca attracting literary, artistic, musical, and political genius from all over the United States and the Caribbean. At no other time before or since has there been such a concentration of major black intellectuals, writers and artists in one community. Zora Neale Hurston, Langston Hughes, Alain Locke, W. E. B. Du Bois, James Weldon Johnson, Arthur Schomburg, Marcus Garvey, Claude McKay, and Paul Robeson: all had established their home bases in Harlem. These personalities came to Harlem with countless others among the great migration from the South to Northern cities. This movement northward was instigated by the combined factors of perceived greater economic opportunity in the north and persistent repression in the south. The large concentration of blacks in specific areas of the northern cities they migrated to facilitated more militant political strategies than those advocated by Booker T. Washington and his followers. In Harlem was headquartered the National Association for the Advancement of Colored People (NAACP) and later the United Negro Improvement Association (UNIA) headed by Marcus Garvey. Similar to the black consciousness movement of the 1960s there was talk of the "New Negro." No longer ashamed or apologetic about their racial heritage, blacks were giving it positive value. The claim that the African American culture, while distinctive, was also of equal worth to Euro-American culture had reciprocal developments in the political realm. Thus, it is no coincidence that James Weldon Johnson the author of the Negro National Anthem "Lift Every Voice and Sing" and *God's Trombones* also happened to be the head of the NAACP. *God's Trombones* is comprised of seven black folk sermons Johnson heard and transcribed while traveling through Kansas City. That Aaron Douglas, whom we will discuss in more detail shortly, was the "illustrator" of *God's Trombones* demonstrates the necessity of reading an African American text in dialogue with it peers and in the context of its performance.

Johnson tried to describe the performance context out of which his sermon-poems arose in the preface to *God's Trombones*: "At an evening church service the preacher had gotten off to a slow start." And the minister intuited correctly that he was not connecting with the congregation. At that point he switched abruptly switched gears and "closed the Bible, stepped out from behind the pulpit and began to preach." He went on to explain the logic for the way the poems are structured by writing:

> The tempo of the preacher I have endeavored to indicate by the line arrangement of the poems, and a certain sort of pause that is marked by a quick in taking and an audible expulsion of the breath I have indicated by dashes. There is a decided syncopation of speech-the crowding in of many syllables or the lengthening out of a few to fill one metrical foot the sensing that must be left to the reader's ear. The rhythmical stress of this syncopation is partly obtained by a marked silent fraction of a beat; frequently this silent fraction is filled in by a hand clap.[4]

Johnson was instructing his reader how to read his poems in a way resonating with Bakhtin's advocacy of hearing the polyphony of voices speaking in any given text. Aaron Douglas's paintings are, yet, another voice and his personal vision. But, Douglas's paintings articulate, in addition to his own personal vision, the voices of Johnson, the black preacher, the congregation's amens, handclaps, singing, and so on. Douglas's task was also one of discovering in his personal style the proper visual vocabulary and structure for representing the narrative content, rhythm, and syncopation of black life. The artistic achievement of William H. Johnson and Romare Bearden can likewise be explained in terms of the way they resolved this issue. But before we discuss Johnson and Bearden, we will focus our attention on Douglas.

Aaron Douglas

Aaron Douglas was not simply an artist of the Harlem Renaissance but *the* Harlem Renaissance artist and is referred to by his peers as "the Dean." Born in Topeka, Kansas Douglas studied art at the University of Nebraska and then, after obtaining a master's degree in Fine Arts from Columbia University, settled in New York City in 1925. With the encouragement of Reiss and the Afrocentric emphasis of Harlem intellectuals, such as Alain Locke, Douglas began deriving his artistic inspiration from African sculpture.

From these beginnings Douglas would evolve his own unique style able to not merely quote African art but also innovate its formal principles into a blend of art deco and synthetic cubism. Developing this style liberated Douglas's paintings from mimetic depictions of black existence and, thus freed, to explore its ontological content. Douglas was able to perfect his craft in this direction with the invitation of W. E. B. Du Bois for him to work on the NAACP's journal the *Crisis* magazine. Douglas also worked for Alain Locke in providing numerous illustrations for *The New Negro*. *Vanity Fair* and *Theater Arts Monthly* and the Urban League Journal *Opportunity* are other magazines that featured Douglas's art. His paintings illustrating *God's Trombones* were completed in 1927. In 1934 he completed a mural for the 135th Street branch of the New York Public Library titled *Aspects of Negro Life*. Then in 1937 Douglas joined the faculty of Fisk University to found and chair its art department until his retirement in 1966.

As mentioned in the preceding discussion, an intertextual interpretation of African American art requires us to hear as well as see the art in its representation of the black experience. Just as James Weldon Johnson's poems were literary signifiers of a dimension of the African American oral tradition—the black sermon—the visual images invoked in the context of the original performance—black worship—take shape and form in Douglas's canvases. In other words, his paintings sing, shout, moan, and preach the idiom of African American religious consciousness.

What the collaboration of Douglas's and Johnson's talents accomplished parallels Langston Hughes innovation in American poetry when he constructed some of his poems in the repetitive AA-B pattern of the blues. The relationship between the spirituals, the work song, the blues, and the black sermon has been well-documented. Many songs cannot be neatly classified as blues, spiritual, or work song but function as all three depending upon the setting of their performance. Some spirituals were originally "sung sermons" that were maintained in the memory and oral performance of the congregation beyond the initial worship event; others were originally work songs whose pathos was maintained in the memory and performance of the community in the context of a subsequent worship event. Part of this process entailed the phenomenon of "wandering verses"; a verse of one song would migrate to appear in an entirely different song during the process of transmission and recombination.

This is important for our understanding of Douglas's art as well as that of other African American artists. In African American oral art, the new is created through recombination and improvisation of the familiar. This principle is also present in African American music and could be paraphrased to define jazz and African American dance as well. Thus, another way we understand how Douglas's art and also that of Johnson and Bearden is related to other African American texts is through their manner of embodying this common mode of creativity and recreativity. In other words, Douglas is not merely illustrating the explicit content of *God's Trombones*; he is making a commentary that results in a proto-black theology as he adds his own voice to those he hears in Johnson's poem. In this way Douglas and Johnson anticipate artistically what James H. Cone did theologically. Cone enumerated the black experience, black history, black culture, revelation, scripture, and tradition among the sources for doing black theology. The norm of this theology, according to Cone, is the hermeneutical principle determining the use of these sources. Black theology—like African American art—should not devise a norm that is not related to the black community's actualities.[5] African American art at its best incarnates, posits, and express the collective memory and imagination of the folks it depicts. Douglas explicates the revelation of God in African American experience through an aesthetic derived from that experience and, in so doing illustrates not only Johnson's poems but also Cone's hermeneutical principle.

One of Douglas's paintings, for example, associates the archangel Gabriel in Johnson's poem "Judgment Day" with a jazz musician. In Johnson's poem Gabriel does not descent from the sky but emerges from the black community. Douglas's illustration made this association in a manner analogous to the manner by which Africans in the Caribbean and South America superimposed African God on Roman Catholic saints. Gabriel's posture is duplicated in the stance assumed by the blues musician depicted in the fourth panel of the mural *Aspects of Negro Life*. Just as the Spirituals and blues contain wandering verses here is an instance of a wandering image with a theological message: the Day of Judgment brings about the destruction of the powers and principalities of evil incarnated in the structures of white supremacy. The eschatology of the black church, particularly during slavery, was one that welcomed and longed for the Day of Judgment. The Spiritual "My Lord What a Moanin" reflects this longing and the slave rebellions lead by such leaders as Nat Turner, Gabriel Prosser, and Denmark Vesey confirm the extent to which slaves were willing to assist judgment day's advent. That a black musician would sound the trumpet announcing God's judgment of the wicked is quite appropriate given America's history of slavery and oppression. Those who long for Judgment Day participate in its arrival. There is also an ironic trope in this image identifying Gabriel with a jazz musician. Jazz, as played in juke halls and clubs, was officially off-limits for people considering themselves "saved" because of the other illicit activities associated with such places. Was Douglas suggesting that Gabriel might appear incognito in some juke joint privileging sinners as the first to hear Gabriel's horn sounded? Were these black sinners to be judged along with their white oppressors or was Gabriel sanctifying them and their dance hall with his presence? Douglas's painting raises provocative questions about the dualistic thinking of twentieth century-black preachers regarding the saved and unsaved. By coordinating ecclesiology with the eschatology imaged in this painting, new ways of thinking about both are provoked. If the true church (ecclesia) is the community chosen to hear Gabriel sound his horn, then the black church in preparing for this event (the eschaton) must attend to the blues and jazz idioms in black culture by bringing them into the church.

On the other end of salvation history's spectrum is Douglas's illustration of Johnson's "The Creation." The preacher overhears the internal dialogue taking place within the Godhead at the beginning of time. Johnson wrote:

> And God stepped out on space
> And he looked around and said:
> I'm lonely—
> I'll make me a world

The poem continues with a description of God's creation of the stars, planets, hills, and valleys....But when God looked on all that was created God said, "I'm lonely still." Then God sat down and began to think—and think until God thought "I'll make me a man!"

> Up from the bed of the river
> God scooped the clay;
> And by the bank of the river
> He kneeled him down
> …
> This great God,
> Like a mammy bending over her baby,
> Kneeled down in the dust
> Toiling over a lump of clay
> Till he shaped it in his own image;
>
> Then into it he blew the breath of life,
> And man became a living soul. Amen. Amen.[6]

This sermon offers a host of possibilities for elaborating a black theology of salvation based on the preacher's insight concerning the motive of creation being God's loneliness. The incarnation and crucifixion become additional episodes in God's attempts to satisfy Divine loneliness. Consistent with the Yahwist or "J" strain in the Old Testament, God must labor to bring about the creation of humanity. Although our sensitivity to Womanist concerns makes us less than satisfied with the preponderance of masculine imagery, there is a redeeming feature in the poems shift to a feminine metaphor when God appears "like a mammy bending over her baby." The profundity of this poem's theology is enhanced by Douglas's painting in which God creates black women and men in God's own image. In his book *Troubling Biblical Waters*, Cain Hope Felder discusses the way racist misreadings of the Bible, for example, the curse of Ham, were used to legitimate the enslavement and colonization of Africans. In Douglas's painting *The Creation*, Africans are present in the account not as an afterthought but in God's intentional primal act.

We can further explore Douglas's theology by viewing his painting *The Crucifixion* (illustrating Johnson's poem by the same title) alongside his 1944 painting *Building More Stately Mansions*. In the foreground of the latter, a black woman with an arm around her two children looks upward with the palm of her other hand turned outward as if seeking Divine intercession and deliverance. Four black men are also shown in the foreground engaged in constructing a modern metropolis that rises above them. Looming above them in the background is the silhouette of a giant pyramid and sphinx.

In *The Crucifixion* another black man is engaged in toil; he is carrying Jesus's cross. The Roman crucifixion shown in this painting signifies the identity between those who crucified Jesus and those who oppress African Americans. God's identification with black suffering and toil is suggested by the theme of labor running through Johnson's poem. Johnson describes a God who works with his or her hands and Douglas's paintings showing black people at toil both on the day of Christ's crucifixion and presently under exploitive capitalism. America is both Egypt and Rome and African Americans are identified respectively with the Hebrews and Christ. Douglas critiques America's self-understanding as a chosen nation by biblically interpreting the experiences of the black rural poor and urban masses.

Even though Douglas was subversive, he did not think many people suspected the "power" invested in these black paintings. But had Douglas not led the way in using African orientated imagery during the Harlem Renaissance, Alain Locke's charge to black visual artist to "return to the ancestral art of Africa for inspiration" would have taken even longer for African American artists to realize. It was Douglas who affected the crucial move toward affirming the validity of the black experience and thereby made one of American's most worthy contributions to art and this art, has great value for black theology and black religious studies.

William H. Johnson

William H. Johnson is another painter who contributed significantly to American art and his paintings, like Aaron Douglas's, lend themselves to the projects of black theology and black religious studies. Born in Florence, South Carolina W. H. Johnson arrived in Harlem in 1918 and studied at the National Academy of Design with George Luks and Charles Hawthorne. In 1926 Johnson traveled to Paris where he studied Cezanne, Roualt, Soutine, Van Gough, and other modern European artists. Under these influences, Johnson began to paint in an expressionistic manner. In 1932, however, after a trip to North Africa and, perhaps, expressing the trend in certain sections of the European artistic community, Johnson made a decision to adopt a more "primitive" or direct style of painting. In *Homecoming: The Art and Life of William H. Johnson,* Richard J. Powell reports Johnson's comment to an interviewer in 1932 that: "even if I have studied for many years in New York and all over the world and know more about Scandinavian literature and classical music than my wife does, I have still been able to preserve the primitive in me." During this interview Johnson stated that his aim was to "express in a natural way what I feel, what is in me, both rhythmically and spiritually, all that which in time has been saved up in my family of primitiveness and tradition, and which is now concentrated in me."[7]

In 1938, Johnson returned to Harlem, realizing that this earlier understanding of primitiveness was too subjective and his need of a reference beyond his own emotional experience for realizing his artistic aims. Its scenery gave him the subject matter he needed. As he devoted his attention exclusively to Harlem's sights and scenes, Johnson was able to work his way back to a style of direct painting appropriate for expressing the African American experience. *Street Life-Harlem*, *Cafe*, and *Nude* demonstrate Johnson's change in style. The minimally modeled figures and flat brightly colored surfaces of these paintings resemble folk art. There is, however, a great amount of sophistication in Johnson's use of primary colors, the way he harmonized them with their compliments, and in his outlining of object and figures to establish linear and rhythmic patterns in his paintings. The exhilaration Johnson experienced in being surrounded by throbbing, bustling black life put him in touch with forgotten memories of growing up in Florence, South Carolina. These memories were translated into other paintings from this period of rural life such as *Going to Market* (Oil on wood, 33 1/8 × 37 7/8") and *Sowing* (Oil on burlap, 38 1/2 × 48 3/4").

The folks shown in these paintings were the same people who migrated to the North's urban centers carrying their religion with them; but in this new context the symbols of black faith needed to meet new requirements. What was hoped would be a promised land proved itself, as Douglas showed in his art, to be only another Egypt. The black church had difficulty putting its spiritual resources and symbols in the service of meeting the growing complexity of political, social, and economic needs in the African American community. Gayraud S. Wilmore characterized this period in his *Black Religion and Black Radicalism* as the black church's "deradicalization" as it focused more on the hereafter and less on the here and now.[8] While this description may be generally true, indicated in William H. Johnson's paintings is the presence of a remnant reflecting on the religious meaning of black suffering.

Jesus and the Three Marys (ca. 1939–1940. Oil on wood, 37 1/4 × 34 1/4") shows three black women in grief and agony at the scene of the crucifixion. The figures in this painting are similar to one done around the same time titled *Lynch Mob* and this helps in our interpreting the political significance of its crucified black Christ.

This black Christ startles the viewer. The largeness of Christ's hands and feet in proportion to the rest of his body draws attention to the nails piercing them. The blue cross on which Christ is being crucified compliments the yellow halos surrounding the heads of each figure and the orange robe of one of the Marys. Although the composition is based on Matthias Grunewald's *The Crucifixion of Christ* (ca. 1510–1515. Tempera on wood, 28 3/4 × 20 3/4"). Johnson has not merely colored Christ black. The gestures of the figures created with thick impasto layers of paint work together to convince the viewer of the scene's veracity and all this implies. In this depiction of a black Christ, God has made black suffering a revelatory event. This revelation of Christ's blackness is a bold confrontation and indictment of white racism for which the black Christ is a stumbling block and offense. The painting is in accord with the religious views of W. E. B. Du Bois who around the same time wrote a short story titled "Jesus Christ in Georgia" and those of Marcus Garvey who advocated the creation of such images as an antidote for black self-hatred. Two other crucifixion scenes Johnson painted were *Lamentation* (Oil on fiberboard, 29 1/8 × 33 1/4") and *Mount Calvary* (Oil on paperboard, 27 1/4 × 33 1/8").

Chain Gang (Oil on wood, 45 3/4 × 38 1/2") is another painting done by Johnson in 1939. It depicts three black convicts working by the roadside with pick, shovel, and wheel barrel in hand under a blazing orange hot sun. Two of the convicts are placed in the center of the painting. One of them is bending over with a shovel in both hands while the other stands upright swinging an axe. The bodies of these two convicts seem to interlock due to their proximity to one another and the black and white stripes on their uniforms. They appear attached to each other like Siamese twins and our eyes try in vain to untangle them by determining whose arms and legs belong to whom. As we struggle to visually disconnect the two convicts we become identified with them—part of these sculpted images—and experience this metaphor of the black predicament viscerally. Finally, it occurs to us that this was the desired effect Johnson wanted this painting to have. We are made to reconsider Jesus's words in Luke 4:16f about releasing the captives—although, we thought of ourselves as free, we are incarcerated by racial "injustice." The black church is, therefore, called to address the issue of black liberation.

Woman in Calico (1944. Oil on paperboard, 26 1/2 × 20 1/2") made during a visit to his hometown Florence, South Carolina in 1944 is of his Aunt Lillian. It captures the way black faith embodied in African American women sustained the black community through-out its years of struggle. It is a Womanist statement. Richard J. Powell wrote:

> Aunt Lillian perfectly epitomizes the concept of complete obeisance to a greater power. The accretion of Christian symbols in this portrait (e.g. the red crosses on the dress and the crossed arms), coupled with the bifurcated background of darkness and light, is certainly a reference to human redemption through the Crucifixion. Like the popular gospel recording of the 1940's "The Sun Didn't Shine"—which recounts, in an upbeat, a cappella arrangement, how absolute darkness fell-over Mount Calvary when "My Lord Was Dyin' on the Cross"—this paint-ing's "good news" is that "God's children" are direct beneficiaries of this ultimate sacrifice.[9]

In other words, the black theology of Johnson's paintings is not only concerned with exploring the Christological significance of the black liberation struggle but also the concept of realized eschatol-ogy in African American women's everyday feats of endurance and hope.

Swing Low Sweet Chariot (ca. 1944. Oil on paperboard, 28 5/8 × 26 1/2") obviously titled after the Spiritual by that name also deals with the theme of eschatology. In this painting's lower center a man with legs and arms stretched wide greets a band of angels—eleven black women of various hues with purple wings—and an orange chariot drawn by a white horse. The river Jordan stretches horizon-tally below the descending angels and chariot. The man's gray hair indicates that he is elderly and his wearing only a pair of yellow shorts devoid of all other earthly possessions communicates his readiness for the death that the white horse personifies. This painting is less militant in political implication than other of Johnson's paintings but commu-nicates correctly and straightforwardly the context of black religious expectation of the vindication of this life's injustices in the next life. In doing this Johnson inserts a secular element into his eschatology by having his young female angels attired in the fashion of the 1940s and in the revitalization suggested by the contrast between their youthful-ness and the man's old age.

The "racial alchemy," as Richard J. Powell termed it, of transmuting biblical characters into African-American types was revolutionary. Like Aaron Douglas, Johnson was at the vanguard of bringing about "the acceptance of Black subjects as part and parcel of the Christian experience in Western art." Johnson discovered that a black artist's "work could be regarded as African American only by embodying the same formal and thematic principles that governed other African American folk expressions."[10]

In making the connection between the above and the endeavors of black theology and Black Religious Studies, the questions it raises are: What are the formal and thematic principles governing the expression of African American folk religion and how can they be demonstrated? What directions should these disciplines follow and what tools must they acquire to parallel the accomplishments of Douglas, Johnson, and Bearden? The questions we are asking here have to do with methodology and even recommend an interdisciplinary approach for studying black religion; but the context framing these questions also emphasizes the necessity for aesthetics to be dealt with by black theology and black religious studies. The method of these disciplines must consider and be appropriate to the black aesthetic because it is among the underlying formal and thematic principles governing the expression of African American religion.

The preceding discussions of Douglas's and Johnson's techniques and the one to follow of Bearden's are quite pertinent to the phenomena studied by black theology and black religious studies. African American art provides another genre of text for helping identify the formal and thematic principles of black religion. This takes us into our discussion of Bearden who was particularly preoccupied with the questions of form and structure.

Romare Bearden

Romare Bearden was a contemporary of Aaron Douglas and William H. Johnson but he did not begin creating the type of art we now associate with his name until the early 1960s. The long, tortuous, and providential path leading to the integration of Bearden's artistic and racial identities is a fascinating story and one worth telling because of its relevance for the black theologians' search for method. Romare Bearden's artistic career begins in the mid 1930s. After graduating from New York University, he enrolled at the Art Students League and studied with George Grosz. Around the same period as Bearden's study with Grosz, he was associating himself with Harlem-based African American artists, particularly, the Harlem Artists Guild, its outgrowth, the Harlem Community Art Center, and later an informal association that met regularly at 306 West 141st Street called the 306 Group. Bearden came in contact with all the major African American artists of that era under the guidance of such first generation practitioners as Aaron Douglas, Augusta Savage, and Charles Alston. Literary figures such as Richard Wright, Langston Hughes, Alain Locke, and Ralph Ellison were also visitors to "306" gatherings.

Leopold Seyfert, a Harlem intellectual, was another influence on Bearden. Seyfert lectured in Harlem on African and African American history and it was he who introduced Bearden to the study and appreciation of African sculpture when Bearden, along with several other artists, accompanied him to an exhibit at the Museum of Modern Art. This helped Bearden conceive of the human form in nonnaturalistic terms of design and pattern and added to his understanding of Cezanne and the Cubists. Bearden's concern for structure and design would carry over into his study of such Renaissance artists as Duccio and Giotto that he translated into a cubist genre in his *The Passion of Christ* series (1945).

In *The Passion of Christ* series, consisting of twenty-two oils and watercolors, Bearden demonstrated mastery over his struggle with problems of design and composition with the use of curves and counter curves to form geometric patterns. A little before this series was exhibited, he had written to a close friend, "I finally think I'm beginning to understand what makes a picture move—what time sense in a picture means—leading plane by plane—step by step in a series of counterpoints—rather than a focusing to give an immediate reaction."[11] Bearden wanted his art to lead the viewer's eye onto and around its surface rather than allowing it to become fixed on one spot. We can also recognize in Bearden's statement the analogy he was making between his art and music. This analogy was confirmed years later in 1986 when alto-saxophonist Jackie McLean and Bearden exhibited together at the Hartford Atheneum in a show titled "Sound Collages and Visual Improvisations." Another validation occurred that same year when Bearden and jazz drummer, Max Roach, met over lunch to discuss the connection between rhythm and art. "My approach to rhythm," Max Roach said, "is the use of space, of silence. It's not that there's necessarily nothing going on. There's always a pulse there....Bearden's paintings are like that. There's the rhythm I see here."[12] Max Roach, as a drummer, brought a special sensibility to his viewing of Bearden's art and one paralleling Bearden's description of its rhythmic content.

As early as 1949, Bearden had corresponded with fellow artist Carl Holty about the discovery that "The intervals can be the sustaining beat of the picture rhythm...The horizontals and verticals can indicate the plane—that is, help bring the moving rhythms back to the flat."[13] Trying to sustain this in representational art is an extremely difficult undertaking, and this may partly explain why during the 50s the subject disappeared entirely from Bearden's works that became nonrepresentational or abstract. A new technique was needed to integrate rhythm and figuration; interestingly, political events would occasion its discovery.

In the early 1960s Bearden came back to representational art almost quite by accident. During the summer of 1963, he and a group of other African American artists calling themselves the Spiral Group began meeting together to discuss the implications of the civil rights struggle for their identity as artists. At one of their meetings someone put forth the idea of producing a collaborative work. As it turned out Bearden was the only member of the group to show up at his studio at the time scheduled to begin this undertaking, He had brought to this meeting a number of pictures he had cut out of magazines with the idea of having them copied on a larger canvas. While waiting for someone else to appear Bearden took his magazine cut-outs and for the fun of it began to experiment with cutting and pasting their images on a board. Bearden later had these images photostatically enlarged and after rolling them up they remained in a corner of his studio until the late spring of 1964. "Then," Bearden reported, "I was painting something in a very non-representational manner and a gallery dealer came and said, 'What are those things rolled up?', I said, I don't think they will be of interest to you: He said, 'Let's see them anyway'. And he said, 'Do a few more, that's your next show.'" Bearden produced another twenty collages that were first exhibited at the Cordier and Ekstrom Gallery in New York in October 1964. With these collages, Bearden had finally discovered his own style and one enabling him to magnificently carry out his artistic aims. As he created his collages an amazing process happened. Ekstrom was fascinated with Bearden's collages which he regarded as "really extraordinary and constitute a sort of re-living and re-telling of his memories as a Negro."[14]

Black theology and black religious studies can benefit tremendously from African American art. It can serve as cultural text in the service of black religious reflection. In Bearden's collages, the problem of defining the complexity and infinite contradictions of blackness are transcended through a hermeneutic of juxtaposition. He provides not only a mirror for looking at what Franz Fanon called the "fact of blackness" but also a way toward its clarification and discovery. Bearden teaches how to look by expanding our gaze to notice more than we would normally see at any given moment in time and space. In his collages, past and present, South and North, sacred and profane, inside and outside overlap, interpenetrate, and intersect to form the contexts of human rituals: bathing, blues singing, dancing, eating, worshiping, loving, and so on. Black theology's and black religious studies' commitment to locating their sources in African American texts does not, in itself, competency in the reading of those texts whose surfaces resist systematic exposition. Many of these texts, like the experience they express, are ephemeral and fragmented; therefore, any attempt to systematize them under an overarching theme risks the danger of superimposing extraneous content upon African American texts. Our hermeneutic must somehow reflect the existential reality of brokenness in the black experience and, simultaneously, the reality of an African American ontology held together, ever tenuously, by faith and hope.

This need is answered by Bearden's collages that contain an implicit hermeneutic—compared with the African American quilt and described as a type of patchwork cubism, they acknowledge the reality of black people's brokenness and, at the same time, celebrate the ever present possibility of creative self reconfiguration. In Bearden's collages, he sculpts the African American anatomy by what seems to be an arbitrary assemblage of eyes, noses, hands, arms, and so on. African masks are often used for the faces of his black subjects and even when not, the case, their faces have a mask-like appearance. Similar to the way the African sculptor regards his statue, Bearden saw black folks as more than flesh and bones who could be scared and broken but as mythical types and incarnations of Spirit. In his creations Bearden played the role of Isis in the Egyptian myth who after Horus's dismemberment by Seth searched throughout Egypt collecting his scattered organs and limbs. After they all were collected and reassembled, Horus was resurrected. At the symbolic level Bearden's art functions in this fashion in the way it assembles and juxtaposes deeply lodged memories from the black psyche.

Bearden achieved this not only in the way he sculpted the black anatomy but also in his depiction of objects from the black experience. A social theorist, Walter Benjamin, who experimented with this medium observed how the collage is able to "interrupt the context into which it is inserted." The objects inserted into Bearden's collages interrupt their context and take on a numinous quality that provokes narration; at the same time, however, these objects remain recognizable to the black viewer. The importance of this is in how it leads to self-discovery. Interpreting the meaning of objects associated with one's everyday reality elicits self-interpretation. For example, one writer said Bearden's 1964 collage *Mysteries* (11 1/4 × 14 1/2″) was "no mystery to the black viewer-Jesus, watermelon, 'Alaga Syrup,' (only the word 'syrup' is visible, but readers of Ebony Magazine will recognize the lettering from the advertisements) are but stereotypes at best of the black world to the white viewer, but completely real to the black viewer."[15] The black viewer will ask upon seeing in "Mysteries" the tattered picture of Jesus (a white one) tacked to the interior wall of a shack, a train passing by in the distance, staring black faces, a watermelon, and so on—"what is the relationship between all these disconnected images?"

Each of the objects shown in the collage has a history of its own that is a history of their use and the desires projected on to them by their users. The function of these objects in Bearden's collages is similar to what Susan Buck-Moss said concerning Walter Benjamin's collages

> As fore-history, the objects are prototypes, or phenomena that can be recognized as precursors of the present, no matter how distant or estranged they now appears...In the traces left by the object's after-history, the conditions of its decay and the manner of its cultural transmission, the utopian images of past objects can be read in the present as truth. Benjamin was counting on the shock of this recognition to jolt the dreaming collective into a political "awakening." The dialectic allowed the super-imposition of fleeting images, present and pat, that made both suddenly come alive in terms of revolutionary meaning.[16]

In light of the above parallel drawn between Bearden and Walter Benjamin, the preponderance of objects in Bearden's collages suggest his operating from a materialistic theological orientation—but not according to the usual connotation of the term "materialistic." For Bearden, ordinary objects can be transfixed by our gaze into the realm of the extraordinary because he saw spiritual energy and force permeating all of life. Thus, it would be disingenuous to ransack Bearden's collages looking for explicit religious or Christian symbols since he was more interested in the mythic element found in the mundane rituals of black folk culture than in what we usually define as religious. Therefore, when Christian symbols appear in Bearden's collages they are part of and belong to the context of neighboring objects that would customarily be seen as profane.

This was illustrated in the collage *Mysteries*. In Bearden's collage *The Street* (1975. 37 1/2 × 51″) we have another illustration of the point we are making in the above. This collage shows a lot of people in front of a brick tenement. On a closer viewing, however, we notice that one of the men standing in front of the tenement is playing a guitar and how with the two other men standing to his left they seem to form a trio. They seem displaced and to more appropriately belong to a Southern landscape. The windows opening onto the street in the upper right side of the picture place us in the role of voyeurs. We can see a woman ascending the stairs. In the second-floor window we see a nude woman reclining on a bed or couch. Through the first floor window another woman holds a baby in a pose directly quoted from Italian Renaissance depictions of the Madonna and Child. In this painting the Christian icon is hidden and not made explicit. Just, as Jesus appeared incognito in as unlikely a place as a stable, the child held tenderly in its mother's arms in this picture takes on Christological significance.

A Christology signified in the black Christ is hinted at whenever we encounter the tender images of black men or women holding infants in Bearden's collages but this is not the only occasion where he sees Spirit becoming flesh—this is also signified in the numerous works that conjure women appear. For example, Bearden is talking about the Obeah water colors, based on the acquaintance he made with conjure women during his frequent trips to the Caribbean, said that

> They are living in a now that is a "not now" because their antecedents may have been witch doctors—all of these rituals that point to other forces, or ways of looking at the world that we have no for the most part rejected. But they are forces that are still in a certain sense inchoate within us.[17]

This statement resonates with Process Theology's presupposition of the interchangeability of mass and energy expressed in Einstein's formula $E = MC^2$ Bearden was fascinated with the practical application of this principle in traditional African religions. Bearden's collages, thus, capture his theme of interrelatedness between flesh and Spirit, matter and energy, and the natural and supernatural realms of reality. In agreement with Melville Herskovits, Bearden sees evidence of the persistence of African beliefs and religious practices in North American black communities as well as in the Caribbean. When, for instance, we view Carolina Shout (1974, 37 1/2 × 51″) beside the "Obeah Watercolor" series, the African origins of black religion become obvious. The former shows a southern baptism scene. The black preacher and his congregation are—as sung about in the Spiritual "wading in the water"—to immerse one of the newly saved. The descent of the Holy Spirit into the midst of the congregation is signified by the crimson colored sky that touches the blue colored creek at the horizon. The upraised arms of the celebrants signify their ecstasy and the ascent of the human spirit during this rite.

The trance state of the Obeah women is similar to that of their Christian counterparts. Furthermore, religious ecstasy is difficult to distinguish from other cathartic African American communal rituals such as the rent parties and jam sessions that Bearden shows in his "Blues series" and "Jazz series." The black musician is also a conjurer of sorts because in the African metaphysic spiritual forces are not abstractions but realities invoked and experienced through sound and music. Hence, Bearden's structural and compositional concern with rhythm during the earlier phase of his career paid off later by equipping him with the method he needed for capturing the essence of black life.

Bearden apprehends a spiritual unity beneath the brokenness of black life. In looking at the entire corpus of Bearden's works, we note how the faces of his conjurers are indistinguishable from the ordinary folk in these urban street scenes and those of the rural south. Life can be made whole and this possibility becomes realized—if but momentarily—for black folks in their communal celebrations and rituals. Since the term "salvation" from the Greek root *soter* means to make whole, the spiritual unity of black existence celebrated in Bearden's art has theological relevance.

Aesthetic and Ethnic in African American Art

One of the primary values of African American art for black theology and black religious studies is in the way it provokes these disciplines into considering the connection between aesthetics and ethics. The moral vision encountered in Douglas's, Johnson's, and Bearden's art interpreted intertextually with other black cultural expressions provides an opportunity for contemplating this relationship. In the creative act, according to Bakhtin, the artist transcends the immediacy of his/her present situation and is addressed by the reality of an "ought" that critiques his life in its situation. This is where aesthetics and ethics intersect. When the vision glimpsed is embodied (even partially) in the work of art, it encompasses a realized eschatology—the almost but not yet dimension of the artistic vision. The artist's vision is not consummated in the individual consciousness of the artist or even in the work of art itself. Consummation is a communal event and is relativitized by the viewer's perspective—for Bakhtin this fact answers the operative question of "consummated-by (for) whom and consummated-when." In our study of African American art, the black community is the locus of artistic consummation. In his 1946 exhibit at the 135th Street Branch of the New York Public Library, the children of Harlem were the most enthusiastic viewers of Johnson's art. African Americans recognized themselves in exhibits of Douglas's and Bearden's art as well. These instances of artistic consummation evidence the presence of a black aesthetic.

Without this black aesthetic, African American art could not exist—nor black preaching, song, dance, and so on—because such art would lack a validating community of interpretation. The existence of this black aesthetic demonstrates a counterhegemonic cultural practice maintained among black folks because the logic of slavery and the discrimination persisting after slavery aimed at obliterating all traces of independent judgment from the black psyche. The black person's entire existence was conditioned to be orientated toward the Master; for example, Slave catechisms, the whip, minstrel shows, advertisements, and the film industry all conspired to reinforce this ontology. Under such an onslaught of cultural aggression, in the case of a weak psychic structure one could observe, according to Franz Fanon, "A collapse of the ego. The black man [sic] stops behaving as an actional person. The goal of his [sic] behavior will be the other (in the guise of the white man), for the other alone can give him worth. that is on the ethical level: self esteem."[18]

Ethics entails choice and the volition to act upon one's judgments. Aesthetics also encompasses judgments—those pertaining to preferences regarding, among other things: goodness, truth, and beauty. In Fanon's analysis, earlier, if black people become nonpersons, for example, lack self-esteem, ethical behavior is preempted. Thus, ethical practice, aesthetic sensibility, and self-esteem are mutually dependent terms that are for African Americans always threatened with annihilation by the dominant culture. Alain Locke recognized this when in

1935 he authored a paper titled "Values and Imperatives" that argued against the "tyranny of absolutes" and advocated, instead, "cultural relativitism." Beauty, truth, and goodness Locke regarded as historically bound categories and not timeless entities. The artist Locke said, in making the connection between ethics and aesthetics, "may feel duty toward his [her] calling, obligation toward his [her] unrealized idea because when he [she] feels conflict and tension in that context, he [she] occupies an entirely different attitude toward his [her] aesthetic material."[19]

Locke felt African American artists had a moral obligation to draw from their African heritage and his desire to provide a rationale for black poets, writers, artists to do so was what motivated his writing of that paper. The issue Locke discussed was politically significant because he saw cultural texts as supplying the moral vision necessary for the guidance and nurturance of African American strivings. Certainly, at this point in our discussion, we can see how the art of Douglas, Johnson, and Bearden substantiate Locke's views. Douglas, Johnson, and, to a lesser degree, Bearden, were influenced by Locke who regarded himself as, and indeed was, the "philosophical mid-wife" to the Harlem Renaissance. Locke was keenly aware of the role popular culture plays in a people's quest for liberation; another way of discussing the cultural dimension of political struggle is in terms of aesthetics and ethics.

Such a discussion is important for black theology and black religious studies to consider. It becomes unavoidable when attempts are made to carry out Cone's admonishment that we derive our hermeneutical principle for interpreting black sources from those sources themselves. This implies some deep structure at work determining the ultimate form and thematic expression assumed in those sources. Identifying, however, the hermeneutical principle lodged in black sources still requires a conceptual orientation to assist in its discovery. In the case of the artists we have been discussing, the hermeneutical principle helping us interpret their works rests upon the black aesthetic. As Douglas, Johnson, and Bearden made black folks and black folk culture the subject of their art, they were required to make stylistic innovations, according to their own genius, which could accurately depict the black experience they sought to represent and interpret. These artists did not merely do with paint brush and canvas what could be done with film and camera—they each in their own way recovered and improvised a visual idiom paralleling the syntax of black music, dance, storytelling, and poetry. The patchwork and appliqué quilt quality common to the art of Douglas, Johnson, and Bearden points to their having independently tapped into the black aesthetic.

The black aesthetic, which contains elements of rhythm, syncopation, repetition, plasticity of form, call and response, and so on, is the formal and thematic principle underlying the diversity of black cultural expressions. No single African American text can be interpreted independently of an informed listening to the voices speaking through other texts in the black tradition. Each text improvises and repeats themes and rhythms established in their predecessors through a call and response spiral. Black social ethics can also be developed within the framework of this model. For instance, integrationist ethics must be open to influence from black nationalist ethics in a dialectical mode and both must understand the urgency of being creative. Cone's latest work *Malcolm and Martin: Dream or Nightmare* moves in this direction.

African American creativity's emergence from the context of exploitation lends itself to a Marxian analysis of its connection with ethics. The Russian philosopher Nicolai Berdyaev understood the creative act and the ethical act as almost synonymous when he wrote:

> The mystery of creativeness is the mystery of freedom...It presupposes, first, man's [*sic*] primary, meonic, uncreated freedom; secondly, the gifts bestowed upon man [*sic*] the creator by God the Creator, and, thirdly, the world as the field for his [*sic*] activity....The awakening of creative energy is inner liberation and is accompanied by a sense of freedom..."The products of creativeness remain in time, but the creative act itself, the creative flight communes with eternity."[20]

Berdyaev undoubtedly derived his understanding of aesthetics from Hegel and Marx's theories about alienation—the separation of one class of humans by another from the product of their own labor. Hegel talks about this in his *The Phenomenology of Mind* and his *Encyclopedia of Philosophy Manuscripts*; Marx in his *Economic and Philosophic Manuscripts*. What young Marx did was to analogize labor to what the artist does when he/she objectifies his own essential powers and then internalizes the artistic product contemplation. When the producer is separated from his/her product through slavery or the intervention of the wage, according to Marx, the producer becomes alienated from himself and the artistic work or product. The fate of the cultural producers in an oppressed community is similar to that of other workers whose labor becomes exploited. Without necessarily having read the above theories, Bearden showed an acute intuition of the relationship between labor exploitation and artistic practice in his 1946 article "The Negro Artist's Dilemma" in which he wrote:

> the Negro aside from his folk expressions, is a latecomer into the visual arts in America. As slave and serf, the Negro has had to struggle for his very existence. The visual arts are in a sense a sophisticated expression...That the innate capacity existed is evidenced in the elegant iron-grill work created by Negro slave artisans. About the only expression allowed the Negro was religion, so it is understandable that his first artistic achievement would be a vocal one—the spirituals.[21]

The point Bearden makes is very insightful. African Americans had to gather in clandestine meetings to create their first cultural product in America—the Spirituals—and these songs, as we know, contain a great deal of ethical instruction. In the Spirituals, aesthetics and ethics intersect. The vision they posit for African American contemplation is simultaneously aesthetic as it pertains to the order of God's cosmos and ethical as it suggests a remedy for the disorder introduced into the world by white oppression. After slavery, as Bearden noted, African American creativity was able to express itself through more varied channels. Although African Americans enjoyed more diverse options for expressing their creativity after slavery, they were still oppressed and, as such, their creativity retained an ethical urgency to which the art of Douglas, Johnson, and Bearden bear witness. Along with a personal sense of inner freedom ad transcendence, their art also expresses an ethical vision they glimpsed in the creative act itself. We can see in the lives of Douglas, Johnson, and Bearden the point of intersection between ethics and aesthetics described earlier by Bakhtin and Berdyaev. The creative act confronts us with another world and instigates the quest for freedom.

In the context of slavery, attempts at cultural genocide, "Jim Crow" legislation and de facto discrimination, African American creativity in all its varied manifestations is a sign of grace with salvic significance. Therefore, black theology and black religious studies must reflect on the miracle of African American creativity with African American art its primary texts. This should include among other things an application of: Marx's theory of value, Charles Longs insights about linguistic conquest, and Cornel West's description of black culture's commodification. Through such an approach to African American artistic texts we can deepen our analysis of the social-cultural-economic contexts of blacks' oppression and the spiritual-artistic or ethical-aesthetic practices African Americans employ in seeking emancipation from these contexts. Black people's oppression in America entails not only joblessness, prison incarceration, substandard housing, and inadequate education; it also entails a deeper spiritual dehumanization and the deadening of their sensibilities through drugs, despair, and hopelessness. But the technological society that would crush the black spirit has already had a negative impact on white sensibilities. The pragmatist, philosopher, and educator John Dewey complained in 1935:

> We undergo sensations as mechanical stimuli without having a sense of the reality that is in them and behind them.... We see without feeling, we hear, but only a second hand report, second hand because not reinforced by vision. Prestige goes to those who use their minds without participation of the body and who act vicariously through the control of the bodies and labor of others.[22]

The spiritual question for black theology and black religious studies is how to prevent the above diagnosis from becoming more true of African Americans than it may be already-albeit for different reasons. Part of the solution, again, brings us back to aesthetics because of the new vision Dewey spoke of cannot be signified with the categories of the old discourse. Breaking from the parameters of the old discourse requires a return to the counterhegemonic language of African American slave religion and, then, its improvisation and recreation to meet present day requirements for faith and hope. In this undertaking, African American art is indispensable. With African American art contributing both to the archaic and modern symbols of black religious consciousness, it provides black theology and black religious studies with interpretive visual metaphors for developing what Charles Long called "a new and counter-creative signification and expressive deployment of new meanings expressed in styles and rhythms of dissimulation."[23] As black theology and black religious studies endeavors the constriction of a new emancipatory discourse, African American art will be indispensable as a dialogue partner.

Conclusion

African American art is vital to the projects of black theology and black religious studies because it: (1) supplies them with an additional text for entering into their sources, that is, black culture, the black experience, and black religion; (2) reinforces the methodology advocated by these disciplines; (3) as an intertextural dialogue partner, it raises questions and clarifies some others that might elude black theology and black religious studies; and (4) provides a mirror for scholars of black religion to see their own efforts reflected and consequently acquire new understandings of their own disciplines.

What we have seen in our discussions of Douglas's, William H. Johnson's, and Romare Bearden's art are several commonly held features: their return to African American folk culture as a source of artistic inspiration and content; the centering of the black subject in their canvasses; stylistic innovations both embodying and interpreting the black aesthetic; creating artistic products through intertextual influences from the black experience. Thus, African American art not only provides material for reflecting on the black religious experience, but it also models a hermeneutic for interpreting that experience; therefore, it is an essential text for black theology and black religious studies.

8

The Meaning of the Moan and Significance of the Shout in Black Worship and Culture and Memory and Hope

This type of structuring of the primary religious expressions does not arise from the metaphysical desire to construct the world. The intent of this structure is a more modest one. Through this structure a pattern, a "language" of the sacred, is revealed, a language that describes human immersion in life—in this case as a confrontation with the sacred. It is through this language that the human being deciphers the meaning of the sacred in history. This language or structure of the sacred is the medium through which historians insert themselves into the historical being of others. The use of every structure, whether biological, aesthetic, or religious, points to the endeavor to find a common form for the self and the "other" which is the object of interpretation. Structure is thus a mode of communication...

This communication of the "intelligible something" (in our case religious structures) should lead to an opening of ourselves and permit us to order unexplored areas of our lives. Our return to the archaic and traditional religious forms does not express a desire merely to trace casual connections. It is a return to the roots of human perception and reflection undertaken so that we might grasp anew and reexamine the fundamental bases of the human presence. (*Significations*, p. 46)

Introduction

In black worship we hear uttered the "language of the sacred" Long wrote of in the above quote taken from *Significations*. Black worship, of course, has no monopoly on this language of the sacred, but it does have its own way of speaking this language. This language is rooted in the signification of silence referred to earlier in chapter four, "Being, Nothingness, and the 'Signification of Silence' in African American Religious Consciousness." I tried to show in chapter seven, "'The Signification of Silence' Revisited: African American Art and Hermeneutics," how this language is given visual expression in that medium. In this chapter, I will engage in a phenomenology of the language of the sacred that is uttered in black worship but which, I also argue, structures the whole spectrum of black experience.

Black Worship

Describing black worship is no easy task even when, as in the present case, the discussion is focused upon the interaction between the preacher and congregation in black worship. One difficulty arises from the fact that, presently, there are as many black worship styles as there are denominational affiliations among African Americans. The designation from this array of one particular worship style as "black" entails risks that I would like to avoid. Nevertheless, certain characteristic features, rightly or wrongly, come to mind when qualifying the noun "church" with the adjective "black" and, needless to say, these associations insinuate themselves in discussions about black preaching. A way of circumventing this difficulty is through an explication of the historical factors that produced a peculiar matrix of psychological need, political aspiration, and spiritual disposition addressed by black worship and black preaching. In this way we might sidestep the debate concerning what qualifies as exemplary of these categories.

In calling the black church by a different name, Zora Neale Hurston wrote: "The Sanctified Church is a protest against the high-brow tendency in Negro Protestant congregations as the Negroes gain more education and wealth." "Those congregations," according to Hurston, were regarded as "unbearably dull to the more primitive Negro who associates the rhythm of sound and motion with religion."[1] If Hurston's use of the term "primitive" is understood in its nonpejorative sense as signifying something whose chronological appearance was earlier than its comparison, her statement is accurate insofar as the polarity she describes indicates the two extremes of the continuum encompassing black worship. Our attention will focus on one end of this continuum.

What we will signify in speaking about black worship and black preaching are certain features in the contemporary black church's liturgical practices representing the greatest continuity with the folk religion of the nineteenth-century rural slave population. Here, as Melville J. Herskovits and, later, Albert Raboteau, Gayraud Wilmore, and others have asserted, can be found the greatest influence and number of African "retentions" such as spirit possession, dance, polyrhythmic music, and an all pervasive "call and response" pattern structuring the participation of the worshiping community's members. In discussing the call and response pattern found in black worship, this chapter attempts to get beneath its surface by describing the mood and modality constituting the substance of this worship form. Their signifiers are the moan and the shout; but before saying more about this, some additional caveats must be introduced regarding how we conceptualize black worship.

As already discussed in previous chapters, it was the peculiar history to which African Americans were subjected, and which they made, that determined the diversity now extant in their styles of worship and preaching. Within this history, there evolved what W. E. B. Du Bois termed a "double consciousness" among African Americans—a consciousness torn by the tension between the competing needs for self-definition and external validation; a consciousness ever incarcerated behind the veil of color. Different forms of black worship and black preaching can be understood, therefore, as offering alternative solutions to this existential dimension of the African American predicament in North America. It was Calvin who said in his *Institutes*: without knowledge of self there is no knowledge of God; without knowledge of God there is no knowledge of self. Since African Americans have never enjoyed unanimity regarding self-definition, there, understandably, has always been diversity in their religious practices. Shortly after slavery ended, Bishop Payne, for example, tried to stamp out every instance he encountered among African Methodist Episcopalians of the ring dance or ring shout that he regarded as undignified and heathen. One A. M. E. Minister, in defending the practice, told Bishop Payne that without it people would not become converted. At issue were conflicting assumptions about African American's identity—one abhorring and the other requiring the moan and the shout.

The Moan

By following the thinking of Charles H. Long, we can locate the moan's origin and epiphany somewhere along the route of the Middle Passage. Captives boarded the slave ships as members of one or

another of the numerous ethnic groups found on the African continent to assume an identity during and subsequent to the voyage
that would become hyphenated in the Americas. The efficacy of deities associated with one's clan or nation were called into question or
reinterpreted in the Americas. Even language, the vehicle of thought
and communication, began to lose its capacity to generate meaning
due to the barbarity of the Middle Passage and New World slavery.
Whatever African retentions are found in black worship did not get
there by a direct route but were transmuted and filtered by the Middle
Passage's incommunicability. Meaning had to be uttered rather than
spoken through something more primal than the particularity of language—the moan. The moan became the first vocalization of a new
spiritual vocabulary—terrible and wonderful, it was a cry, a critique,
a prayer, a hymn, a sermon, all at once. The moan facilitated and
expressed the captive's vague intuition of what latter would be identified with the Exodus God who hears the groans of the oppressed and
intervenes on behalf of their liberation. Although the captives could
not name this God, the Divine was invoked and acknowledged in the
moan. Pneumatology preceded Christology in the religious history
of African Americans. It was not until the Second Awakening during
the early nineteenth century or later that the Holy Ghost began to be
associated with the personality of Jesus in the slave mentality. On the
slave ship, before reaching the Americas and before conversion, slaves
prayed in the sighs and groans too deep for words written about the
Apostle Paul.

Before they could name him, the moan invoked the Exodus God
who heard the Hebrew's cry and brought about a new perception of
God's redemptive action on their behalf. The moan expressed loneliness, pain, and the inchoate hope that would, later, fuse with biblical imagery. Its rhythm was not only the syncopated beat of the
West African drum as the rock and sway of the sea-faring vessel
that contained their bodies. As the human cargo was rocked and
swayed beneath the slave ship, the singularity of the individual suf-
ferer's utterance lost its opacity within the harmony constituted by
the utterances of other sufferers! This is not an abandoned expression; the pneumatology of the moan remains extant in the African
American community. It can be heard in the work song, the Spirituals,
blues, gospel, jazz, the black deacon's prayer, the black preacher's sermon, and the responses from the "Amen Corner." The late Reverend
Carl Bennett shared with me his grandmother's remark regarding
what can be heard between the hymns and prayers of many Baptist

worship services. "We moan," she said, "because that-way the devil can't understand what we're talking about."

What Instigates the Moan

Yet the preacher has to know and be able to communicate in this modality. Accordingly, to be effective, the black preacher must construct sermons that resonate to the congregation's spiritual sensibilities and social strivings. He or she must strike the right chord in the community by victoriously representing to it the faith born from its struggles. Black preachers who emerged during the Second Awakening camp meetings of the early nineteenth century often accomplished this task through the "sung sermon" or "preaching spirituals." After the official services ended, the slaves in attendance then gathered separately to hold their own services to, according to a contemporary observer, "sing for hours together short scraps of disjointed affirmations, pledges lengthened out with long repetitive choruses." Sometimes, one or another of the scraps would be developed into a song by an excited exhorter during the course of the sermon. William Wells Brown witnessed this at a church in Nashville, Tennessee when the preacher took a piece of paper from his pocket at a point in the sermon and told the congregation that when they reached heaven and looked for their mothers "the angel will read from this paper." The preacher's voice increased in pitch "until he was almost singing"; in their excitement folk began saying:

> "Let this angel come right down now and read that letter,
> Yes, yes. I want to hear the letter," ... "Amen."
> "Glory. Hallelujah," "Yes. Lord."[2]

The corporateness of black worship indicated above has to do not just with sound and rhythm but also theology. All black preaching does not involve "hooping" but it must, of necessity, speak to and about what occasions the community's moans—it must dwell and then rise with the congregation from the valley of the shadow of death. Like the blues that does not make you sad even though it is about that emotion, black preaching, while having its point of departure in the depths of the moan's historicity, moves beyond that to a joyful and courageous affirmation of being. The shout is the opaque utterance expressing what more trained black clergy were saying in standard English. For example, Presbyterian minister and Abolitionist Henry

Highland Garnet would say in his 1843 "An Address to the Slaves of the United States of America":

> While you have been oppressed, we have also been partakers with you; nor can we be free while you are enslaved.... Many of you are bound to us not only by the ties of a common humanity but we are connected by the more tender relations of parents, wives, husbands, and sisters, and friends. As such we most affectionately address you.

Garnet went on in that speech to urge slaves to rebel against their masters saying, "Let your motto be resistance! resistance! resistance!"[3] This was an ethical imperative for Garnet. The slaves, of course, were capable of obtaining this hermeneutical insight from any number of biblical sources. In 1859, Jackson Whitney, an escaped slave who made his way to Canada, wrote his former master a letter wherein he jubilantly said: "I rejoice to say that an unseen, kind spirit appeared for the oppressed and bade me take up my bed and walk—the result of which is that I am victorious and you are defeated."[4] This is "realized eschatology" at its best! Black preaching, at its best, addresses the political and economic situation confronting the congregation while simultaneously bringing about an emotional catharsis among the worshipers. This catharsis should, by no means, be explained reductionistically, in other words, solely in terms of psychological processes. It is something brought about by a profound and overwhelming experience of God's love. That's what makes one shout. This happens when the preacher communicates the Gospel in such a way that, in addition to the hearing of Divine speech, the congregation recognizes its own voice in the preacher's.

Slaves sang "Nobody knows the trouble I see," and contradicted themselves by saying, "nobody knows but Jesus." In this one line, we have dual references to what instigates the moan as well as the shout. Embodying both frames of reference is what black preaching somehow accomplishes partly in practicing the distinction between speech and voice. The distinction between speech and voice in black preaching corresponds with the distinction between the "what" from the "how" of what is said.

Euphony and Resonance

Describing the old-time black preacher, James Weldon Johnson wrote in *God's Trombones*:

> He knew the secret of oratory, that at bottom it is a progression of rhythmic words more than it is anything else. Indeed, I have witnessed

congregations moved to ecstasy by the rhythmic intoning of sheer inco-
herencies.... The old-time Negro preacher loved the sonorous, mouth
filling, ear filling phrase because it gratified a highly developed sense
of sound and rhythm in himself and his hearers.[5]

Of the preacher whose sermon inspired those put to verse in *God's
Trombones*, Johnson wrote that the preacher "strode the pulpit up
and down in what was actually a very rhythmic dance, and he brought
into play the full gamut of his wonderful voice, a voice...not of an
organ or a trumpet, but rather of a trombone."[6]

What Johnson observed in the old-time black preacher can also be
observed in its more contemporary exemplars. In Hortense J. Spillers'
analysis of Martin Luther King's sermons, she pointed out how their
success in utilization of certain phrases to elicit desired congregational
responses "was more attributable to his sense of euphony and reso-
nance than to gesture and movement." King and Spillers observed,
"often brought together words that ended in the same sound to create
a kind of rhythm and cadence." For example: the southern upholders
of segregation with their "lips dripping in interposition and nullifica-
tion." The call and response pattern characteristic of black worship
also helped sustain the sermon's rhythmic pattern characteristic of
black worship. By placing some of the congregation's responses during one of King's sermons in parenthesis, Spillers attempted in written
form to convey the dynamic interaction between the preacher and
congregation in black worship.

> The same man (same man!) who sits high and looks low, who rounded
> the world in the middle of his hands (who rounded the world in the
> middle of his hands!), This same man who fed five thousand and still
> had food left over. (Yessuh! Had some left).[7]

A similar literary device was used in a poem by Samuel Allen titled
"Big Bethel (Call and Response)" wherein the two voices, the preacher's and the congregation's, are lain beside each other in parallel col-
umns. The congregation's voice appears in parenthesis.

> Dearly beloved (Alright)
> Brethren in spirit (Alright now)
> Children in sorrow (O Yes)
> When we have come to the (Weellll)
> last hour of the journey (Unnhn)
> So let us move on together
> On the road to the kingdom

> The heart of the kingdom
> The sweet scent of Canaan
> ....
> So let us move on together Alright)
> On the road to the kingdom (Road to the Kingdom)
> The heart of the Kingdom (Heart of the Kingdom)
> The sweet scene of Canaan (Preach now)[8]

The rhythm or cadence of this type of call-and-response pattern closely resembles that of the work song. Parenthetically, it should also be pointed out how the "hoop" of certain black preachers resembles the work song as well. What is suggested in the similarity is the fact that African Americans had to expend tremendous amounts of energy to worship. The clandestine "brush arbor" meetings took a lot of work and planning. The similarity can also be explained by the similarity of the breathing mechanics of the work song and the "hoop." In analyzing the latter, Zora Neale Hurston made the following observation:

> The well-know "ha!" of the Negro preacher is a breathing device, the tail end of the expulsion just before the inhalation. Instead of permitting the breath to drain out...the wind is expelled out violently. Example: (inhalation) "And oh!"; (full breath) "my father and my wonder-working God"; (explosive exhalation) "ha!"[9]

In its written form, such as in Allen's previously quoted poem, the preacher-congregation interaction almost looks like the responsive reading or call to worship of mainline Protestant liturgies. White churches, however, provide few other opportunities in worship for active congregational participation and when they do occur they remain structured and inhibited. We should note, of course, that socioeconomic factors may have as much to do with this generalization as race. There is no formal structuring to the call and response pattern of black worship—it is dictated by the visitation of the Holy Ghost in interaction with the preacher's gifts and the overall mood of the congregation. What the folks bring to worship, influences what they need to take from it, what they hear, and what they will say "amen" to.

In Allen's poem, we have a set of stock phrases that have high probability of eliciting "amens" but those "amens" will be merely politeness unless the preacher exercises ingenuity in employing them in the task of creatively and intelligibly improvising the telling of the

Gospel story. The masters of the art can intersperse and interweave these phrases throughout the sermon to drive home the points being illustrated. For example, after explaining or illustrating a point, the black preacher might exclaim: "That's why they say he'll make a way out of no way!" Someone in the congregation may then say, "That's right," as the verbal equivalent to the nodding of the head in informal conversation. But it could happen that with the identical exclaim by the preacher, several people in the congregation begin saying things such as: "Come on now!" "Alright preach!" "Preach, preach!" Then the preacher might find him or herself inspired to go into a "run" of repetitions beginning with, for example, "That's why."

The moan and shout grow out of the complexity and severity of the African American existential situation. James Baldwin describes this situation in the notes to his play *The Amen Corner*. He explains that he wanted to communicate the reality of ordinary black church folk as he knew them growing up in Harlem as the son of a minister. He wrote the play thinking about his father but "to think about my father meant that I had also to think about my mother and the stratagems she was forced to use to save her children from the destruction awaiting them just outside her door." And he thought about all the people Sister Margaret represented.

> She is in the church because her society has left her no other place to go. Her sense of reality is dictated by the society's assumption, which is also her own, of her inferiority. Her need for human affirmation, and also for vengeance, expresses itself in her merciless piety; and her love, which is real but which is also at the mercy of her genuine and absolutely justifiable terror, turns her into a tyrannical matriarch. In all this, of course, she loses her old self—the fiery, fast-talking little black woman whom Luke loved. Her triumph, which is also, if I may say so, the historical triumph of the Negro people in this country, is that she sees this finally and accepts it, and, although she has lost everything, also gains the keys to the kingdom. The kingdom is love, and love is selfless, although only the self can lead one there. She gains herself.[10]

One moans the loss of self and shouts at its reacquisition—but, where do we demark the boundary between the two? The moan and shout can only be comprehended through empathy with the persons giving them utterance. Such empathy allows the listener to understand how the moan and shout are the only vehicles, under those circumstances, able to articulate and give release to the pain, longing, fear, expectation, faith, confusion, and hope bundled up and attached to the stories that become one's burden. Therefore, empathy—in this case—presumes an a priori understanding of what cannot be spoken or thought. The moan and shout are vocalized significations of silence or flashes of light briefly revealing what lies darkly hidden in the Baroque convention of chiaroscuro. The secular analogue to this is described in Matthew V. Johnson, Sr.'s novel *The Cicada Song* where two of the characters, Anna Mary and Bird experience mutual ecstasy.

> A shaft of light, a solid beam, sliced through the shadows in the barn and fell close by. Dust particles played in the light rising, some falling and swirling about. The life draining fro his limbs ebbed from his body and dissolved into the flow. They conveyed him through the murky atmosphere of the barn, up along the beam. He followed them up and out of the barn through the roof and into the open air; into a universe free and unchained. He had found a window and passing through it, discovered another world.[11]

But these descriptions are ones that skirt the surface of the phenomenon of black worship and render it still opaque. We are still struggling with what we having been discussing all along—the problem of language or its inadequacy when it comes to describing the nature of religious experience. How can any words capture what it is like to be present when the folks are gathered in "a community listening to the sounds and words of each other [and] in this one moment of experience the immediacy of experiencing outside the veil is afforded."[12] This ineffable experience of immediacy is related to the community's memory and hope discussed in the next section.

Black Religious Consciousness

Charles H. Long made the following statement in Significations regarding the "religious consciousness of blacks."

> Insofar as society at large was not an agent of transformation, the inner resources of consciousness and the internal structures of the black's own history and community became not simply the locus for new symbols but the basis for a new consciousness for blacks. It is therefore the religious consciousness of the blacks in America which is the repository of who they are, where they have been, and where they are going. A purely existential analysis cannot do justice to this religious experience. A new interpretation of American religion would

come about if careful attention were given to the religious history of this strange American.[13]

Consciousness is a troubling and ambiguous term and qualifying it with the designation African American makes it no less so; however, it is the best term to use in clarifying what comprises African American subjectivity. This is due to the term "consciousness" having certain nuances not connotated by the term "psychology" which, if used, would not only limit our method to that discipline but, also, preclude any discussion of the political, cultural, historical, religious, and ontological features essential to an understanding of the African American experience. These features are often elaborated in isolation to one another by separate disciplines and to the real actors whose consciousness determines and is determined by such realities. Hence, I will endeavor, in this chapter, to describe how African American consciousness is objectively and subjectively constituted through an interplay of these factors.

Preliminary Definitions and Considerations

Structuralism, as I am using the term, refers to the way in which the interplay of the above factors is conceptualized. It refers therefore not to the structuralism of Barthes, Foucault, models to the explication of social reality but to the earlier forms of structuralism related to functionalism and exemplified, for example, in the works of Wilheim Dilthey and Karl Mannheim. Both Dilthey and Mannheim believed that consciousness could be indirectly apprehended through an interpretation of its "objectifications" but the difference between them and the more contemporary figures named earlier is that the latter tend to so widen the distance between text(s) and author(s) that the subject (consciousness) becomes inaccessible to interpretation and insignificant to the meaning of the text(s). This chapter, therefore, does not presume any autonomy of the text (African American culture) but, to the contrary, regards it as the highest expression of African American consciousness. Elucidating the connection between the interpretive text and the consciousness it objectifies is the task of a structuralist phenomenology. According to Dilthey "the category of structure originates from the analysis of life's recurring features... this is an abstraction and its concept is only valid when it is linked to the consciousness of the context of life in which it is contained."[14] The most brilliant and, as yet, unsurpassed product of this type of analysis is exemplified in the work of the Martiniquian psychiatrist Frantz Fanon in his *Black Skin, White Masks* and *Wretched of the Earth*. Henry F. Ellenberger traces this type of phenomenology back to the work of Eugene Minkowski whose "structural analysis" (as Minkowski termed his method) sought "to define the basic disturbance (trouble *generateur*) from which one could deduce the whole content of consciousness and the symptoms of the patients."[15] Fanon's phenomenology was similar to Minkowski's in that he attempted to describe the gestalt (connections and interconnections) he observed within the consciousness of the colonized native. Like Dilthey, Fanon was influenced by Hegel in his belief that self-consciousness arose through the experiencing of the outside world in terms of resistance. Phenomenology imputes intentionality to consciousness thanks to Husserl's insistence that consciousness is consciousness of an object but it is not Husserl's "transcendental ego," which Fanon will posit as standing over and above an alienated, objectified self revealed in the eyes of the other. Fanon's phenomenology is closer to Sartre's than Husserl's in that his can be described (like Sartre's) to be "the reflexive study of consciousness of things, of himself, and of other selves."[16]

This philosophical method of understanding existence through a description of experience is related to epistemology because experience necessitates cognition or knowing. Hermeneutics is also called upon since consciousness, as such, is not immediately available to philosophical observation and, therefore, must be restructured or interpreted through a description of its products—language and symbols. Discernment of the deeper level incarnated and expressed in language and symbols (behind which lies hidden consciousness and being or conscious being) is what a structuralist phenomenology seeks to accomplish. In saying this, I do not mean to imply that consciousness is not shaped and qualified by language and symbols and must therefore add, as a caveat, that this relationship is reciprocal. In addition, it should be said that this reciprocity is not automatic but, indeed, problematic for people who are racially oppressed; this brings about the need for ontological resistance on their part against the language and symbols that would distort and even destroy the integrity of their being. Hence, to develop a structuralist-phenomenology of African American consciousness, we must not fail to clarify its historical context or, more accurately, its historical-existential-cultural context.

African American Culture as Text

For a definition of culture, I am relying upon Heinrich Rickert's understanding in *Science and History*, of history being comprised of activity directed toward valued ends and culture of "whatever is produced directly by men [and women] acting according to valued ends or, if it is already in existence, whatever is fostered intentionally for the sake of the values attached to it."[17] According to Rickert's definition, culture (and history) can be seen as the projection and concrete expression of consciousness.

Rickert's definition of culture better lends itself to our task than the ambiguous definition of it as "everything people think and do as members of a particular society" being more dynamic than the latter and suggesting explanations of how culture can function in a people's historical quest for freedom. African American culture is comprised of slave narratives, the blues, jazz, folk tales, folkways, sermons, Motown, dance art, literature, and so on. Culture is not a metaphysical entity acting on a people; people are the creators of their culture. The collective subjectivity of African Americans is what I am terming African American consciousness. Consciousness shapes and is shaped by culture. African American culture, for example, African American art can be seen as the objectification of consciousness. In its interpretation, however, this chapter seeks to avoid the hermeneutical flaw of explaining the work of art genetically or reductionistically. Karl Mannheim argued that cultural products, for example, the novel, or the painting, as objectifications of *Weltanschauung*, have three levels of meaning: objective, expressive, and documentary. In his essay "On the Interpretation of Weltanschauung" he wrote:

> objective interpretation is concerned with grasping a completely self-contained complex of meaning—pervading the "representation" of the subject matter as well as the "shaping" of the medium—which is ascertainable from the work alone as such…Expressive meaning has to do with a cross-section of the individuals' experiential stream, with the exploration of a psychic process which took place at a certain time; documentary meaning…is a matter…of the character, the essential nature, the "ethos" of the subject which manifests itself in artistic creation.[18]

Mannheim utilizes Dilthey's distinction between explanation (*erklaren*) and understanding (*verstehen*) in making the case that a documentary interpretation of *Weltanschauung* cannot be derived reductionistically. In his essay "A Review of George Lukacs' Theory of the Novel," Mannheim opposes the method of interpreting "from below upward" by advancing the opposite approach "from up downward" to grasp what he calls the "spiritual element" in the work of art which is an "objectification of the spirit"... "deeper explanation can be attained only by a discipline that takes as its object the full spiritual context of the work as a whole: metaphysics or philosophy of history."[19]

In this chapter, with regard to interpreting African American consciousness, I am adapting Mannheim's procedure for interpreting *Weltanschauung* and, toward the end of this discussion, will offer a model for engaging in such interpretation that identifies the various components of this "hermeneutic circle." For the present, suffice it to say: African American culture serves as the interpretive text for a structuralist-phenomenology of African American consciousness.

Objective and Subjective Dimensions of African American Experience

At the outset let it be said that to view African American consciousness as merely the product and reaction to racial exploitation would rob African Americans the dignity of being the subjects of their own history and deny the fact that they have been making history but, on the other hand, to ignore the degree to which their existence has been determined by racial oppression is to render a full appreciation of the former impossible. To avoid either pitfall, it is helpful to distinguish between objective and subjective realities of the black experience and understand history and culture as playing a dual role of mediation and transformation (figure 8.1). Objective reality refers to the Middle Passage, the slave ship, bondage, toil, the whip, bloodhounds, rape, murder, and all the other horrors designed to obliterate any trace of humanity in the African psyche. Subjective reality refers to the existential dimension of blackness—the way African Americans experienced America—both the way African Americans were broken and crushed by oppression as well as the way they, in resisting oppression, maintained a sense of wholeness. African American history and culture, while including features of the objective and subjective dimensions, can also be regarded as having synthetic functions of mediation and transformation. In other words, in the dialectical interaction between

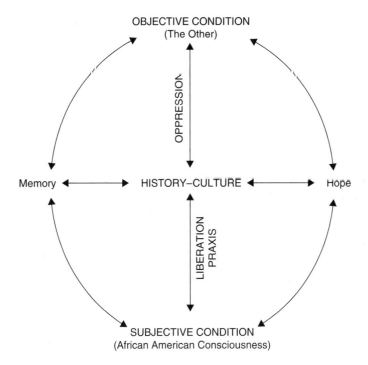

Figure 8.1 Objective/subjective dimension of African American consciousness.

the objective and subjective components of African American reality, the action of the latter on the former is African American history, for example, Nat Turner, Danmark Vessey, Harriet Tubman, Fredrick Douglas. African American history, thus conceived, mediates the activity of African Americans to facilitate resistance against the negative features of objective reality in the process of transforming it and opening it toward the future. In becoming actors in their own history, African Americans are thereby opened to the positive/nonthreatening/self-enhancing features of objective reality that is the product of their own activity that is "African American culture."

Reciprocity and Resistance in Cultural Formation

The subject-object poles in the reality being described are, as I mentioned, in a relationship of reciprocity; and therefore, there must be a mutual opening to one another at both ends of this dialectic. It is this insight that led George Simmel to point out that "cultures exist only if man [and woman] draws into his development something that is external to him"[20] How it is possible to draw into ones development something from the objective realm without being destroyed in the process is what a structuralist-phenomenology of African American consciousness must address. In other words, how does African American consciousness engage, simultaneously, in the act of negation and assent or resistance and reciprocity?

As Freud has shown, repression is the basic ego defense mechanism of negation, the blocking out from consciousness painful and negative aspects of reality. What we discover, however, in a study of the Spirituals, is that through hope African Americans have addressed the horror of the present and projected their consciousness beyond the oppressive immediacy of the "now" toward that "great gettin'-up mornin'." Thus, the barefoot slave is able to sing "I've got shoes, you've got shoes, all God's children got shoes" not because he is denying reality but rather, because its legitimacy has been negated with a hope providing the ground on which to fortify the beleaguered structure of the self against the assault of an oppressive reality. Value, as the *telos* of African American history and the form of its culture, is derived from its hope. To say it differently, hope is the basis of value in the African American experience providing thereby a "categorical imperative" or "ought." This imperative establishes the legitimacy of black existence as well as the basis for ontological resistance before the other's attempt at devaluating the black self.

The history of slavery and colonialism and its rationalizations expressed in a racist ideology that, even today, lingers as an a priori psychic category in the European and American world view is what African American consciousness encounters as "otherness." In the Hegelian sense it is what African Americans experience upon being confronted with the white world. It is what forces on the African American the burden of becoming an existentialist, which is to say, a person (if he/she is to remain a person) whose existence can never be taken for granted for now in his/her encounter with the other he must "experience his being through others... not only must the black man be black; he must be black in relation to the white man.... Overnight the Negro has been given two frames of reference within which he has to place himself."[21] What I have been challenging throughout this study is the existential privilege enjoyed by whites of operating with one frame of reference—whiteness.

This is another way of describing the double consciousness that W. E. B. Du Bois spoke of in his *The Souls of Black Folks*. But the objectification resulting from such an encounter is not one that can be fully appreciated through the description of "twoness." Another feature of this phenomena is brought out in Ralph Ellison's concept of "invisibility":

> I am invisible, understand, simply because people refuse to see me...it is as though I have been surrounded by mirrors of hard, distorting glass. When they approach me they see only my surroundings, themselves, or figments of their imagination—indeed, everything except me. Nor is my invisibility exactly a matter of a bio-chemical accident to my epidermis. That invisibility to which I refer occurs because of a peculiar disposition of the eyes of those with whom I come in contact.[22]

The feature brought out by Ellison's concept of invisibility is similar to Sartre's concept of nausea and nothingness. The self loses its sense of solidity, begins to melt and evaporate. The outcome of this experience will depend upon numerous factors among which is the ego strength of the person undergoing the encounter. Fanon observes that: "If the psychic structure is weak, one observes a collapse of the ego. The black man stops behaving as an actional person. The goal of his behavior will be the Other (in the guise of the white man), for the Other alone can give him worth. That is on the ethical level: self esteem."[23]

Aesthetic and Ethical Dimensions of African American Consciousness

Fanon, in making the connection between self-worth and ethics, indicates that a discussion of the other is not unrelated to a consideration of "value." If the Other is the standard by which value is ascertained, then the African American is doomed, and, therefore, it is in his/her self-interest to discover the means by which he/she can stand above or, at least, on a par with the Other and escape relegation to "thinghood." He/she does this by turning the Other's standard back on the Other. Sometimes this is in code as in Spiritual "everybody talking about heav'n ain't going there," or in the tradition of political oratory:

> By a peculiar logical inversion the Anglo-Saxon ruling class, its imitators, accomplices and victims have come to believe in a Negro problem.

With great zeal and industry those controlling the media of information and instruction have succeeded in indoctrinating the whole world
with this fiction. It is written into the laws, accepted by organized
religion; it permeates our literature, distorts our thinking and is deeply
imbedded in our customs and institutions. So successful has been this
propaganda that even its unfortunate victims often speak of it with
the same conviction with which many people talk of guardian angels,
ghosts and malignant spirits. It is the "stop thief" technique at its
best a great testimonial to the ingenuity of exploiters with a bad con-
science; for while there is actually no Negro problem, there is definitely
a Caucasian problem.[24]

The moral vision of African American consciousness transcends the
giveness of historical (the objective) because, as I have said, so often
it is the very experience of the historical that mitigates against hope
and, also, as Hegel realized, because the categorical imperative, as an
absolute, can never be totally realized in history. It breaks through
and illuminates present striving while even calling one to action. In
the spiritual "O Freedom, O Freedom, O Freedom over me…and
before I'll be a slave I'll be buried in my grave and go home to my-
'Lord and be free" is indicated that such a vision gives implicit value
to life and value to value beyond life. In singing the song, a value is
not only identified but sustained and, in addition, its singing imparts
courage and worth to the singer whose singing embraces the value of
freedom. To overcome its alienation from its past and future, African
American consciousness has sought to gain and maintain an aesthetic
vision of the whole from which to interpret the immediate data of
experience. This vision of a time beyond time when "every tear will
be wiped from the eye, pain and suffering are no more" is its *telos*
and highest value. It is toward this ending—beginning which African
Americans "Lift every voice and sing til earth and heaven ring, ring
with the harmonies of liberty." African American history and culture
and, on the deep structural level, African American consciousness
must be interpreted according to its eschatology; its essence derives
its meaning from the future toward which it is striving. Matthew V.
Johnson referred to the "shout" or "frenzy," discussed previously in
this chapter, as an "eschatological moment."

In the experience of the frenzy the intra-psychic tensions that resulted
from the refractor socialization of the African American into the
warped cultural taxonomy of a racist culture were negotiated in the
hyper-liminal experience of the shout…In the experience the subject

undergoes a euphoric experience of wholeness and well-being. The "as if" nature of the experience, experience in the subjunctive sense provides a centering moment in which the state of freedom (not defined exclusively or even predominately in political and economic terms) as experienced vicariously and its reality or more accurately the reality of its possibility affirmed.

The eschatological moment, implicated in the experience, lent itself naturally to a utopian sensibility that prevailed throughout African American Christian consciousness. This utopian sensibility, as I have called it, found its quintessential symbolic expression in the notion of Heaven and crystallized in what some have identified, over simplistically, as a counter productive other-worldliness.[25]

Johnson goes on to observe the tendency among a number of black theologians to create a false dichotomy between conservative (otherworldly) and progressive (this worldly) types of African American religiosity due to a "premature conflation of theological reflection and social ethics." Like myself, however, he recognizes "There is a more fundamental unity in African American Christian consciousness (religious experience), the examination of which provides for a fuller richer theology than traditional black theology has provided up to now."[26] It is this future/eschatology/hope/value that provides the ethical unity of African American art, music, religion, literature, drama, dance, and so on. Alain L. Locke provided the foundation for this conceptualization in the essay "Values and Imperatives" in which he postulates four categories of form qualities or feeling references (exaltation, tension, acceptance or agreement, repose or equilibrium) corresponding respectively with the religious, ethical and moral, logical and scientific, aesthetic and artistic value modes. Locke wrote:

To my thinking, the gravest problem of contemporary philosophy is how to ground some normative principle or criterion of objective validity for values without resort to dogmatism and absolutism on the intellectual plane, and without falling into their corollaries, on the plane of social behavior and action, of intolerance and mass coercion....It raises the question whether the fundamental value modes have a way of setting up automatically or dispositional their end-values prior to evaluation judgment. Should this be the case, there would be available a more direct approach to the problem of value alternates...We should then be nearer a practical understanding of the operative mechanisms of valuation of the grounds for our agreement and conflicts over values.[27]

Locke's theory is useful in helping to explain both the unity and diversity among African American leaders in terms of the similarity or differences on the feeling reference predetermining the corresponding value type. Such differences, however, will always reside within certain parameters due to the objective condition of racial oppression that affects all African Americans to varying degrees. Locke's agenda, though, was that of promoting in his own words: "cultural racialism as a defensive counter-move for the American Negro." This agenda led Locke to fight on several fronts for the salvation of African Americans. Locke assumed the role of creating the philosophic space for the cultural achievements of African Americans. A people's humanity requires such space but this is not recognized in a racist society that denies the existence of any culture but its own. Locke, like other Harlem Renaissance and post-Harlem Renaissance figures, understood cultural activity as liberation-praxis and for all the failures and limitations of the 1920s and 1930s that are well documented in Harold Cruse's *The Crisis of the Negro Intellectual*. The cultural achievement of people such as Locke, Dubois, Schomburg, Robeson, Woodson, Hughes, Zora Neale Hurston, and yes, Garvey, was that the historical and cultural hegemony of the Other was deprived of its center. This independence was expressed in the manifesto of Langston Hughes who wrote in 1922: "We younger Negro artists now intend to express our individual dark-skinned selves without fear or shame. If white people are pleased, we are glad. If they are not, it doesn't matter. We know we are beautiful and ugly too...We build our temples for tomorrow strong as we know how, and we stand on top of the mountain free within ourselves."[28]

Catharsis, Memory, and Eschatology

For African Americans history is cathartic and serves not only to describe facts but also to penetrate the data of experience with the understanding that can guide a praxis aimed at social transformation. Arthur Schomburg wrote that the African American "must remake his past in order to make his future." To return to Simmel's definition of culture which he said "exists only if man [woman] draws into his development something that is external to him," it can be said that in the case of the African American it is his/her own past that has become externalized. Colonialism, as Fanon noted in *The Wretched of the Earth*: "is not satisfied merely withholding a people in its grip and emptying the natives brain of all form and context.

By a kind of perverted logic, it turns to the past of the oppressed people and distorts, disfigures, and destroys it. This work of devaluing pre-colonial history takes on a dialectical significance today."[29] And therefore Arthur Schomburg was absolutely correct in stating that African Americans must reconstruct their past to make their future.[30] This is the fact African Americans consciousness endeavors to accomplish becoming conscious—a consciousness for itself rather than the pathologic consciousness for others. It is not that a knowledge of Egypt, Ghana, Mali, Songhai, and so on. will automatically bring about a direct change in the objective condition of African Americans. Such a view would be naive. If, however, the objective conditions of African American oppression are to be altered through their own historical activity upon those conditions and if history is actually directed toward some value, then the historical consciousness of African Americans as subjects of their own history will be a crucial factor determining its outcome. The importance of overcoming the foreshortened perspective imposed on the African American psyche was discussed almost mystically by James Baldwin in the preface to his *The Evidence of Things Not Seen* where he wrote:

> I do not remember, will never remember how I howled and screamed the first time my mother was carried away from me…yet, what the memory repudiates controls the human being…what one does not remember contains the only hope, danger, trap, inexorability of love— only love can help you recognize what you do not remember….My memory stammers: but my soul is a witness.[31]

Conclusion

The hermeneutical axis required in constructing a structural-phenomenological understanding of African American consciousness cuts across its objective and subjective condition and its history culture that forms the midterm and has in its horizon hope on one end and memory on the other. African American consciousness is determined by the dialectical interplay between the trinity of its objective condition (the present), the memory (the past), and hope (the future) and that the interaction between these terms is reciprocal in that this trinity is affected by their liberation praxis as agents of history-culture. History and culture do not exist in a metaphysical/ethical vacuum nor is isolation to real subjects or concrete material conditions. Negatively speaking, this diagram suggests how African

American consciousness loses its subjectivity in proportion to the loss or obscuring of memory and/or hope. In this negative instance, African American consciousness would be determined by objective conditions not of its own making. Thus this model makes possible the viewing of integrationist, cultural nationalist, and revolutionary nationalist strategies within the black movement as being complementary, all being relativized before the absolute posited as their goal: African American freedom and liberation defined objectively and subjectively. Hence the Washington-Du Bois, Du Bois-Garvey, Malcolm-King controversies must be interpreted not only in terms of the objective condition confronting them but, in addition, in terms of their respective interpretations of it that mediated their praxis. And, despite the political differences epitomized in the earlier dichotomies, there remains an underlying unity stemming from an overall common milieu of oppression the experience of which, being differentiated intersubjectively, remains, nevertheless, within the boundaries of a certain world view.

To posit African American consciousness is not to epidermalize the ephemeral but to tentatively establish for the African American the spiritual basis of his/her psychology and the material basis of his/her culture and history. This model, therefore, provides a preliminary structure for elaborating a phenomenology of African American consciousness that avoids (without being either antihistorical or antipsychological) the limitations of mechanistic historico-genetic approaches on the one hand and reductionistic psychoanalytic approaches on the other hand. It will be useful for one who takes Karl Mannheim's admonishment seriously in which he said: "In the realm of the mental, we cannot understand the whole from the parts; on the contrary, we can only understand the parts from the whole."[32]

The Salsa/Jazz/Blues Idiom and Creolization in the Atlantic World

I am not african. Africa is in me, but I cannot return.
I am not tiano. Tiano is in me, but there is no way back.
I am not european. Europe lives in me, but I have no home there.

I am new. History made me. My first language was spanglish.
I was born at the crossroads
and I am whole.

—Aurora Levins Morales, *Getting Home Alive*

The oppressed have faced the hardness of life. The world has often appeared as a stone...Hegel spoke of a form of consciousness as the lithic imagination, that mode of consciousness which in confronting reality in this mode formed a will *in opposition*...This hardness of life or of reality was the experience of the meaning of the oppressed's own identity as opaque. Reality itself was opaque and seemed opposed to them...The matter of God is what is being experienced. This may be an old god (but all old gods are new gods). The expression of this god cannot be in the older theological languages. This god has evoked a new beat, a new rhythm, a new movement. (Charles H. Long, *Significations*, p. 197)

Introduction

This chapter seeks to investigate the salsa/jazz/blues idiom as a means of discerning the nature of creolization in the Atlantic World as a feature of modernity. This term—salsa/jazz/blues—is definitely not stated in historical order but indicates the fact that by the time salsa received its label there was a mutual and reciprocal interrelationship between it and jazz and blues that continues to this day. I place salsa first in this term because had I started with the blues or jazz I would have been force to privilege the North American experience of creolization and then had to endeavor to include the Caribbean and other areas of the Atlantic World. To start with salsa brings us immediately into a discussion of migrations of Afro-Cubans and Afro-Puerto Ricans from the Caribbean to New York and other cities in Europe. The meaning of the term creolization will be elaborated on later. Suffice it to say at this point that its importance has to do with understanding the nature of modernity whose temporal structure I am situating in the Atlantic World. That world did not come into being until the extreme western end of Asia called Europe made contact and entered into a series of sustained and nonreciprocal exchanges with Africa and the Americas. Creolization was the biological and cultural product of this temporality. Because this phenomenon has not been privileged in the West's conception of itself as "modern," it is only now being abstractly described and acknowledged in the discourse about postmodernity wherein hybridity is experienced as something new and startling.

Religion, Race, and Space

Salsa is not a pure sound. Those who want to study Salsa must abandon the fallacies of purity as well as singularity of origin. Its rhythm is not purely of one African group because the Africans that established its fundamental conventions or the ingredients that would constitute them were undergoing mutation during the process of their creativity. In one sense Africa was invented during and through the invention of the underlying rhythms constituting Salsa. The *Mandingo, Fon, Yoruba, Ibo, Ki-kongo* peoples who were transported to the Americas through the Middle Passage were recreating themselves as they created their rhythms. It was the Atlantic World as a whole and not the place of Africa where the echo of these rhythms can be traced. Salsa's archaic source is multiple. It appears simultaneously with the new epistemological category of western ontology—race. In Iberian terms, the concept of race was founded upon the prior notion of purity of blood (*limpieza de sangre*) etched into Iberia's collective consciousness during the long centuries of fighting crusades against the Moors. Originally having to do with the absence of Jewish ancestry, *limpieza de sangre* was easily applied to degrees of Africanness as miscegenation occurred and categories were invented to assign status to its multicolored offspring.

The first group of slaves that were imported to Americas in the early sixteenth century had undergone various degrees of creolization. They came from Spain and not directly from Africa. Some of the religious and cultural manifestations of their creolization established patterns of religious life that were continued by the slave population that arrived directly from Africa. Enslaved Africans in Spain's urban areas formed their own religious confraternities and mutual aid societies to assist with burials, participate in numerous saint's days associated with Iberian Christianity, and help to raise funds for their member's manumission. Such organizations were replicated in the Americas and provided a structure through which Africans organized various aspects of their religious and social life. These organizations—called "*cabildos*"—were noted for the songs and dances they performed at fiestas and holidays according to their respective "nacions." The first arrivals from Spain established certain patterns of religious life that were continued by the slave imported directly from Africa. Thus the *cabildos* provide us with one historical site for discernment and generalization regarding the way African ethnic groups in the Spanish colonies had to adapt, blend, and reinterpret the rituals, meanings, and practices drawn from Traditional African Religions and Roman Catholicism to further their survival in the Americas. At one end of the spectrum—depending on a number of factors—there were slaves who would become more thoroughly converted to Roman Catholicism. This was rare because there was no concerted policy or effort on the Spaniard's part to indoctrinate the slave population with Christianity. On the other end of the spectrum, there were African Caribbean cults whose Christian content was superficial at best or nonexistent as in Santeria and its pantheon of "*orishas*" or Yoruba gods such as *Chango* and *Obatala* that were invoked with specific drum rhythms and dances. This aspect of Salsa's history is usually omitted from most accounts since it is studied under the category of "secular" music that it indeed is but as a model of creolization its rhythms were not always so. Even today contemporary Salsa musicians such as vocalist La India are not adverse to singing in praise of *Yemaya* or some other *orisha* that remains potent in the substratum of Afro-Caribbean religiosity. Therefore, in present day Puerto Rico, Roman Catholic and Protestant Evangelical consternation and vocal condemnation as "pagan" of the "*fiesta Patronales*" celebrated annually in every town where Salsa, Merengue, and now, Raggaeton are played is not totally without theological warrant. However, within the broader historical context of this chapter we must mention, as noted in chapter two, that neither the Roman Catholic or Protestant branches of Christianity ever lodged a coherent and efficacious critique of the oppressive conditions within which the creolization of which salsa is an expression occurred. The religious dimension in Salsa's roots stems from fact that the rhythms made by Africans who worked in Cuba and Puerto Rico's sugar and coffee plantations helped them resist dehumanization by providing them with a modality of simultaneously experiencing concreteness and transcendence. In *World Music: A Very Short Introduction*, Philip V. Bohlman refers to the nameless persons who began creating various African American musical genres as the "musicians of the Middle Passage."[1] The Middle Passage, for Bohlman, "marked the historical and cultural distance between the West and the others created during the Age of Discovery which persisted through the Age of Enlightenment and beyond to the modern and post-colonial eras and still farther beyond into the landscapes of the African diaspora." This is the space not only where "alterity" was created "but enforced through the exercise of power. *It was also a space in which world music was and, in the racial imagination, is forged*" (my emphasis). Concerning the pivotal importance of the musics of the African diaspora for the contemporary study of world music, Bohlman writes:

> African music did survive the Middle Passage, and in the course of world music history, that music, indeed in the form of the popular musics of the West during the past century and a half, has shaped and influenced world music perhaps more than any other... African musics developed into a boundless spectrum of genres and forms, through isolation of distinctive markers of selfness and creative hybridization of otherness.[2]

Creolization, Miscegenation, and Hybridity(?)

Salsa literally means sauce. This music did not receive this designation until the 1960s. Legend has it that a DJ began using the label Salsa or sauce to what people had been calling variously Latin music, charanga, pachanga, boogaloo (indicating the Blues influence), Latin jazz, mambo, and so on. Although this term did not please everyone it stuck. Salsa denotes a mixture of no precise proportions whose flavor is hot and spicy. Like barbecue sauce in African American soul food, there are numerous recipes and proportions based on several basic ingredients that make it recognizable as barbecue sauce. Like African American soul food, one can debate whether particular regional variations represent the most authentic versions of different dishes. The debate around Salsa has to do with whether one privileges Cuba or Puerto Rico in one's historical account. I would like to avoid this issue by simply stating that both islands played and continue to play crucial roles in Salsa's development. The fact that these two islands—"los dos Antilles"—have different political structures but similar cultural orientations is very significant for our discussion. But with regard to Salsa's genealogy, we should avoid the fallacy of uni-causality and operate with a multicausal framework. This framework pushes Salsa's genealogy off the shores of "los dos Antilles" into the waters of the Atlantic. Upon those water were carried the bodies of slaves from diverse parts of West Africa.

The basic ingredient of Salsa was created on the bottom of slave ships when Africans from different part of the continent articulated vocal and somatic rhythms to express and address the terror and trauma of their capture and enslavement. One can discern even amidst the Salsa's intense, syncopated rhythms the muted wail and lament that expresses the vague memory of and longing for the place from which one's body was severed as in "Africa" sung by Azilia Cruz. So too, can one can discern even amidst the heat and fire of Salsa's maddening tempo the signification of the Middle Passage and other Afro-Caribbean rites of passage as in Azilia Cruz's patented exclaim "*Azuca*!" or sugar—the commodity whose demand fueled the trade in human bodies. "It don't mean a thing if it ain't got that swing" and one can discern even amidst the dizzying rhythms of the congas, bongos, and timbales the base line whose pulse evokes the sway of those ships that carried the original inhabitants from their African homelands and the heart beats of those carried on the bottom of those ships. The first—or, should we say, primal?—of the ingredients in the sauce are black bodies and the rhythms they articulated during their ordeal. Salsa was not made in a bottle but on the ships of the Middle Passage and the heat that cooked this sauce was provided by the friction of suffering. The stubborn persistence of the fundamental rhythms that now define Salsa's genre were founded upon the concrete necessity of psychic survival—not any high brow, formal, aesthetic theory—and this is what connects it so closely to the essential, dynamic, dimension of existence and experience called life. The fact that the underlying rhythms constituting Salsa's essential ingredient were excreted out of the throbbing flesh of black bodies representing diverse cultural groups from West Africa cannot be over-emphasized. This means the process of creolization, to be discussed shortly, was already at work while these people were undergoing the Middle Passage. Furthermore, I have also, already complicated the picture by indicating that the first group of Africans to arrive at Cuba and Puerto Rico were those that had already become assimilated to Iberian culture coming from Seville and not West Africa. Creolization occurred at another level when, as we shall see shortly, when these Iberian Africans reconnected with those transported directly from different parts of West Africa.

The term creole occurs in Spanish, Portuguese, and French. One prominent definition of "creole" is a person of Spanish, Portuguese, or French descent who was born in another, usually a tropical colo-nial territory. This was extended to include the English settler in colo-nial lands, thus the English colonists in North America before the American Revolution could be called "creoles." However, creole is much more than an issue of place of birth. Creole is the result of a process of creolization that expresses the complex and various mean-ing of the nature of contact, subordination, and settlement of peoples and cultures within the Atlantic World. This term, as already sug-gested, connotes also the result of biological as well as cultural con-tacts and exchanges. Creolization in this sense was something that started even before Africans were transported across the Atlantic. It occurred on the islands off the coast of Africa and on the Iberian Peninsula. At Cape Verde—where the initial racial classification con-sisted of: *broncos*, people of European origin who ruled the island; *capitaos*, the administrators, nobleman, settlers and their families; and *pretos* ("blacks") who were the enslaved population—a *crioulo* class emerged that was also referred to as *mestico*. Power relations as well as physical characteristics always determined which classifica-tion one fell under.

Notwithstanding what has been stated earlier, as early as the six-teenth century the term *"criollo"* was being used in Puerto Rico and Cuba to distinguish Africans born in those islands from those who had come directly from Africa who were referred to as *"bozales."* In *El Elemento Afronegroide En El Espanol De Puerto Rico*, Manuel Alvarez Nazario cites sixteenth-century documents listing the names of different slaves designated them as for example: "Ambrosio *negro criollo*," "Andres, *criollo de Santo Domingo*," "Beatrice, *negra cri-olla*," and so on. One document written in 1590 by Father Abbad defined a *"criolla/o"* as any African *"a los nacidos de espanoles en Indias."* As late as 1826, Governor De la Torre to notice a difference in the recreational preferences between *"criolles"* and *"boazales"* Africans. The *"boazales"* danced and played the bomba whereas the criolles layed the guitar. He wrote: *"Estas diversiones y recreaciones las tendran…hombres y mugeres, pero con la misma separacion, sus bailes de bombas de pellejo u otras sonajas de que usan los boazales, o de guitarra y vihuela que suelen tocar los criollos."*[3]

These power relations determining the degree to which one assimilated the religio-cultural practices and beliefs of the dominant group were more complex than usually imagined and these power relations had musical consequences. Some of the verses in "El Jibaro" (1849) by Manuel A. Alonso allude to the racial mixing that was occurring on the island of Puerto Rico:

> *Y se ponga a beriguay*
> *Si soy cristiano, judio,*
> *Tuico, mandinga o canga.*

Manuel Alvarez Nazario explains also in *El Elemento Afronegroide En El Espanol De Puerto Rico* how the preoccupation with race that was a part of Puerto Rican sensibilities manifested itself in the popular satirical expression *"el que no tiene dinga, tiene mandinga,"* which *"insinuador de la inevitable mezcla de sangres en la sociedad criolla."*[4] Today, more than one hundred and fifty years later one hears references, as terms of endearment and praise to *"mi mullata"* or *"mi negrita"* in Salsa lyrics. In *Caribbean Currents: Caribbean Music from Rumba to Raggae*, Peter Manuel documents how the creolization resulting from the cultural and biological miscegenation of Taino, African, and Spanish elements eventually produced a more definitive sort of creolization when this process reached a level of acceptance by Cuba and Puerto Rico's upper classes. *A creole national musical culture exists when all of a society's population embraces the musical expression of its creolization process as reflective of its common yet diverse identity.* It is at this point where the music does perform the role of organizing subjectivity in terms of nationality over against the metropolis. The negritude movement of the 1930s and 1940s played no small part in enabling Cuban and Puerto Rican elites to embrace the African elements in their cultures and, thereby, celebrate and incorporate the rhythms derived from Santeria, *rumba*, *bomba*, and *plena* into *son*, *danzon*, and *guajira*.

So too, did the civil rights and black consciousness movements of the 1960s play a similar role in influencing an acceptance and emphasizing of the African-Caribbean ingredients of Salsa. Salsa was one of the cultural vehicles that popularized pride in a new cultural sensibility. According to Manuel in Cuba during the early to mid-twentieth century:

> One important challenge for the country was the need to develop a national cultural identity that would unite the entire population—white, black, mulatto. Insofar as this goal has been achieved, music has played an important role in the formation of such an identity. From the 1920s on, hostility to Yankee domination and corrupt dictators like Gerardo Machado fueled the growth of a vibrant cultural nationalism that gradually came to embrace Afro-Cuban culture as well, as is reflected in the work of intellectuals like Fernando Ortiz and poet Nicolas Guillen...most important for our purposes was the emergence of dance-music genres that synthesized European and Afro-Cuban elements.[5]

If were not for the non-European elements in Cuba, there would have been no basic to posit a distinct national identity through which political independence could be asserted and Cuba's African presence could not be ignored under that necessity. Whether the political power of blacks in Cuba corresponds equally to the ideological value assigned to their presence is another and highly debatable matter that raises the question of whether something equivalent to commodification is possible in a socialist context. On the other hand, the expectation of a direct correspondence between cultural potency and political agency could risk reducing the former to propaganda and the instrumental rationality of which it serves as a critique.

Rhythm and Emotion

Recently when attending a conference in Paris, I ventured to a place on the River Seine where I was told people danced Salsa outdoors every evening. I made my way to the spot—about two or three city blocks up from the Notre Dame on the left bank. Just as I was beginning to suspect that my directions were wrong or I had been led on a wild goose chase, I began to hear a faint sound that revived my hopes in my adventure. As I quickened my pace, the sound became more definite and recognizable as Salsa. After continuing for another half block, I could see a crowd of people gathered on the sidewalk in front of where the music seemed to originate. After reaching that spot and navigating through a wall of spectators, I beheld one of the most marvelous sights to behold by any Salsa aficionado. Here in a large square opening between the street and above the walkway below at the banks of the River Seine were at least two hundred and fifty people representing the Rainbow Coalition all dancing in sync to some of the greatest percussive Salsa I have ever heard. Everybody on the floor was good but not at all in the ballroom sense of the term. Everybody was good because everybody was really enjoying and feeling the groove. After dancing for a while I found myself talking with another person of African ancestry, Mongo, who DJs there on certain evenings who asked me how I liked their scene and how their dancing compared with what we do in San Francisco. I told him: "Man, on a good night the spots I frequent are just like this but at some places people are into different orthodoxies about dancing on the 'One' or the 'Two' and what have you." Mongo then exclaimed: "Man, I am not into that...I have to feel and dance to the rhythm!" I said: "Exactly my brother!"

Rhythm is the most distinguishing feature of African and African derived music and the way Salsa combines African rhythms with European musical conventions constitutes its uniqueness as a genre. The structure of Salsa's rhythm is usually simply described as "syncopation"—the interaction of pulse patterns that are punctionated with off-beats. How the punctuation happens is not as easy to explain or conceptualize as it is to feel. Therefore, by itself, the term "syncopation," according to Peter Manuel, is far too simplistic to do Salsa justice. The way Salsa is syncopated is somewhat complex. Salsa's rhythm is not only syncopated; it is polyrhythmic that means two or more pulse rhythms are combined as they are in African music. In, *Emotion and Meaning in Music*, Leonard B. Meyer offers another way of explaining the distinctiveness of African music's temporal organization. Meyer bases his remarks on the studies of Richard Wasterman.

Wasterman begins by observing that in order for there to be a regular "off-beating," a series of regular recurring pulses, a normative beat, must become established in the mind of the listener. This beat, which Wasterman calls the "metronome sense," is primarily mental: "The regular recurrence of rhythmic awareness involves expectancy." The off-beats are deviants from this normative pulse. They must be irregular or else they too will become normative; for "complete 'off-beating' has the same effect as complete lack of off-beat patterns; it is in this sense meaningless."[6]

The rhythms in Salsa are structured into "cells" of twelve beats that instrumental patterns play in aggregates of twos and threes. This structuring is not possible to achieve "with the four- or eight-beat meters that pervade most contemporary North American and Caribbean pop music." The reference point that holds the complex polyrhythmic pattern together is provided by the playing of an iron bell in African music. This is called the "clave" in Salsa. The European element was provided in the form of "instruments, chordal harmony, sectional formal structures (rather than the reliance on cellular osti-natos), concepts of ensemble orchestration and arrangement, the practice of notating music," and so on.[7] Cuba's population consisted of almost equal proportions of blacks, whites, and mulattoes since the beginning of the early nineteenth century. Spanish musical traditions that included those of white farmers, *guajiros* (*jibreos* in Puerto Rico), were an indelible part of Cuba's cultural musical vocabulary. The guitar and mandolin type instruments were used in *Guajiro* music to play ten-line stanzas called the "*decima*". The other Spanish music that was played in Cuba was called the "*guajira*" the most famous being "Guantanamera" whose lyrics are based on a poem written in 1895 by Cuban nationalist Jose Marti. As we continue with this description, it should be understood that a similar process occurred also in Puerto Rico with some differences whose details we need not go into other than to point out that in Puerto Rico the Bomba is somewhat equivalent to what the Rumba is in Cuba. Bomba like its Cuban counterpart, Rumba, is the music (and dance) that happened in the slave quarters. However, in Puerto Rico the black population was not as numerically significant throughout the island as it was in Cuba. Blacks were concentrated primarily in those sections of the island where sugar cane was cultivated—the areas of Loiza in the northeast near San Juan and in the Guyama-Arroyo-Patillias area in the southern part of the island.

By 1800 Havana was the third largest city in the Americas with a flourishing bourgeois culture based, of course, on the exploitation of unfree black labor. As Cuban bourgeois culture was becoming more and more alienated from Spain, it was becoming heavily influenced by at this time by cosmopolitan French culture via Franco-Haitian immigration. Another influence was Italian style canto singing popularized by Donizetti and Bellini's operas. Viewing the Spanish style group dances as archaic and stiff, the Cuban bourgeois adapted the British and French trends of couple dancing that became the "*contradanza*" danced to music played in salons by chamber groups or pianists. This form of dance redounded back to Europe where it became popular by the 1830s. Guaguanco, a subtype of rumba that became distinct from other forms of rumba, such as yambu and columbia, also in the mid-1800s, consists of three conga drums, claves, a woodblock, solo singer, a chorus, and a male and female dancer. All of these elements of guaguanco interact in an intricate and complex manner. The couple interact in a sexual cat and mouse game with the woman enticing the male dancer while avoiding his attempt, while circling around her, to make contact with her through his execution of a pelvic thrust called the "*vacunao*." These movements have insinuated themselves into modern Salsa.

By the 1880s the "*danza*" had incorporated more of the depreciated African rhythms into its structure as it mutated into what would be called "*danzon*." In the 1920s, another type of music appeared on the Cuban scene called "*charanga*" that included two violins and a wooden flute. "*Bolero*"—a slower music sung in European bel canto style also appeared in the 1920s. Also during the 1920s, when even more African rhythms were added to the *danzon* that we pointed out had evolved from the *danza* we get the Cuban music called "son." It can be thought of as a cross between the raw and percussive rumba and the smooth and genteel *danzon*. The "son" was actually being played in the eastern part of Cuba at the beginning of the nineteenth century. When it first was played the European element was more prominent in its moderate tempo and reliance on string instruments. However, even at its early stage of development it included the bongo and marimbula and an extended "montuno section" during which "vocal call-and-response pattern were sung over a simple harmonic ostinato." In addition, "most of the soneros themselves were black or mulatto, and their songs texts were rooted in Afro-Cuban life." In the 1920s groups started to incorporate more sophisticated jazz harmonies into their "son" and also add horn sections to their groups. Manuel writes:

> One of the most distinctive features of the composite rhythm of the modern son (including most salsa songs) is the bass pattern. In most North American and Afro-American popular musics, from rock and rap to disco and doo-wop, the bass emphasizes the downbeat, falling strongly on the "one" beat of the four-beat measure. In son, by contrast, the base usually omits the downbeat entirely, in a pattern known as the anticipated bass. You can get the feel of this rhythm by repeatedly counting "one-two-three-one-two-three-one-two" and clapping

on the underlined "ones" (not the first "one"!). The pattern is called "anticipated" because the note of the last "one" indicates the chord of the following measure.[8]

This is where the point of contention arises between those who insist that the correct way to dance Salsa is what they call "on the Two" as opposed to those who dance "on the One." Then, to make matters worse, there are different ways of hearing the "Two" and the "One." The unfortunate result of the debate is that at some clubs people will be segregated into different sections based upon the accident of the preference of one's teacher. Basically speaking, the people who dance on the "One" have internalized a way of hearing and moving to Salsa based on a count that goes "one-two-three-And-four-five-six-And." This provides eight beats to the measure but the feet move only six steps to which are added two pauses (the "And") that makes eight. But the problems still remain of when one starts one's count—on the actual "one" or the anticipated "one" that puts you on "two." The younger generation of Cuban style dancers keep an eight count beat with their feet and move their shoulders and hips in a more pronounced fashion from side to side rather than in a forward-backward pattern of the "on-One" and "on-Two" stylists. Everything works depending on the music and the dancers. It not only takes two to tangle; it also takes two to Tango; and, as well, it takes two to Salsa. Briefly mentioning how Salsa is danced because in the Salsa scene the dancers are as important as the musicians themselves. The timbale player of a local San Francisco Salsa group, Boriquen, once told me that the group plays a lot better when dancers are on the floor who know what they are doing because visually the way they play is affected by how the audience feel and dance to the music. He said when a bunch of bad dancers are on the floor it throws their rhythm off or, at least, prevents them from really kicking in to the groove. And it all is based on catching that anticipated "One" that is discussed earlier. If the dancer does not catch it he/she will often wind up trying to dance to what occurs on top of the pulse and not only move too fast but get lost in the frenzy. Legend has it that once when Dizzy Gillespie got completely lost in a jam session comprised of mostly Cuban musicians while they were recording one of his Latin Jazz albums he shouted in desperation, "Where is beat one?" For the readers who are completely unfamiliar with what Salsa, in my view, should look like, I recommend that they check out the way Juan Matos and/or Frankie Martinez dance at the YouTube Web site because these two dancers have remained very close to the dance's rumba/bomba roots in their styling and are absolutely exquisite in their performance.

Motion, Rhythm, and Commotion

By the 1940s, many Cubans and Puerto Ricans were migrating to New York as well as other U.S. cities bringing their music with them. Global historical-political-economic factors would determine the deferential between Cuban and Puerto Rican immigration. Cuba became independent after the Spanish American War whereas Puerto Rico became a U.S. Commonwealth (some would say "colony"). After Cuba became Communist under Fidel Castro, immigration from Cuba became virtually impossible but remained an option for any Puerto Rican who could scrape up the amount of money needed for a plane ticket. But during the early 1940s, Arsenio Rodriquez pioneered the "conjunto format" of playing "son" that laid the basic foundation for Salsa that appeared later. When Afro-Cuban rhythms fused with the big-band jazz bands that played swing something else appeared that Perez Prado (who was based both in Mexico and New York) is credited as having invented called "mambo." Benny More continued to innovate by combining the mambo format with son and guaracha. In the 1950s Machito was the number one band leader along with Tito Puente and Tito Rodriquez (both Puerto Ricans).

In the 1950s Puerto Rico's governor, Luise Munoz Marin elevated the island's economy through a combination of public works projects and the type of capitalists investments that made its standard of living the highest in Latin America at the cost of urbanizing the poor, rural population and forcing to seek work in San Juan, New York, and other U.S. cities. About half of the Puerto Ricans who came to the mainland settled in New York City in East Harlem (Spanish Harlem). Once in the United States, Puerto Ricans were forced by discrimination and economic necessity to live in the "barrio" alienated from mainstream North American society by language and culture. Puerto Ricans in the same family discovered that on the mainland their chances of assimilation differed depending upon skin color—a factor that did not hold nearly the same significance on the island. The civil rights and black consciousness movements of the 1960s and 1970s provided a model for Puerto Ricans to begin to assert the value and worth of their own ethnicity especially in New York City where African American and Puerto Rican neighborhoods, culture and political interests overlapped. African American and Puerto

Rican youth went to the same schools and danced to the same music even if they did not hear it in the same way. The new social consciousness called for its musical expression. Cuban dance music became the vehicle. *"In the process, the son's Cuban origin, like that of the rumba now so avidly played by barrio street drummers, was deemphasized, and the genre became resignified as a symbol of Newyorican and, by extension, pan-Latino ethnic identity"*[9] (my emphasis). It was "hip" for African American youth to be into jazz and artists such as Dizzy Gillespie, Cal Jade, and Herbbie Mann were playing Latin Jazz at the same time that other artists such as Willie Bobo and Ray Barretto were playing the more danceable "boogaloo." If you were old enough to go to the Palladium, you knew you were cool and would have a host of admiring peers waiting to learn how to do the dance then called the Palladium before it was called Salsa. Then there were all the albums Fania Records put out, particularly those by Johnny Pacheo (his parents were actually Dominican). On the whole, Puerto Ricans came to dominate the Salsa scene. According to Manuel:

> It was not that Puerto Rican music per se took New York by storm but rather that Puerto Rican musicians and audiences came to dominate the city's Latin music scene. One music historian describes the resulting paradox: *"The bulk of what we today call popular Puerto Rican music was written and recorded in New York. Puerto Rico is the only Latin American country whose popular music was mainly created on foreign soil. The curious thing about this phenomenon is that it was precisely in those years that the popular Puerto Rican song became more Puerto Rican than it ever been before or since."*[10] (my emphasis)

If one goggles any major city in the world and the word Salsa, one will find several spots to listen and dance to this musical genre: San Francisco, Los Angeles, San Antonio, Seattle, Miami, New York, Toronto, London, Paris, Stockholm, Tokyo, Sydney, Berlin, Frankfurt, and so on. At major concerts and many night clubs, it is common at some point in a groups performance for the band leader to shout out the different places in the Caribbean and South America represented in the audience to the cheers of representatives of those places made in a call and response pattern. The leader will shout: "Puerto Rico!" and the Puerto Ricans will yell. Then "Columbia" and the Columbians will yell sometimes until the entire geography of the Caribbean and Central and South America is covered.

Theoretical/Musicological Considerations

The study of music as an expression of what is distinctive of a culture is not new. Indeed Max Weber wrote a short study of western classical music to illustrate his thesis regarding "rationality" as one of the deep structural features distinguishing western and eastern societies. For Weber the logical development of western music expressed the underlying mentality and ethos of western society. However—as Michael P. Steinberg points out in *Listening to Reason: Culture, Subjectivity, and Nineteenth Century Music*—given the subsequent developments in Germany that resulted in the uses put to musicology to undergird a subjectivity of national exceptionalism and finally a fascist ideology, the study of music as a mode of cultural particularity was for a long time discouraged because of its negative possibilities. Theo Adorno of the Frankfurt School set the precedent for modern musicologists to engage in cultural analysis but his Eurocentricism determined that jazz would be condemned to his category of regressive music. As an advocate for interrogating music's cultural history, Steinberg's methodological question, posed in the present tense, is: "What is the music trying to do?" And he argues that music has its own mode of subjectivity—its own agenda. Moreover, "this agenda involves the making of subjectivity...insofar as music can be understood to possess a quality of simulated agency, it would appear to achieve a condition of subjective experience for itself." Steinberg's use of the term subjectivity is distinct from such related terms as: the self, selfhood, the subject, and their associations with the political discourse of John Locke and John Stuart Mill and the epistemological discourse of Descartes on the one hand and on the other Kant. According to Steinberg's usage, the term subjectivity refers to "the subject in motion, the subject in experience and analysis of itself and the world...at once redolent of contingency yet inherently critical of self-understanding in terms of a fixed position." Such a subject "and its genealogy posit a more ambiguous relationship between the world and the self, and consequently between power and freedom, authority and autonomy."[11]

Even though Steinberg does not qualify the noun "music" with the adjective "European" in the title of his book that I said is *Listening to Reason: Culture, Subjectivity, and Nineteenth-Century Music*, his focus *is* European music. Nevertheless, if his thesis about music's function and ability to organize subjectivity has any broader application then what—particularly, in light of his notion of subjectivity—is the Salsa/Jazz/Blues idiom doing in this regard? What is especially provocative in Steinberg's distinction between subjectivity as something in motion with no fixed location and the subject or self derived from the Lockean connection of this notion to the body and private property as its extension. If we entertain this distinction as it relates to Africans brought to the New World as chattel, it means we must think of them as not possessing selfhood in this Lockean sense but, nevertheless, being capable of subjectivity through their cultural creativity. Hence, we turn to the Salsa/Jazz/Blues idiom as a cultural modality having its roots in earlier cultural practices that organized a creole subjectivity within the contacts and exchanges of Atlantic World that eventuate in modernity.

Modernity? Whether the modern period in western history begins with the Renaissance, the Reformation, the Enlightenment, or the Industrial Revolution is still open for debate among historians. In addition, when one tries to amass evidence supporting one scenario over another one is confronted by fact that there are lags due to the autonomy enjoyed by different spheres of art, literature, music, politics, law, religion, the economy, philosophy, and so on even though they all are related. As per what has been discussed already, I am locating the beginning of modernity in the "long sixteenth century" when the Americas were contacted by Europeans, the slave trade began, and the Atlantic World emerged with its miscegenated prodigy. This period is also described by scholars of European cultural history as the Baroque Period. Steinberg uses the term baroque in opposition to the term modern to connote different historical periods as well as styles of culture, politics, and aesthetics. The baroque emerged after the breakdown of a unified cosmology in Western Europe in the wake of the Protestant Reformation. According to Steinberg: "Baroque culture involves the power of visuality, which also means the tendency of visuality to metastasize into visual ideology." On the other hand, "the critical drive of music involves the critique of the assumed authority of the visual worlds." To get to the point; the baroque is not indirectly related to where I am situating modernity as two distinct or parallel phenomena. The historian who made a direct connection to the baroque, slavery, and the Atlantic world was Robin Blackburn whom Steinberg cites in a footnote. In Michael P. Steinberg states:

> One term for evoking the ethos and aspirations of early European colonialism is "the baroque"…The baroque appears in a Europe confronting Ottoman might and discovering the material culture of Asia,

Africa, and America. It is first sponsored by the Jesuits, the Counter-Reformation and the Catholic monarchs and courts in an attempt to meet the challenges of the Puritans, though subsequently some Protestant monarchs also adopted some aspects of the baroque...The baroque favored a sanitized and controlled vision of civil society. While the baroque as spectacle a link to the world of colonial slavery, it exhibited a public entrepreneurship, the positive face of mercantilism, which contrasted with the private enterprise that was the driving force behind the New World's civil slavery.

For Steinberg, the baroque/modern opposition or dialectic is something that "remains available and relevant to later periods as elements of cultural vocabularies and ideology." The other opposing tendencies or styles that appear in European cultural history during the neoclassical period in art are those of the Enlightenment and Romanticism. What this suggests is that the west has for a long time been vexed by its inability to integrate the oppositions of: formal structure/freedom, surface/depth, distance/immediacy, reason/intuition into a stable cultural convention. It has always oscillated between these different poles and narrated it through the trop of progress. "The category of the modern usually signifies either the true or false claim of emancipation—from nature (via industrialization), from religion (via secularization), or from unearned authority (via political reform and revolution)." The excess of the Baroque was diverted into the service of absolutism and the emancipatory potential of the modern is used to reify through commodification new forms of tyranny. What then can modernity learn about itself when it attends to the culture made by those had no illusions about the scope of their agency—whose culture emerged from within the liminal space between freedom and necessity, spontaneity and determination, subjectivity and objectification, individuality and community?

The musical genre of Salsa developed in the same world in which modern European music was developing because the Atlanticization of the world through slavery, colonialism made the world "global" for the first time in history. This meant that increasingly everything that occurred any where in the world had the entire world as its context. Consequently, we can view things happening in different parts of the world as being interrelated not due to simple linear causality but to the influence of the broader global context of those event's occurence. Salsa, as we have shown, as a phenomenon of creolization is a musical genre that drew from European as well as African instruments and conventions.

European conventions were not static but in rapid flux due, in no small measure, to the speed of cultural change that was connected with the societal changes caused by war, revolution, and creation in Europe and in its colonies. The people making the music that became untimely Salsa were on the outer fringes of European society—in the colonies of Cuba and Puerto Rico. But even though everyone occupies the same historical context does not mean we cannot periodize everyone in the same way culturally. This is something most postmodernist fail to appreciate. Although diasporic Africans and Afro-Caribbeans were not unaffected by the political and cultural changes occurring in Europe as it moved from the baroque to the modern, they were becoming modern through different cultural modalities than their European counterparts. Africans in Cuba and Puerto Rico were dancing the rumba and bomba, respectively, while Europeans were dancing the waltz. The waltz was taken to the Americas where it was danced in aristocratic salons under the observation of domestic slaves. The waltz became popular Europe in very interesting political circumstances.

Take for instance the Congress of Vienna and let us look briefly at the musical preference of Chancellor Metternich. No one can argue against the importance of Austrian Chancellor Metternich to modern Europe. Although he embodied the force of reaction against the French Revolution and its aftermath or logical development in Napoleon, the success of reaction in the balance of power established at the Congress of Vienna established the basic pattern for the "new world order" of European political hegemony over its own peasants and proletariat and the rest of the colonized world. One of the things he oversaw at the Congress of Vienna were the evening balls. The kind of dance one engaged in, like fashion and hairstyles, revealed one's political orientation. The "cotillion" that was French and Republican was popular in Washington. In Vienna the minuet was abandoned as too outdated and replaced with a dance of its own creation. Vienna "produced its own extravaganza, new, exhilarating, daring, erotic and intensely athletic—the waltz...the intimate close contact between the couple made it an entirely new kind of dance, a sexual break with the past." There were dozens of waltz orchestras and composers in Vienna to supply a sufficient amount of music to meet the aristocratic demand—Muzio Clementi and his students, Cramer and Kalkbrenner; Mozart's students Ebert and Hummel; Carl Maria von Weber, to name a few. Ludwig van Beethoven (1770–1827)—the embodiment of musical innovation—gave a performance of Fidelio two days before the Congress on October 28 by imperial command and another concert when the Congress was in full swing on November 29. He had written his Battle Symphony in celebration of Wellington's victory at Vitoria and had become a patriotic cultural icon before the Congress convened. He wrote his Chorus to the Allied Princes during the Congress. Beethoven's flattery, however, did not place him beyond the constant surveillance of Vienna's secret police who surveilled him and constantly measured the public reaction to his music. Even though Beethoven praised the victory of the Allied Princes over Napoleon, the forces of reaction were right to sense something in his music and personality that was subversive. The project he conceived in 1793 of setting Friedrich Schiller's An die Freude to music by 1817 had developed into a more ambitious nationalistic one of a "German Symphony." He began composing in 1823 and it was first performed in Vienna on May 7, 1824 at the Theater of the Kaerntnertor. Almost one hundred years after Beethoven had conceived of his Fifth Symphony, its opening bars were played at the beginning of BBC broadcast to Nazi-occupied Europe and a century and a half after his death his musical interpretation of An die Freude became the official anthem of the European Community. "The world, which were taken to celebrate the universal brotherhood of Man [sic], linked a pre-nationalist with a post-nationalist age."

Perhaps we should be talking about "paradox." In implying a correlation between the cultural anthropological notion of "creolization" and the term "heterogeneity" from postmodernist discourse, I may have inadvertently been suggesting the meaning of these terms to concern themselves primarily with how difference is resolved through combination. Upon further reflection, however, my analysis of creolization—even with the attention it gave to miscegenation—allows us to see it as having to do with the way difference is constructed in modernity as binary oppositions. There exists no firm ontological status to these differences apart from the epistemological categories attributed to them in modernity due to the way it seeks to value the nature of the contacts and exchanges from which this epoch ensues. They correspond to the basic binary of "primitive vs. civilized." In modernity, and, perhaps, before modernity as well, categories of difference were made to appear neutral so as to often mask and legitimate the violence and genocide that went into their making and maintaining. In the awareness of paradox is the condition of possibility for ideology's unraveling because ideology functions to make sense of contradiction or project its resolution exclusively into the future.

Meanwhile differences, inequalities based on them, apartheids constructed to maintain them all seem natural. We might, therefore, conclude that the predominance or privileging of harmony in an aesthetic easily succumbs to functioning in either utopian or reactionary modes by projecting the resolutions of contradiction into the future or making us oblivious to them in the present.

Thus, going back to the notion of *"limpieza de sangre"* and moving through the distinctions of *"boazales"* and *"criolles negroes"* and arriving finally to the difference—that now seems natural and ontological—between black white we see at work the assigning of value that is inherent in the binary. Therefore, postmodernist discourse is severely limited in its ability to illuminate the historical and phenomenological experience of those who may have had to skip over modernity by undergoing it through slavery and colonialism because while acknowledging heterogeneity it never narrates how that occurred in our case. Hence, for the postmodernist heterogeneity is a condition without a history and does not signify the cultural spontaneity and creativity of creolization. Indeed, much in postmodern discourse winds up being a fatalistic abandonment of "depth" and capitulation to the meaninglessness of "surface" meaning void of a determining "subject." The reality of which postmodern theorist do not attack directly and to which they have been incapable of providing a satisfying aesthetic and existential response is something that first appeared in the sixteenth century around the time of the Baroque—paradox. But in announcing postmodernity, its theorist are still profoundly indebted to a rather linear notion of time and history—or, at minimum, one that is as naive as all attempts at historical periodizations as in the division of western history into the periods of Ancient, Medieval, Renaissance/Reformation, Age of Reason, Romantic, and so on.

Paradox is central to Arnold Hauser's explication of sixteenth-century European art in *Mannerism: The Crisis of the Renaissance and the Origin of Modern Art.* Hauser points out that the distinctive artistic style of mannerism coexisted with the baroque before being overtaken by the later. Its achievement, however, provided the clues for modern artist to appropriate later. What was its achievement? It devised a means of paradoxical expression for stating and addressing the problems that arose from the contradictions of its era. Mannerism was based "not merely on the conflicting nature of occasional experience, but on the permanent ambiguity of all things, great and small, and on the impossibility of attaining certainty about anything." A, therefore, mannerism's underlying and distinguishing epistemological characteristic was to "show that we live in a world of irreducible tensions and mutually exclusive and yet inter-connected opposites." The opposites or tensions of the era to which mannerism chose (so to speak) not to remain oblivious were those of "classicism and anti-classicism, naturalism and formalism, rationalism and irrationalism, sensualism and spiritualism, traditionalism and innovation, conventionalism and revolt against conformism." The theological paradox that galvanized the break up of Christiandom's universal synthesis was the Augustinian doctrine of grace emphasized by Luther and further elaborated on by Calvin in terms of predestination. Hauser writes:

> However, in the age of mannerism it is not only Protestantism that created paradoxes with its doctrine of irrational choice of the elect. Paradoxes abounded in the field of economics, with the worker's alienation from his work; in that of politics, with its "double standard" of morality, one for the prince and the other for his subjects; in literature, with the leading role allotted to tragedy, which created a counterpart to the "predestination of the elect" with the idea of guilt without sin, and with the discovery of humor, which enabled a man [sic] to be looked at and judged simultaneously from two different and contradictory aspects.

Along these lines, can we not imagine that African slaves would be conscious of the paradox of having their bodies enslaved in the worldly temporal order so that their souls could be saved in eternity? If so, the genius of creolization and its cultural products was in its ability to consciously address the same set of paradoxes listed by Hauser albeit at another location in modernity because it was concretized in the bodies of people who made those cultures. This might be what is signified in the name of Monk's tune, "Round About Midnight," and the reference in the blues to what transpires at the crossroads.

Conclusion

From the time of the Greeks, western music theory has been unable to overcome the dichotomy between its conception of music as either a divine or demonic art. So too, has western music theory been ambivalent regarding music's ability and purpose to be either that of evoking emotions or signifying thought. "Whereas Enlightenment rationalists had almost universally dismissed instrumental music for its inability to incorporate and convey ideas, their Romantic successors, particularly in Germany, were quick to embrace music without words precisely because of its ability to function outside the strictures of language."[12] Both conceptions of music's religious dimension recognized music's mysterious power to signify and evoke realities lying in the realm of the unseen—either divine or demonic. This distinction about music's potential laid the basis for arbitrarily assigning the music of the "other" in the negative category. Without narrating the long history of music theory in the West from the time of the Greeks, through the Middle Ages, the Reformation, the Baroque Period, the Enlightenment Period, the Romantic Period and the like, suffice it to say western music theory has posited western music as its theoretical object and relegated the music of the world's other peoples to the field of ethnomusicology. In the process western musicology and the philosophical discourse related to it pertaining to aesthetics has remained oblivious to the phenomenon of creolization. This phenomenon began when the West made its first contacts with the rest of the world's peoples and cultures. However, because slavery and colonization governed the nature of these contacts the epistemological structure determining their meaning conformed to the aforementioned binaries in terms of: primitive/civilized, pagan/Christian, and low-culture/high-culture.

> The space between the West and its others has vexed ethnomusicology since its inception. Indeed, we might even go so far as to say that the field has developed by attempting to shape the types of encounter that occur within this space and thus define the space. Depending on the historical moment and the disciplinary focus, it becomes the space between "high" and "low" culture, "oral" and "literate" culture, "popular" and "elite," peoples "with history" and those "without history," "premodern" and "modern," or, in our own age, "modern" and "postmodern." The paradox here becomes even more troubling when we realize that all these terms and the conceptual pairs they form have distinctly Western origins.[13]

These epistemological binaries ignored the creolization that was occurring all along in between the space defined by the opposing terms within each category—linguistically, musically, biologically, and so on. The current recourse to the term "hybridity" does scant justice to the historical and phenomenological complexities actually involved in creolization or its paradoxes. This chapter posits creolization as the modality constituting black and white identities. Black religion and African American culture can be seen as occasions wherein subjectivity is organized in a manner similar to Steinberg's discussion of the symphony. Thus we can concur with Robert Gooding-Williams's statement in *"Look, A Negro": Philosophical Essays on Race, Culture and Politics*:

> The distinction between being authentically a black person and being inauthentically a black person makes no sense in my view, since one becomes a black person by, and only by, acting under certain descriptions...I postulate no black personhood apart from a black person's actions I do not suppose that, prior to the performance of discursively shaped actions, there exist black selves or persons that such actions could authentically or inauthentically express.[14]

Conclusion

Here we are speaking not of fantasies but of a community, a community listening to the sounds and words of each other, and if there is something fantastic about this experience, such must obviously be present...For in this one moment of experience the immediacy of experiencing outside the veil and double consciousness is afforded.

—Charles H. Long, Significations, p. 169.

Although very few scholars of black religion have heeded his advice, Charles H. Long has been recommended situating the study of black religion within the Atlantic World's geo-temporal framework for quite some time. In 1983 Winthrop S. Hudson had called for situating the study of black religion within its broader American context. One foci of his criticism were scholars who, in his estimation, overemphasized the African roots of black religion. Hudson felt this trend would only produce diminishing returns due to, among other factors, the limited amount of historical data pertaining to African religions during the period of African's transport to the Americas. Hudson felt historians should "shift their focus from possible distant antecedents to less remote forebears who adopted Christian faith in the midst of desperate circumstances and fashioned from it a church life of their own."[1] He noted that this preoccupation with African retentions has its parallel in the tendency among white church historians, particularly Protestants, to attribute the character of their ecclesiastical bodies to as remote historical origins as possible. What Hudson does not say, but something we can easily observe, is that the preoccupation with origins lying somewhere in antiquity—that is, the Apostolic period—conforms very easily with white supremacist's preoccupation over purity. Afro-centric scholars can fall into a trap of reacting to their exclusion from standard Church History texts by unwittingly adopting the same fallacy of their white counterparts. Thus the phenomenon of black religion has been interpreted in isolation to the broader context of its formation. In this regard Hudson's observation is still apropos. He wrote:

> America blacks forged something new, the product of their own experience in a new land. An overemphasis on American survivals obscures their accomplishment. It also distorts the story of the black churches. By focusing attention on that which is largely unknowable, it diverts attention from a rich heritage of faith and courage, knowledge of which can be recovered. At bottom it is a question of which generation of forebearers one wishes to honor: the forebearers of a distant, shadowy past who can be known only obscurely…or those known ancestors (named and identified) who, with great heroism and remarkable creativity, fashioned out of the Christian faith a strategy of survival and mutual care…In the quest for a distant past, it would be sad for the remarkable achievements of known ancestors to be left unhonored and unsung.[2]

I addressed the issue Hudson was raising in chapter one of this volume in the discussion of continuities and discontinuities in black religion. Hudson, however, does not focus as much on black religion as much as he focuses on the black church as his object of study. These two terms are by no means synonymous. Whether Hudson's admonition was excessive has to be judged over against the scholarship against which he was reacting when he wrote his article. More recently, the scholarship of Lawrence Levine, Albert Raboteau, Marcel Sobel, and others makes a much more nuanced argument about African retentions than the one Hudson was criticizing.[3] This book's focus has been the way blacks in the Americas imagined and invoked Africa through their various religio-cultural practices. Our concern as it pertains to Africa was not the identification of African retentions as artifacts that can be objectively traced back to Africa. Rather, we have been describing the way New World Africans imagined themselves as occupying a temporal space that included Africa, the Americas, and the waters of the Atlantic Ocean. This study has not been narrowly focused on the black church and its ecclesiastical practices but more broadly on the broader category of black religion. We have described black religion in terms of Charles H. Long's concept of "the imagination of matter." This activity was described as something different from the Descartean ego's objectification of matter. Rather, the "imagination of matter" as a religious act entails how humans intuit themselves in relation to other humans, nature, and the invisible forces of the cosmos and the exchanges occurring therein. Therefore, the concept of materiality we have borrowed from Long's writing is very different from the modern epistemological stance of "materialism."

I have tried to situate black religion within a broader geo-temporal framework than America and place it within the Atlantic World—a world comprised of Europe, the Caribbean, South America, and North America. In situating the study of black religion within the Atlantic World, a number of larger questions emerge. Not only is there the basic question of the nature of religion; there is the question of how the character of the religion of whites was determined by its contact with its black counterpart. Although it is evident how the presence of enslaved Africans in the Americas was necessary for the construction of race in terms of a white-black dichotomy; the relationship between white religion and black religion has not been understood in an analogous fashion. In other words, if Hudson wants to insist that historical accounts of black religion attend to the affect of its contact with whites, then the same must be done in historical accounts of white religion. This is no trivial matter. Roger D. Hatch discussed this problem in an article titled, "Integrating the Issue of Race into the History of Christianity in America." In this article he examined Sydney E. Ahlstrom's *A Religious History of the American People*; Martin E. Marty's *Righteous Empire: The Protestant Experience in America*; and Robert T. Handy, *A Christian America: Protestant Hopes and Historical Realities* for their ability to achieve their stated aim of integrating the issue of race into their texts. Handy found all these attempts seriously wanting primarily because the authors sought to include African Americans here and there into an already established narrative of American Church History or American Religious History. Race, therefore, was regarded as external to the main object of study—Christianity.

> Thus the most important step in adequately integrating the issue of race into the story of Christianity in America comes at the beginning, it comes in defining the subject matter. As long as the issue of race is not adequately integrated into an understanding of what the subject of a history is, it will not be integrated into the story. As long as race is assumed to be something external to Christianity, the issue of race will not be adequately integrated into the story of Christianity in America.[4]

The problem we immediately face in trying to follow Hatch's recommendation is not only the problem of definition but also the problem of determining the narrative structure of one's history. Inserting the black presence into the existing narrative strengthens the fallacy that race is only an issue for blacks and other's who have been marginalized from the mainstream. Accordingly, African Americans have appeared in the narrative at only two or three points: in discussions of slavery during the periods of the Great Awakening and the Civil War and during the civil rights movement. White identity is not implicated or seen in its reciprocal relationship to blackness. The problem that no one has solved is how to present the simultaneous appearance of white and black religious identities. Long addressed this problem in recent lectures wherein he has talked about "non-historical temporalities." These are the lived, experienced, and remembered histories of the Other that cannot be integrated into the master narrative. Long does not even think it should be so integrated if it is to be done justice. What Long is calling for is a history of the "contacts and exchanges" between Europeans and Others in modernity. In "Research Plans For 1991–92" he stated:

> The goal of this inquiry is an attempt to substitute the opposite of colonialism as an alternative meaning of thought for what was the reigning content and style of thought of the cultures of European colonizers. I shall, rather, seek to raise the issue of thinking out of those relationships, reciprocities, and meanings that were attested to but hidden and obscured during the long period of colonialism.[5]

This necessarily means getting beyond the nation-state paradigm for studying religion and particularly black religion. Considering events and histories in a "broad transoceanic framework" brings Africa—as well as Europe, the Caribbean, and South America—into the picture not for the sake of uncovering African retentions but as a unit of analysis that transcends political boundaries.[6] Bernard Bailyn point out that although the paradigm of Atlantic History rules out "a uniform chronology across the entire area." It is still possible to discover "a common morphology." Long had already described his research orientation in these terms:

> I shall make use of Marcel Mauss' theory of gift exchange and the cycle of prestations as total social phenomenon as the theoretical basis for establishing the locus for those relationships that must bear upon the colonizer and the colonized during the colonial period. The structure

and norm of the "gift" and its reciprocities will, for, example, revolve around the meaning of the commodity and the creation of the fetish and "fetishism" as well as the materiality of physical and social bodies (races, the underprivileged, primitives, civilized, etc.).

In other words, I shall locate Mauss' theory within a methodological space of mediation. This space of mediation will allow for deciphering and critique of the reciprocities, relationships, and discourses between Europeans and their *others*. In so doing I emphasize methodologically that there is no place outside of otherness for a new science of the human.[7]

This volume has attempted to apply Long's insights and methodological orientation to the history of religion to the study of black religion in the Atlantic World. It has sought to explicate how race as a constitutive phenomenon in modernity is also constitutive of religion in the modern world—it affects everything thought and unthought and informs the meanings and significations of modernity's articulations and silences (see: chapter six). The notion of "non-historical temporalities" also communicates the fact that due to the different modes by which various peoples entered into and had their identities formed by modernity, they can occupy the same space white undergoing a different temporality. Temporality has to do with experienced time. This relates to my discussion of African American consciousness in terms of "Memory and Hope" in chapter eight. In short, situating black religion with the framework of the Atlantic World is not merely a matter of moving a particular subject of knowledge from one compartment to another. It entails redefining the subject of knowledge in relationship to other phenomena that appear in making such a move. We do not know what anything is until we view it in relationship with other materialities that account for its appearance. Still there will always be something that escapes description in the realm of religion. Hence our recourse to Long's epistemological categories: silence, nothingness, otherness, arche, and opacity.

The condition of possibility for comprehending what is signified in the earlier epistemological categories is captured in a white photo journalist's recollection of what he experienced when he spoke at a worship service of an African American Holiness church he had been documenting.

When I talked from my head they had no way of relating to what I said . . . But when I spoke from my heart they understood and responded openly…The congregation—even the pianist and drummer, with their instruments—had gradually established a subtle, rhythmic accord, supporting my speech. Our beings had gradually intermingled in a strange, interactive dance of consciousness toward understanding.…As far as they were concerned there had been a visitation of the Spirit.[8]

The author of the above comment was not—in the moment he referenced—describing black religion as an observable empirical item. He described the perception of observing himself being observed during his attempt to communicate with those who constituted his original object of study. His initial failed attempt to establish verbal contact with the congregation required him to attempt to express more than ideas but what he was feeling in that moment of being apprehended. In other words, he was forced to allow his subjectivity to be shaped by that of the Other. When this occurred, there was communication and a discerning of something that transcended the mere content of the communication. The black parishioners had terminology available to them to signify the nature of the shared experience that he did not share but also did not contest—"a visitation of the Holy Spirit." The experience of immediacy was only possible when the journalist becme completely present to himself and the community. He was only able to interpret and understand that community when he became transparent to their mutual interpretation of him. What he discerned and intuited was simultaneously absence and presence, nothing and something, Being and Nothingness, me and them. The actuality of the experience whether named or unnamed still eluded precise linguistic description and therefore requires a hermeneutic on this side of the veil. The methodological implication brings us back to Long's statement quoted earlier: "I emphasize methodologically that there is no place outside of otherness for a new science of the human."

Introduction

1. Charles H. Long, "Mircea Eliade and the Imagination of Matter," Journal for Cultural and Religious Theory 1, no. 2 (2000).
2. Anthony Pinn's *Terror and Triumph* (Minneapolis: Augsburg/Fortress, 2003) purports to be an extension of Long's thought and method. An excellent treatment of Long's thought is Jennifer I. M. Reid, ed., *Religion and Global Culture: New Terrain in the Study of Religion and the Work of Charles H. Long* (New York: Lexington Books, 2003).

I. Studying Black Religion: Contacts/Exchanges and Continuities/Discontinuities

1. M. Malowist, "The Struggle for International Trade and Its Implications for Africa," in *General History of Africa* vol. 5, ed. B. A. Ogot (Berkeley: University of California Press, 1992), p. 1.
2. Bernard Bailyn, *Atlantic History: Concepts and Contours* (Cambridge, MA: Harvard University Press, 2005), pp. 85, 95.
3. Charles H. Long, *Significations: Signs, Symbols and Images in the Interpretation of Religion* (Philadelphia: Fortress, 1986), p. 91.
4. Ibid., p. 32.
5. V. I. Mudimbe, *The Invention of Africa: Gnosis, Philosophy and the Order of Knowledge* (Bloomington: University of Indiana Press, 1988).
6. Bailyn, *Atlantic History,* p. 96.
7. George E. Brooks, *Landlords and Strangers: Ecology, Society, and Trade in Western Africa, 1000–1630* (Boulder, CO: Westview, 1993).
8. E. J. Alagoa, "Fon and Yoruba: The Niger Delta and the Cameroon," in UNESCO, *General History of Africa*, vol. 5 (San Francisco: University of California Press, 1992), pp. 449–450.
9. John M. Janzen, *Lemba, 1650–1930: A Drum of Affliction in Africa and the New World* (New York: Garland Press, 1982), p. 135.
10. Ibid., pp. 19–20.
11. Ibid., p. 21.

12. Melville Herskovits, *Dahomean Narratives* (Evanston, IL: Northwestern University Press, 1970), p. 189.

13. John Thornton, *Africa and Africans in the Making of the Atlantic World, 1400–1800* (Cambridge: Cambridge University Press, 1992), p. 6.

14. Charles Wagley, "Plantation-America: A Culture Sphere," in *Caribbean Studies: A Symposium,* ed. Vera Rubin (Seattle: University of Washington Press, 1960), pp. 3–5.

15. Richard Price, *Maroon Societies: Rebel Slave Communities in the Americas* (New York: Anchor Press, 1973), pp. 27–28.

16. M. G. Smith, "The African Heritage in the Caribbean," in *Caribbean Studies,* ed. Rubin, p. 37.

17. Price, *Maroon Societies,* pp. 28–30.

18. Onaiyekan, "The Priesthood among the Owe Yoruba," in *Traditional Religion in West Africa,* ed. E. A. Ade Adegbola (Ibadan: Daystar Press, 1983), pp. 42–43.

19. Bernard Maupol, *La Geomancie a L'Ancienne Cote des Esclaves* (Paris: Institute D'Ethnologie, 1961), p. 60.

20. Ibid., p. 71–72.

21. Melville Herkovits, *An Outline of Dahomean Religious Belief* (Menasha, WI: The American Anthropological Association, no. 41, 1933), p. 52.

22. Rev. Samuel Johnson, *The History of the Yorubas from the Earliest Times to the Beginning of the British Protectorate* (London: Routledge, 1921), pp. 32–34.

23. Gonzales-Wipplers and Metraux, *Santeria: The Religion. A Legacy of Faith, Rites, and Magic* (New York: Harmony Books, 1989) pp. 120–121.

2. The Age of Discovery and the Emergence of the Atlantic World

1. Charles H. Long, "Indigenous People, Materialities, and Religion: Outline for a New Orientation to Religious Meaning," in *Religion and Global Culture: New Terrain in the Study of Religion and the Work of Charles H. Long,* ed. Jennifer I. M. Reid (New York: Lexington Books, 2003), p. 177.

2. C. A. Baly, *The Birth of the Modern World, 1780–1914* (London: Blackwell, 2004), pp. 62–63.

3. Eric Williams, *From Columbus to Castro: The History of the Caribbean* (New York: Vintage Books, 1970), p. 78.

4. J. H. Elliott, *Imperial Spain: 1469–1716* (New York: Penguin Books, 1963), pp. 101–102. The 1516 concordat between France and the Papacy then enabled Charles V to negotiate from Pope Adrian VI the right to present to all bishoprics in Spain and finally fulfill Ferdinand and Isabella's ecclesiastical ambition.

5. Luis N. Rivera, *A Violent Evangelism: The Political and Religious Conquest of the Americas* (Westminster/John Knox Press, 1992), p. 25. What exactly was meant by *donamus* (give), *concedimus* (grant), and *assignamus* (assign) would be debated for years to come. The debate between Juan Gines de

Sepulveda and Bartolomeau de Las Casas at Valladolid in 1550 over the treat-ment of the Indios was in many ways a debate over how to correctly interpret the Treaty of Alcacovas and the aforementioned terms in particular.

6. Ibid., p. 30.
7. Nicholas Canny, *The Origins of Empire. British Overseas Enterprise to the Close of the Seventeenth Century* (Oxford: Oxford Press, 1998), p. 20.
8. Williams, *History of the Caribbean*, pp. 71–72. "Sir William Cecil (later Lord Burleigh) the Elizabethan statesman, told the Spanish Ambassador to England in 1562 that 'the Pope had no right to partition the world and to give and take kingdoms to whomsoever he pleased.' The British Government countered Spanish claims with the doctrine of effective occupation."
9. Colin Kidd, *The Forging of Races: Race and Scripture in the Protestant Atlantic World, 1600–2000* (London: Cambridge Press, 2006), p. 25.
10. Joseph Fontana, *The Distorted Past: A Reinterpretation of Europe* (Oxford: Blackwell, 1995) pp. 113–14; see also Charles H. Long's earlier discussion in *Significations* in "Primitive/Civilized: The Locus of the Problem."
11. Edward Reynolds, *Stand the Storm: A History of the Atlantic Slave Trade* (Chicago: Ivan R. Dee, 1985), p. 59.
12. Eric R. Wolf, *Europe and the People without History* (Berkeley: University of California Press, 1982), p. 134.
13. Williams, *History of the Caribbean,* p. 33.
14. David Armitage, *The Ideological Origins of the British Empire* (Cambridge: Cambridge University Press, 2000), p. 90.
15. J. H. Elliott, *Empires of the Atlantic world: Britain and Spain in America 1492–1830* (New Haven, CT: Yale University Press, 2006), p. 184.
16. See Gordon Connell-Smith, *Forerunners of Drake* (London: Longmans, green, 1954).
17. W. Elliot Brownlee, *Dynamics of Ascent: A History of the American Economy* (New York: Alfred A. Knopf, 1974), p. 12.
18. Jane H. Ohlmeyer, " 'Civilizing of Those Rude Partes': Colonization within Britain and Ireland, 1580s–1640s," in *The Origins of Empire,* ed. Nicholas Canny (Oxford: Oxford Press, 1998), p. 146.
19. Hilary McD. Beckles, "The 'Hub of Empire': The Caribbean and Britain in the seventeenth century," in *The Origins of Empire,* ed. Nicholas Canny (Oxford: Oxford Press, 1998), p. 239.
20. W. E. B. Du Bois, *The Suppression of the African Slave Trade, 1638–1870* (Baton Rouge: Louisiana State University Press, 1896/1969), p. 4.
21. Quoted in Wolf, *Europe and the People without History,* p. 198.
22. C. J. Abbey and J. H. Overton, *The English Church in the Eighteenth Century* (London, 1898), II, p. 107 quoted in Williams, *History of the Caribbean,* p. 43.
23. Beckles, "Hub of Empire," p. 227.
24. Williams, *History of the Caribbean,* pp. 145–147.
25. Beckles, "Hub of Empire," p. 227.
26. Sydney E. Ahlstrom, *A Religious History of the American People* (New Haven, CT and London: Yale University Press, 1972), p. 191.

27. Cotton Mather, "The Negro Christianized" (1706) quoted in *The Arrogance of Faith: Christianity and Race in America from the Colonial Era to the Twentieth century,* ed. Forrest G. Wood (New York: Alfred A. Knopf, 1990), pp. 117–118.

28. See Andrew F. Murray, *Presbyterians and the Negro* (Philadelphia: Presbyterian Historical Society, 1966).

29. Williams, *History of the Caribbean,* pp. 237–238.

30. Ibid., pp. 156–157.

31. Thornton, *Africa and Africans,* pp. 244–245.

32. J. Vansina, "The Kongo Kingdom and Its Neighbors," in *General History of Africa, vol. V. Africa from the Sixteenth to the Eighteenth Century,* ed. B. A. Ogot (Berkeley: University of California Press, 1992), p. 573.

33. Michel Beaud, *A History of Capitalism: 1500–2000* (New York: Monthly Review Press, 2001), pp. 44–45.

3. The Imagination of Matter in the Atlantic World's Political Economy

1. Cheryl Harris, "Whiteness as Property," *Harvard Law Review* 106, no. 8 (June 1993), pp. 1720–1721.

2. Istvan Hont and Michael Ignatieff in *Wealth and Virtue: The Shaping of Political Economy in the Scottish Enlightenment* (Cambridge: Cambridge University Press, 1986).

3. Donald Philip Verene, *Vico's Science of Imagination* (Ithaca, NY: Cornell University Press, 1981), p. 86.

4. Long, "Mircea Eliade and the Imagination of Matter."

5. Long, *Significations,* p. 135.

6. Ibid.

7. Charles H. Long, "Research Plans For 1991–92," unpublished.

8. Daniel Chirot, *Social Change in the Modern Era* (New York: Harcourt, 1986), p. 20.

9. Ibid., p. 20.

10. Ibid., p. 23.

11. R. W. Southern, *Western Society and the Church in the Middle Ages* (New York: Penguin, 1990), pp. 138–139.

12. Ibid., p. 226.

13. William Pietz, "The Problem of the Fetish," *RES* 9 (Spring 1985): pp. 6–7.

14. Karl Marx, Capital.

15. Arend Theodor Van Leeuen, *Critique of Heaven and Earth* vol. 2 (New York: Charles Scribner's Sons, 1974), p. 230.

16. Nell Painter, "Thinking about the Languages of Money and Race: A Response to Michael O'Malley," *American Historical Review* 99, no. 2 (April 1994), p. 398.

17. A number of forces and tendencies that were percolating in Europe galvanized and were released through the Reformation. Reason became unfettered by

dogma and freed to not only engage in an independent reading of the Holy Scriptures but also reality in general. This freeing of reason according to some scholars such as Robert K. Merton, *Science, Technology and Society in Seventeenth Century England* (New York: Fertig, 1970) contributed to the birth of modern science.

18. Long, *Significations*, p. 9.
19. In Reid, *Religion and Global Culture*, p. 170.
20. R. C. Young, *Colonial Desire: Hybridity in Theory, Culture and Race* (London: Routledge, 1995), pp. 181–182.

1. Being, Nothingness, and the "Signification of Silence" in African American Religious Consciousness

1. Matthew V. Johnson, "The Middle Passage, Trauma and the Tragic Re-Imagination of African American Theology," *Journal of Pastoral Psychology* 53, no. 6 (July 2005).
2. Martin Heidegger, *An Introduction to Metaphysics* (New Haven, CT: Yale University Press, 1959), p. 19.
3. Stanley J. Tambiah, *Magic, Science and Religion and the Scope of Rationality* (Cambridge: Cambridge University Press, 1990), p. 86.
4. Louis Dupree, *Passage to Modernity: An Essay in the Hermeneutics of Nature and Culture*. (New Haven, CT: Yale University Press, 1993), p. 3.
5. Bernard Bailyn, *The Ideological Origins of the American Revolution* (Cambridge, MA: Belknap Press, 1992), pp. 235–246.
6. Dupree, *Passage to Modernity*, pp. 10–11.
7. Paul Gilroy, *The Black Atlantic: Modernity and Double Consciousness* (Cambridge, MA: Harvard University Press, 1993).
8. Placid Temples, *Bantu Philosophy* (Paris: Presence Africaine, 1959), pp. 50–51.
9. Olaudah Equiano, *The* Interesting *Narrative of the Life of Olaudah Equiano or Gustavus Vassa The African. Written by Himself. 1971* in *In Their Own Words: A History of the American Negro*, ed. Milton Meltzer (New York: Cromwell 1964).
10. Johnson, "The Middle Passage."
11. Nathan Huggins, *Black Odyssey: The African American Ordeal in Slavery* (New York: Vintage Books, 1990), p. 53
12. Elain Scarry, *The Body in Pain: The Making and Unmaking of the World* (Oxford: Oxford University Press, 1985), p. 7.
13. John D. Caputo, The *Mystical Element in Heidegger's Thought* (New York: Fordham University Press, 1986), p. 26.
14. Huggins, *Black Odyssey*, p. 52.
15. Long, *Significations*, p. 60.
16. Ibid., p. 61.
17. Rudolph Otto, *The Idea of the Holy: An Inquiry into the Non-rational Factor in the Idea of the Divine and Its Relation to the Rational,*

trans. John W. Harvey (London: Oxford University Press, 1923, 1950, 1958), pp. 113–114.

18. Martin Heidegger, *Being and Time* (New York: Harper Perennial Classics, 2008), p. 485.

19. Edmund Burk, *A Philosophical Inquiry into the Origin of Our Ideas of the Sublime and the Beautiful* (Oxford: Oxford University Press, 1998).

20. Otto, *The Idea of the Holy*, p. 63.

21. James Walsh, ed., *The Cloud of Unknowing* (Mahwah, NJ: Paulist Press, 1981).

22. Ibid., p. 202.

23. Ibid., p. 205.

24. Andrew Louth, *The Origins of the Christian Mystical Tradition* (Oxford: Oxford University Press), p. 186.

25. Kirean Kavanaugh, *Selected Writings of John of the Cross* (Mahwah, NJ: Paulist Press, 1987), p. 85.

26. Richard Polt and Gregory Fried, *Heidegger's Introduction to Metaphysics* (New Haven, CT: Yale University Press, 2001), p. 81.

27. James Baldwin, *Go Tell It on the Mountain* (New York: Dell Book), pp. 199, 207.

5. Epistemologies Opaque:
Conjuring, Conjecture, and the Problematic of Nat Turner's Biblical Hermeneutic

1. Thornton, *Africa and Africans*, pp. 64–66.

2. Theophus H. Smith, *Conjuring Culture: Biblical Formation of Black Culture* (New York: Oxford University Press, 1997).

3. Du Bois, *Suppression of the African Slave Trade*, 1903, p. 190.

4. Joseph Washington, *Black Religion, the Negro and Christianity in the United States* (Boston: Beacon Press, 1964), p. 33.

5. Nat Turner, *Chronicles of Black Protest* (New York: The New American Library, 1969), pp. 64–74.

6. Raymond Brown, "Hermeneutics" in *Jerome Biblical Commentary* (Englewood, NJ: Prentice Hall), pp. 605–623.

7. Edgar I. McKnight, *Post-Modern Use of the Bible* (Nashville, TN: Abingdon Press, 1988), p. 39.

8. Fredric Jameson, *The Political Unconscious* (Ithaca, NY: Cornell University Press, 1982), p. 31.

9. Joseph Murphy, *Santeria* (New York: Original, 1989), pp. 17–18.

10. Jameson, *The Political Unconscious*, pp. 9–10.

11. Karl Mannheim, *Ideology and Utopia* (Orlando, FL: Harvest Books, 1955), p. 4.

12. Terry Eagleton, *Literary Theory* (Minneapolis: University of Minnesota Press, 1996), pp. 54–55.

13. Robert Coote, *The Bible's First History* (Minneapolis, MN: Fortress, 1989), pp. 129–130.

14. Schubert M. Ogden, *On Theology* (San Francisco, CA: Harper and Row, 1982), pp. 53–54.
15. Ibid., p. 64.
16. Paul de Man, *Blindness and Insight* (Minneapolis: University of Minnesota Press, 1983), pp. 135–136.
17. Ibid., pp. 109–110.
18. Jonathan Culler, *On Deconstruction* (Ithaca, NY: Cornell University Press, 1983) p. 81.
19. Turner, *Chronicles of Black Protest*, pp. 72–74.
20. Coote, *The Bible's First History,* p. 103.

6. The Mulatto as Material/Sexual Site of Modernity's Contacts and Exchanges

1. W. E. B. Du Bois, *The Souls of Black Folks* (New York: W. W. Norton, 1999).
2. W. E. B. Du Bois, "The Souls of White Folks," in *Darkwater: Voices from Within the Veil* (New York: Schocken Books, 1972), p. 37.
3. Edward J. Blum, *W. E. B. Du Bois: American Prophet* (Philadelphia: University of Pennsylvania Press, 2007), p. 54.
4. Edmund Husserl, "Expression and Meaning," The Essential Husserl: Basic writings in Transcendental Phenomenology (Bloomington: Indiana University Press, 1999), pp. 41–42.
5. Du Bois, *Souls*, p. 11.
6. Ibid., p. 17.
7. Frantz Fanon, *Black Skin, White Masks* (New York: Grove Press), p. 110.
8. W. E. B. Du Bois, *The Autobiography of W. E. B. Du Bois: A Soliloquy on Viewing My Life from the Last Decade to Its First Century* (New York: International, 1968), p. 99.
9. He obtained two B. A. degrees: one from Fisk University in Nashville, Tennessee in 1888 and the other from Harvard University in Cambridge, Massachusetts. in 1890. In 1891, Du Bois received his M.A. degree and in 1895, his Ph.D. degree from Harvard University.
10. Du Bois, *Autobiography of W. E. B. Du Bois*, p. 107.
11. Ibid., p. 112.
12. Ibid., p. 120.
13. Ibid., pp. 170–171.
14. Fanon, *Black Skin*, p. 109.
15. Favor, Martin *Authentic Blackness* (Durham, NC: Duke University Press, 1999).
16. W. E. B. Du Bois, "Jesus Christ in Georgia," in *The Seventh Son: The Thought and Writings of W. E. B. Du Bois*, vol. 2, ed. Julius Lester (New York: Vintage Books, 1971).
17. Ibid.
18. Abraham L. Davis and Barbara Luck Graham, *The Supreme Court, Race, and Civil Rights* (Thousand Oaks, CA: Sage, 1995), pp. 50–53.

19. Joel Williamson, *Rage for Order* (New York: Oxford University Press, 1984), p. 238.

20. Susan Gubar, *Racechanges: White Skin, Black Face in American Culture* (New York: Oxford University Press, 1997), p. 211.

21. Williamson, *Rage for Order,* p. 239.

22. Thomas J. Davis, "Race, Identity, and the Law: Plessy v. Ferguson," in *Race on Trial: Law and Justice in American History,* ed. Annette Gordon-Reed (Oxford: Oxford University Press, 2002), pp. 61–63.

23. Cheryl I. Harris, 'Whiteness as Property," *Harvard Law Review* 106, no. 8 (June 1993), p. 1746.

24. Ibid., p. 1748.

25. Davis, "Race, Identity, and the Law," p. 72.

26. Harris, "Whiteness as Property," p. 1749.

27. Derrick Bell, *Race, Racism and American Law* (Boston: Little, Brown, 1973), p. 260.

28. Ibid., p. 262. The distinction in the above quoted Virginia Statute of 1662 is between a Christian and a slave. This wording reflects a situation wherein the majority of whites had been baptized but the majority of the Africans arriving to the colony had not. There were several instances, however, where black slaves successfully sued for their freedom based on the fact that they had been baptized. In 1667, Virginia took measures to prevent any Negro slaves from ever again being freed through this loophole.

    "Whereas some doubts have risen whether children that are slaves by birth and by the charity and piety of their owners made partakers of the blessed sacrament of baptism, should by virtue of their baptism be made free, it is enacted...that the conferring of baptism does not alter the condition of the person as to his bondage or freedom." see Paul Finkelman, *The Law of Freedom and Bondage: A Casebook* (New York: Oceana, 1986), p. 16.

29. Bill Maurer, "The Anthropology of Money," *Annual Review of Anthropology* 35 (2006), p. 13.

30. O'Malley, "Specie and Species: The Question of Money," *American Historical Review* 99, no. 2 (April 1994), pp. 391, 395.

31. Painter, "Thinking about the Languages of Money and Race," p. 398.

32. Bell, *Race, Racism and American Law,* p. 6.

33. O'Malley, "Specie and Species," pp. 380–381.

34. Michael O'Malley, "Free Silver and the Constitution of Man," www.Common-place.org 6, no. 3 (April 2006).

35. In Gubar, *Racechanges,* p. 209.

36. John Edgar Wideman, *Fatheralong: A Meditation on Fathers and Sons, Race and Society* (New York: Vintage Press, 1995).

37. David Theo Goldberg, *Racist Culture: Philosophy and the Politics of Meaning* (Oxford: Blackwell, 1993), pp. 53–55.

38. Du Bois, "Jesus Christ in Georgia," pp. 29–30.

39. Myron Schwartzman, *Romare Bearden: His Life and Art* (New York: Harry Adams, 1990).

7. "The Signification of Silence" Revisited: African American Art and Hermeneutics

1. Long, *Significations*, p. 60.
2. Ibid., pp. 54–57.
3. Ralph Ellison, *Shadow and Act* (New York: Signet Books, 1966), pp. 174–175.
4. James Weldon Johnson, *God's Trombones* (New York: Viking Press, 1965), p. 6.
5. James Cone, *A Black Theology of Liberation* (Maryknoll, NY: Orbis Books), pp. 35–39.
6. Johnson, *God's Trombones*, pp. 17–20.
7. Richard J. Powell, *Homecoming: The Art and Life of William H. Johnson* (New York: Rizzoli International, 1991), pp. 77–78.
8. Gayraud Wilmore, *Black Religion and Black Radicalism* (New York: Anchor Press, 1973), p. 188.
9. Powell, *Homecoming,* p. 191.
10. Ibid., p. 228.
11. Schwartzman, *Romare Bearden*, p. 128.
12. Ibid., p. 288.
13. Ibid., p. 157.
14. Ibid., pp. 210–212.
15. In Phyllis Rauch Klotman, ed., *Humanities through the Black Experience* (Dubuque, IA: Kendall Hunt, 1977), p. 179.
16. Susan Buck-Moss, *The Dialectics of Seeing: Walter Benjamin and the Arcades Project* (Cambridge, MA: MIT Press, 1999), p. 219.
17. Schwartzman, *Romare Bearden*, p. 248.
18. Fanon, *Black Skin*, p. 154.
19. Alain L. Locke, "Values and Imperatives," in *Philosophy Born of Struggle,* ed. Leonard Harris (Dubuque, IA: Kendall Hunt, 1983).
20. Nicolai Berdyaev, *The Destiny of Man* (London: Geoffrey Bles, 1948), p. 127.
21. Romare Bearden, "The Negro Artist's Dilemma," *Critique* November 1946, pp. 16–22.
22. John Dewey, *Art as Experience* (New York: Capricorn Book, 1958), p. 21.
23. Long, *Significations,* p. 9.

8. The Meaning of the Moan and Significance of the Shout in Black Worship and Culture and Memory and Hope

1. Zora Neale Hurston, *The Sanctified Church* (Berkeley, CA: Turtle Press, 1983), p. 103.
2. Eileen Southern, *The Music of Black Americans* (New York: W. W. Norton, 1983), pp. 176–177.

3. Carter G. Woodson, ed., *Negro Orators and Their Orations* (New York: Russell and Russell, 1969), pp. 150–157.

4. In John W. Blessingame, ed., *Slave Testimony* (Baton Rouge: Louisiana State University Press, 1977), pp. 114–115.

5. James Weldon Johnson, *God's Trombones* (New York: Viking Press, 1927/1965), p. 5.

6. Ibid., pp. 6–7.

7. Hortense J. Spillers, "Martin Luther King and the Style of Black Sermon," in *The Black Experience in Religion*, ed. C. Eric Lincoln (New York: Anchor Press, 1974), p. 83.

8. Ibid.

9. Zora Neale Hurston, *The Sanctified Church*, p. 82.

10. James Baldwin, *The Amen Corner* (New York: Vintage Books, 1996), pp. xv–xvi.

11. Matthew V. Johnson, *The Cicada's Song* (Atlanta: Publishing Associates, 2006), p. 89.

12. Long, *Significations*, p. 169.

13. Ibid., pp. 182–183.

14. William Dilthey, "The Construction of the Historical in Human Studies," in *W. Dilthey: Selected Writings*, ed. H. P. Rickman (London: Cambridge University Press, 1976), p. 239.

15. Henri F. Ellenberger, "A Clinical Introduction to Psychiatric Phenomenology and Existential Analysis," in *Existence*, ed. Rollo May (New York: Simon and Schuster, 1958), p. 100.

16. Jean Paul Sartre, *The Transcendence of the Ego* (New York: Noonday Press, 1957), p. 25.

17. Hendrich Rickert, *Science and History* quoted in Andrew Arato, "The Neo-Idealist Defense of Subjectivity," *Telos* no. 21 (Fall 1974), p. 125.

18. Karl Mannheim, "On the Interpretation of Weltanschauung," in *Karl Mannheim*, ed. Kurt H. Wolf (New York: Oxford University Press), p. 30

19. Karl Mannheim, "Lukacs' Theory of the Novel," in Ibid., p. 5.

20. George Simmel, "Subjective Culture," in *George Simmel on Individuality and Social Forms*, ed. D. Levine (Chicago: University of Chicago Press, 1971), p. 230.

21. Frantz Fanon, *Black Skin, White Masks* (New York: Grove Press, 1967), p. 154.

22. Ralph Ellison, *Invisible Man* (New York: Vintage Books, 1972), p. 3.

23. Fanon, *Black Skin*, p. 154.

24. George S. Schuyler, "The Caucasian Problem," in *What the Negro Wants*, ed. Rayford Logan (Chapel Hill: University of North Carolina Press, 1944), p. 281.

25. Matthew V. Johnson, "The Middle Passage, Trauma and the Tragic Re-Imagination of African American Theology," *Pastoral Psychology* 53 no. 6 (July 2005), pp. 555–556.

26. Ibid., p. 556.

27. Locke, "Values and Imperatives," pp. 22–23.

28. Langston Hughes, "The Negro Artist and the Racial Mountain," *Nation* 122 (June 23, 1926), pp. 692–694.
29. Frantz Fanon, *The Wretched of the Earth* (New York: Grove Press, 1968), p. 210.
30. Arthur Schomburg, "The Negro Digs Up His Past," *Survey Graphic* VI, no. 6 (March 1925), p. 670.
31. James Baldwin, *Evidence of Things Not Seen* (New York: Holt, Rinehart and Winston, 1985), pp. XII–XIII.
32. Karl Mannheim, "On the Interpretation of Weltanschauung," p. 57.

9. The Salsa/Jazz/Blues Idiom and Creolization in the Atlantic World

1. Philip V. Bohlman, *World Music: A Very Short Introduction* (Oxford: Oxford University Press, 2002), p. 35.
2. Ibid., p. 36.
3. Manuel Alvarez Nazario, *El Elemento Afronegroide En El Espanol De Puerto Rico* (San Juan: Instituto De Cultura Puertorriquena, 1974), p. 335.
4. Ibid., p. 45
5. Peter Manuel, *Caribbean Currents: Caribbean Music from Rumba to Raggae* (Philadelphia: Temple University Press, 1995), pp. 35–36.
6. Leonard B. Meyer, *Emotion and Meaning in Music* (Chicago: University of Chicago Press, 1956), p. 243.
7. Ibid., p. 14.
8. Manuel, *Caribbean Currents*, p. 37.
9. Ibid., p. 73.
10. Ibid., p. 67.
11. Michael P. Steinberg, *Listening to Reason: Culture, Subjectivity, and Nineteenth-Century Music* (Princeton, NJ: Princeton University Press, 2004), pp. 4–5.
12. Mark Evan Bonds, *Music as Thought: Listening to the Symphony in the Age of Beethoven* (Princeton, NJ: Princeton University Press, 2006), p. 10.
13. Bohlman, *World Music*.
14. Robert Gooding-Williams, Look, *A Negro: Philosophical Essays on Race, Culture and Politics* (New York: Routledge, 2006), p. 95.

Conclusion

1. Winthrop S. Hudson, "The American context as an Area for Research in Black Church Studies," *Church History* 52 no. 2 (1983), p. 157.
2. Ibid., p. 171.
3. See for example: Lawrence W. Levine, "African Culture and Slavery in the United States"; Albert J. Raboteau, "African Religions in America: Theoretical Perspectives," in *Global Dimension of the African Diaspora,*

Second Edition, ed. Joseph E. Harris (Washington, DC: Howard University Press, 1993).

4. Roger D. Hatch, "Integrating the Issue of Race into the History of Christianity in America," *Journal of the American academy of Religion* XLVI no. 4, p. 567.

5. Long, "Research Plans," (unpublished), p. 5.

6. Jack P. Greene, "Beyond Power: Paradigm Subversion and Reformulation and Re-creation of the Early Modern world," in *Crossing Boundaries: Comparative History of Black People in Diaspora,* ed. Darlene Hine and Jacqueline McLeod (Bloomington: Indiana University Press, 1999), p. 377.

7. Long, "Research Plans," p. 8.

8. Michael P. Smith, *Spirit World: Photographs and Journal* (Gretna, LA: Pelican, 1932), p. 31.

Bibliography

Ahlstrom, Sydney E. *A Religious History of the American People.* New Haven, CT and London: Yale University Press, 1972.

Alagoa, E. J. "Fon and Yoruba: The Niger Delta and the Cameroon." In *General History of Africa,* vol. 5, UNESCO. San Francisco: University of California Press, 1992.

Armitage, David. *The Ideological Origins of the British Empire.* Cambridge: Cambridge University Press, 2000.

Bailyn, Bernard. *Atlantic History: Concepts and Contours.* Cambridge, MA: Harvard University Press, 2005.

————. *The Ideological Origins of the American Revolution.* Cambridge, MA: Belknap Press, 1992.

Baldwin, James. *Go Tell It on the Mountain.* New York: Dell Book, 1981.

Baly, C. A. *The Birth of the Modern World, 1780–1914.* London: Blackwell, 2004.

Bearden, Romare. "The Negro Artist's Dilemma." *Critique* (November 1946): 16–22.

Beaud, Michel. *A History of Capitalism: 1500–2000.* New York: Monthly Review Press, 2001.

Beckles, Hilary McD. "The 'Hub of Empire': The Caribbean and Britain in the Seventeenth Century." In *The Origins of Empire: British Overseas Enterprise to the Close of the Seventeenth Century,* vol. 1, edited by Nicholas Canny. Oxford: Oxford Press, 1998.

Bell, Derrick. *Race, Racism and American Law.* Boston: Little, Brown, 1973.

Berdyaev, Nicolai. *The Destiny of Man.* London: Geoffrey Bles, 1948.

Blessingame, John W. ed. *Slave Testimony.* Baton Rouge: Louisiana State University Press, 1977.

Blum, Edward J. *W. E. B. Du Bois: American Prophet.* Philadelphia: University of Pennsylvania Press, 2007.

Bohlman, Philip V. *World Music: A Very Short Introduction.* Oxford: Oxford University Press, 2002.

Brooks, George E. *Landlords and Strangers: Ecology, Society, and Trade in Western Africa, 1000–1630.* Boulder, CO: Westview, 1993.

Brown, Raymond. "Hermeneutics." In *The Jerome Biblical Commentary,* ed. Raymond Brown, 605–623. Englewood Cliffs, NJ: Prentice Hall, 1968.

Brownlee, W. Elliot. *Dynamics of Ascent: A History of the American Economy.* New York: Alfred A. Knopf, 1974.

Buck-Moss, Susan. *The Dialectics of Seeing: Walter Benjamin and the Arcades Project.* Cambridge, MA: MIT Press, 1999.

Burk, Edmund. *A Philosophical Inquiry into the Origin of Our Ideas of the Sublime and the Beautiful.* Oxford: Oxford University Press, 1998.

Caputo, John D. The *Mystical Element in Heidegger's Thought.* New York: Fordham University Press, 1986.

Chirot, Daniel. *Social Change in the Modern Era.* New York: Harcourt Press, 1986.

Cone, James. *A Black Theology of Liberation.* Maryknoll, NY: Orbis Books, 1990.

Connell-Smith, Gordon. *Forerunners of Drake.* London: Longmans, green, 1954.

Coote, Robert C. *The Bible's First History.* Minneapolis, MN: Fortress, 1989.

Culler, Jonathan. *On Deconstruction.* Ithaca, NY: Cornell University Press, 1983.

Davis, Abraham L., and Barbara Luck Graham. *The Supreme Court, Race, and Civil.* Thousand Oaks, CA: Sage, 1995.

Davis, Thomas J. "Race, Identity, and the Law: Plessy v. Ferguson." In *Race on Trial: Law and Justice in American History,* edited by Annette Gordon-Reed, 61–63. Oxford: Oxford University Press, 2002.

de Man, Paul. *Blindness and Insight.* Minneapolis: University of Minnesota Press, 1983.

Dewey, John. *Art as Experience.* New York: Capricorn Book, 1958.

Dilthey, William. "The Construction of the Historical in Human Studies." In *W. Dilthey: Selected Writings,* edited by H. P. Rickman. London: Cambridge University Press, 1976.

Du Bois, W. E. B. *The Autobiography of W. E. B. Du Bois: A Soliloquy on Viewing My Life from the Last Decade to Its First Century.* New York: International, 1968.

———. "Jesus Christ in Georgia." In *The Seventh Son: The Thought and Writings of W. E. B. Du Bois,* vol. 2, edited by Julius Lester. New York: Vintage Books, 1971.

———. *The Souls of Black Folks.* New York: W. W. Norton, 1999.

———. "The Souls of White Folks." In *Darkwater: Voices from Within the Veil.* New York: Schocken Books, 1972.

———. *The Suppression of the African Slave Trade, 1638–1870.* Baton Rouge: Louisiana State University Press, 1896/1969.

Dupree, Louis. *Passage to Modernity: An Essay in the Hermeneutics of Nature and Culture.* New Haven, CT: Yale University Press, 1993.

Eagleton, Terry. *Literary Theory.* Minneapolis: University of Minnesota Press, 1996.

Edgar I. McKnight. *Post-Modern Use of the Bible.* Nashville, TN: Abingdon Press, 1988.

Ellenberger, Henri F. "A Clinical Introduction to Psychiatric Phenomenology and Existential Analysis." In *Existence,* edited by Rollo May. New York: Simon and Schuster, 1958.

Elliott, J. H. *Empires of the Atlantic World: Britain and Spain in America 1492–1830.* New Haven, CT: Yale University Press, 2006.

———. *Imperial Spain: 1469–1716.* New York: Penguin Books, 1963.

Ellison, Ralph. *Invisible Man.* New York: Vintage Books, 1972.

———. *Shadow and Act.* New York: Signet Books, 1966.

Equiano, Olaudah. *The Interesting Narrative of the Life of Olaudah Equiano or Gustavus Vassa The African. Written by Himself.* New York: Dover, 1999.

Eric Williams. *From Columbus to Castro: The History of the Caribbean.* New York: Vintage Books, 1970.

Fanon, Frantz. *Black Skin, White Masks.* New York: Grove Press, 1967.

Favor, Martin. *Authentic Blackness.* Durham, NC: Duke University Press, 1999.

Finkelman, Paul. *The Law of Freedom and Bondage: A Casebook.* New York: Oceana, 1986.

Fontana, Joseph. *The Distorted Past: A Reinterpretation of Europe.* Oxford: Blackwell, 1995.

Gilroy, Paul. *The Black Atlantic: Modernity and Double Consciousness.* Cambridge, MA: Harvard University Press, 1993.

Goldberg, David. Theo. *Racist Culture: Philosophy and the Politics of Meaning* Oxford: Blackwell, 1993.

Gonzales-Wipplers and Metraux. *Santeria: The Religion. A Legacy of Faith, Rites, and Magic.* New York: Harmony Books, 1989.

Gubar, Susan. *Racechanges: White Skin, Black Face in American Culture.* New York: Oxford University Press, 1997.

Harris, Cheryl I. "Whiteness as Property." *Harvard Law Review* 106, no. 8 (June 1993).

Heidegger, Martin. *Being and Time.* New York: Harper Perennial Classics, 2008.

———. *An Introduction to Metaphysics.* New Haven, CT: Yale University Press, 1959.

Herskovits, Melville. *An Outline of Dahomean Religious Belief.* Menasha, WI: The American Anthropological Association, no. 41 (1933).

———. *Dahomean Narratives.* Evanston, IL: Northwestern University Press, 1970.

Hont, Istvan, and Michael Ignatieff. *Wealth and Virtue: The Shaping of Political Economy in the Scottish Enlightenment.* Cambridge: Cambridge University Press.

Huggins, Nathan. *Black Odyssey: The African American Ordeal in Slavery.* New York: Vintage Books, 1990.

Hurston, Zora Neale. *The Sanctified Church.* Berkeley, CA: Turtle Press, 1983.

Jameson, Fredric. *The Political Unconscious.* Ithaca, NY: Cornell University Press, 1982.

Janzen, John M. *Lemba, 1650–1930: A Drum of Affliction in Africa and the New World.* New York: Garland Press, 1982.

Johnson, James Weldon. *God's Trombones.* New York: Viking Press, 1927/1965.

Johnson, Matthew V. *The Cicada's Song: A Novel*. Atlanta: Publishing Associates, 2006.

———. "The Middle Passage, Trauma and the Tragic Re-Imagination of African American Theology." *Pastoral Psychology* 53, no. 6 (July 2005).

Johnson, Rev. Samuel. *The History of the Yorubas from the Earliest Times to the Beginning of the British Protectorate*. London: Routledge, 1921.

Kavanaugh, Kirean. *Selected Writings of John of the Cross*. Mahwah, NJ: Paulist Press, 1987.

Kidd, Colin. *The Forging of Races: Race and Scripture in the Protestant Atlantic World, 1600–2000*. Cambridge: Cambridge University Press, 2006.

Klotman, Phyllis Rauch. ed. *Humanities through the Black Experience*. Dubuque, IA: Kendall Hunt, 1977.

Locke, Alain. "Values and Imperatives." In *Philosophy Born of Struggle,* edited by Leonard Harris. Dubuque, IA: Kendall Hunt, 1983.

Long, Charles H. "Indigenous People, Materialities, and Religion: Outline for a New Orientation to Religious Meaning." In *Religion and Global Culture: New Terrain in the Study of Religion and the Work of Charles H. Long,* edited by Jennifer I. M. Reid. New York: Lexington Books, 2003.

———. "Research Plans For 1991–92." unpublished.

———. *Significations: Signs, Symbols and Images in the Interpretation of Religion*. Philadelphia: Fortress, 1986.

Louth, Andrew. *The Origins of the Christian Mystical Tradition*. Oxford: Clarendon Press, 1983.

Malowist, M. "The Struggle for International Trade and Its Implications for Africa." In *General History of Africa*, vol. 5, edited by B. A. Ogot. Berkeley: University of California Press, 1992.

Mannheim, Karl. "On the Interpretation of Weltanschauung" and "Lukacs' Theory of the Novel." In *Karl Mannheim*, edited by Kurt H. Wolf. New York: Oxford University Press.

Manuel, Peter. *Caribbean Currents: Caribbean Music from Rumba to Raggae*. Philadelphia: Temple University Press, 1995.

Marx, Karl. *Capital*, vol. 1. In *The Marx-Engels Reader,* 2nd ed., edited by Robert C. Tucker (New York: W. W. Norton, 1978), pp. 319–320.

Maupol, Bernard. *La Geomancie a L'Ancienne Cote des Esclaves*. Paris: Institute D'Ethnologie, 1961.

Maurer, Bill. "The Anthropology of Money." *Annual Review of Anthropology* 35 (2006).

Meyer, Leonard B. *Emotion and Meaning in Music*. Chicago: University of Chicago Press, 1956.

Mudimbe, V. I. *The Invention of Africa: Gnosis, Philosophy and the Order of Knowledge*. Bloomington: University of Indiana Press, 1988.

Murphy, Joseph. *Santeria*. New York: Original, 1989.

Murray, Andrew F. *Presbyterians and the Negro*. Philadelphia: Presbyterian Historical Society, 1966.

Nazario, Manuel Alvarez. *El Elemento Afronegroide En El Espanol De Puerto Rico*. San Juan: Instituto De Cultura Puertorriquena, 1974.

Ogden, Schubert M. *On Theology*. San Francisco, CA: Harper and Row, 1982.

Ohlmeyer, Jane H. " 'Civilizing of those Rude Partes': Colonization within Britain and Ireland, 1580s–1640s." In *The Origins of Empire,* edited by Nicholas Canny. Oxford: Oxford University Press, 1998.

O'Malley, Michael. "Fire Silver and the Constitution of Man." www.Commonplace. org 6, no. 3 (April 2006).

———. "Specie and Species: The Question of Money." *American Historical Review* 99, no. 2 (April 1994).

Onaiyekan. "The Priesthood among the Owe Yoruba." In *Traditional Religion in West Africa,* edited by E. A. Ade Adegbola. Ibadan: Daystar Press, 1983.

Otto, Rudolph. Translated by John W. Harvey. *The Idea of the Holy: An Inquiry into the Non-rational Factor in the Idea of the Divine and Its Relation to the Rational.* London: Oxford University Press, 1923, 1950, 1958.

Painter, Nell. "Thinking about the Languages of Money and Race: A Response to Michael O'Malley." *American Historical Review* 99, no. 2 (April 1994): 398.

Pietz, William. "The Problem of the Fetish." *RES* 9 (Spring 1985).

Polt, Richard, and Gregory Fried. *Heidegger's Introduction to Metaphysics.* New Haven, CT: Yale University Press, 2001.

Powell, Richard J. *Homecoming: The Art and Life of William H. Johnson.* New York: Rizzoli International, 1991.

Price, Richard. *Maroon Societies: Rebel Slave Communities in the Americas.* New York: Anchor Press, 1973.

Reid, Jennifer. *Religion and Global Culture: New Terrain in the Study of Religion and the Work of Charles H. Long.* Lanham, MD: Lexington Press, 2003.

Reynolds, Edward. *Stand the Storm: A History of the Atlantic Slave Trade.* Chicago: Ivan R. Dee, 1985.

Rickert, Hendrich. *Science and History* quoted in Andrew Arato, "The Neo-Idealist Defense of Subjectivity." *Telos* no. 21 (Fall 1974).

Rivera, Luis N. *A Violent Evangelism: The Political and Religious Conquest of the Americas.* Louisville: Westminster/John Knox Press, 1992.

Sartre, Jean Paul. *The Transcendence of the Ego.* New York: Noonday Press, 1957.

Scarry, Elain. *The Body in Pain: The Making and Unmaking of the World.* Oxford: Oxford University Press, 1985.

Schwartzman, Myron. *Romare Bearden: His Life and Art.* New York: Harry Adams, 1990.

Simmel, George. "Subjective Culture." In *George Simmel on Individuality and Social Forms,* edited by D. Levine. Chicago: University of Chicago Press, 1971.

Smith, M. G. "The African Heritage in the Caribbean." In *Caribbean Studies: A Symposium,* edited by Vera Rubin, 37. Seattle: University of Washington Press, 1960.

Smith, Michael P. *Spirit World: Photographs and Journal.* Gretna, LA: Pelican, 1982.

Southern, Eileen. *The Music of Black Americans.* New York: W. W. Norton, 1983.

Southern, R. W. *Western Society and the Church in the Middle Ages.* New York: Penguin Books, 1990.

Spillers, Hortense J. "Martin Luther King and the Style of the Black Sermon." In *The Black Experience in Religion,* edited by C. Eric Lincoln. New York: Anchor Press, 1974.

Steinberg, Michael P. *Listening to Reason: Culture, Subjectivity, and Nineteenth-Century Music.* Princeton, NJ: Princeton University Press, 2004.

Tambiah, Stanley J. *Magic, Science and Religion and the Scope of Rationality.* Cambridge: Cambridge University Press, 1990.

Temples, Placid. *Bantu Philosophy,* Paris: Presence Africaine, 1959.

Thornton, John. *Africa and Africans in the Making of the Atlantic World, 1400–1800.* Cambridge: Cambridge University Press, 1992.

Van Leewuen, Arend Theodor. *Critique of Heaven and Earth,* vol. 2. New York: Charles Scribner's Sons, 1974.

Verene, Donald Philip. *Vico's Science of Imagination.* Ithaca, NY: Cornell University Press, 1981.

Wagley, Charles. "Plantation-America: A Culture Sphere." In *Caribbean Studies: A Symposium,* edited by Vera Rubin. Seattle: University of Washington Press, 1960.

Walsh, James. ed. *The Cloud of Unknowing.* Mahwah, NJ: Paulist Press, 1981.

Washington, Joseph. *Black Religion, the Negro and Christianity in the United States.* Boston: Beacon Press, 1964.

Wideman, John Edgar. *Fatheralong: A Meditation on Fathers and Sons, Race and Society,* New York: Vintage Press, 1995.

Williams, Eric. *From Columbus to Castro: A History of the Caribbean, 1492–1992.* New York: Vintage Books, 1970.

Wilmore, Gayraud. *Black Religion and Black Radicalism.* New York: Anchor Press, 1973.

Wolf, Eric R. *Europe and the People without History.* Berkeley: University of California Press, 1990.

Woodson, Carter G. ed. *Negro Orators and Their Orations.* New York: Russell and Russell, 1969.

Young, R. C. *Colonial Desire: Hybridity in Theory, Culture and Race.* London: Routledge, 1995.

Index